# WHAT A CHRISTIAN SHOULD KNOW ABOUT *THE SUPERNATURAL*

## McCANDLISH PHILLIPS

VICTOR BOOKS®

A DIVISION OF SCRIPTURE PRESS PUBLICATIONS INC.
USA CANADA ENGLAND

Recommended Dewey Decimal Classification: 235
Suggested Subject Heading: THE SUPERNATURAL: GOD, ANGELS, SATAN, EVIL SPIRITS

Library of Congress Catalog Card Number: 87-62479
ISBN: 0-89693-703-8

VICTOR BOOKS
A division of SP Publications, Inc.
Wheaton, Illinois 60189

# Table of Contents

**PART 1:**
**JOURNEY INTO THE SUPERNATURAL**
The Chariots of Israel:
  More than Meets the Eye                9
The Door That Can Never Be
  Opened Again                          12
The Impenetrable Order                  18
He Comes as Wind                        22
Testing Prophets and Dreamers
  of Dreams                             26
Journey into the Supernatural:
  Knowing What Is                       30

**PART 2:**
**THE BIBLICAL STRUCTURE OF REALITY**
The Invisible God: "I AM"               37
The Invisible God Made Visible          46
Angels                                  57
Satan: The Name Means "Adversary"       67
The Author of Idolatry                  72
Taking Sober Measure                    85
Battle for Allegiance                   91
The Origin of Satan                     96

## PART 3:
### THE THIEVES OF FOREVER
The Angels of the Dragon **105**
Acts of Power and Love:
 Setting Victims Free **111**
Legion: A Trophy of Grace **117**
King Saul Consults a Medium **124**
Mysticism, Mediums, Witchcraft,
 and Magic **133**

## PART 4:
### THE CHALLENGE TO SELF-POSSESSION
Spirit, Soul, Body—Knowing Yourself **147**
Reality, *"Reality,"* and REALITY **158**
Natural to Supernatural—Glimpses
 of the Wider Picture **169**
Guarding the Endowment **177**
Getting to the Nitty-Gritty **185**
Openings to Liberty and Joy **191**
Drugs and the Supernatural **199**

## PART 5:
### CALLED TO CONQUER
God, Government, and the Supernatural **215**
Peace by Conquest **219**

## To the Reader

Welcome to what I hope will be an adventure of discovery for you. You hold in your hand a basic guidebook to the entire supernatural realm, as the Bible reveals it. What lies ahead is designed to strengthen and fortify you in your Christian life.

Here is a book for the believer who needs solid, basic, and biblically accurate knowledge of the supernatural. It starts with a broad overview of the subject in its whole sweep, and it gets down to some practical particulars. It is especially suited for the young or new believer in Christ, who needs to know the great core facts about the supernatural.

Please note that the title of this book is not *"Everything* that *Every Christian* Needs to Know About the Supernatural." Some need to know more than others, especially ministers who deal with victims of the evil supernatural. This is a handbook for the general believer, not for the specialist.

A book of this kind would have been of immense help to me in the earlier part of my Christian walk. After hearing a message in the old Arlington Presbyterian Church in Baltimore on being "willing to go anywhere in the world and do anything that Jesus Christ has for you to do—with no holds barred," I fully and formally gave my life to the Lord, to direct as He desired.

The Lord soon led me to New York City and into daily newspaper reporting, where I found myself in a starkly unbelieving atmosphere. I came into it knowing nothing about the facts of spiritual opposition and buffeting. As I openly bore testimony to Jesus Christ, I found that I was, indeed, "wrestling" with something mysterious and quite powerful, but it was "not against flesh and blood," as Ephesians 6:12 says.

Had I known much sooner what I came to know, I would have been spared years of baffling trouble. It is the keen memory of that early experience that motivated me to write this book.

Christians are told, in 1 Peter 5:8, that "your enemy the devil prowls around like a roaring lion looking for someone to devour." The following verse tells us what to do about it: "Resist him, standing firm in the faith . . ."

The first law of intelligent spiritual warfare and effective resistance to evil is—*know your enemy*. Know who he is, what he is about, how he works, and how he can be overcome.

To use a crude but clear illustration, believers do not need to fear the supernatural any more than they would fear electricity, but they do need to understand it, respect it, and approach it lawfully.

Electricity confers vast benefits, but ignore or break the rules governing it and it can be harmful and deadly dangerous. The same is true of the supernatural.

Christians cannot afford to be naive or ill-informed about this aspect of reality. From the Scriptures we can learn the open secrets of becoming, as we are told to do, as "wise as serpents, and harmless as doves" (Matthew 10:16, KJV).

I hope you enjoy reading the chapters ahead and gain definite help in your life with Christ, for yourself and for those you love, as you turn these pages.

**McCandlish Phillips**

**1**

# JOURNEY
# INTO THE
# SUPERNATURAL

## The Chariots of Israel:
## More than Meets the Eye

Once, when the king of Syria was at war against Israel, his secretly devised plans were repeatedly frustrated because the king of Israel always seemed to know exactly what they were. The Syrian king suspected a spy in his own camp, but one of his servants told him, "Elisha, the prophet who is in Israel, tells the king of Israel the words that you speak in your bedchamber."

Elisha was in a city called Dothan, the servant said.

So the king sent "horses and chariots and a great army, and they came by night and surrounded the city." An army was sent to seize one man.

"When the servant of the man of God rose early in the morning and went out, behold, an army with horses and chariots was round about the city." Elisha was encircled and trapped.

"And the servant said, 'Alas, my master! What shall we do?'" And Elisha answered, "'Fear not, for those that are with us are more than those who are with them.'"

That seemed an odd declaration, because *no* soldiers were with Elisha.

And Elisha prayed and said, "'Lord, I pray Thee, *open his eyes that he may see.*' So the Lord opened the eyes of the young man, and he saw, and behold, the mountain was full of horses and chariots of fire round about Elisha" (2 Kings 6:8-23, RSV).

In this account—and at many other points in the Bible—the Scriptures tell of forces and events in the physical and natural realm and of forces and concurrent events in the spiritual and supernatural realm. There was something visible going on and something invisible going on in the same place at the same time, and both had a bearing on the event. Here, for a brief moment, the unseen veil that separates the two was drawn back, so the young man who at first had seen only the army of Syria saw another army camped in that place, the army of the Lord.

What he saw was not a vision but reality. He saw real horses and real chariots on that mountain, but they existed on a different plane of reality than the physical. They could come into the natural order and affect it, but they were not a part of the natural order. They exist in an order beyond or above that of the natural, called the supernatural. They are not less real because they are normally invisible to man.

The peaceful outcome of this confrontation between natural and supernatural forces hints that the prophet—and most probably the Lord—had a sense of humor in it.

Elisha was not seized or harmed, nor were any of the invading Syrian soldiers killed. The prophet asked the Lord to strike the aliens with temporary blindness, and when the Syrians could not see, Elisha had some sport with them. He told them that they were in the wrong place.

"Follow me," said the man they were after, "and I will lead you to the man whom you seek." Elisha thus offered to lead them straight to Elisha. But he led them like sheep into the center of the stronghold of Israel, where the army of Israel could quickly have cut them all down. Instead, Elisha asked the Lord to take their blindness away, and a bit later he set them all down to "a great feast."

He fed them well, left them with wonderful stories to tell to their grandchildren later in life, and sent them home, baffled but wiser. The last word on it is that "the Syrians came no more on raids into the land of Israel."

They had learned their lesson in regard to raids, but the Syrian king later "mustered his entire army" for an all-out attack on Israel. It was abruptly cut off when the Lord, acting according to a prophecy spoken by Elisha, "made the army of the Syrians hear the sound of chariots, and of horses, the sound of a great army" (2 Kings 7:6). The troops fell into a panic—it sounded to them as if Israel had got the Egyptian army to help them in a counterattack. The Syrians abandoned their camp in haste, leaving all their horses and supplies behind as a spoil for Israel.

This time the Syrians "heard" chariots that were not there. We do not know just how it worked, but what happened in their hearing was entirely supernatural. Yet its effects in the natural-physical realm were direct, immediate, and conclusive.

There had been one previous occasion on which Elisha had seen a sight like the one he saw on the morning when the Syrians tried to seize him. It came while he was serving as a young man under the Prophet Elijah.

Elijah was one of the holiest and mightiest prophets in the history of Israel. He is one of two men in Old Testament times who were taken into heaven without suffering physical death. The other is Enoch.

Elisha had been servant to Elijah. When the day came for Elijah to be taken from the earth, Elisha knew what was going to happen. He followed the older man's steps closely that day, refusing suggestions that he linger behind.

At the end, the old prophet turned to the younger man and said, "Ask what I shall do for you, before I am taken from you." Elisha said, "I pray you, let me inherit a double share of your spirit." He was asking that the power of God that had made Elijah a prophet and a worker of miracles rest upon him—in double measure.

Elijah said, "You have asked a hard thing. Yet, *if you see me* as I am being taken from you, it shall be so for you; but if you do not see me, it shall not be so."

"As they still went on and talked, behold, a chariot of fire and horses of fire, separated the two of them. And Elijah went up by a whirlwind into heaven.

"And Elisha saw it and he cried, 'My father, my father! The *chariots of Israel and its horsemen!*' And he saw him no more" (2 Kings 2:1-12, RSV).

The condition had been fulfilled. For a moment Elisha had seen hidden things, and that made him call out in astonishment and awe. He saw forces assigned as protectors of Israel—real, powerful, efficient forces that the human eye cannot see, because they are not physical but spiritual, not natural but supernatural.

Because they are on a different plane than that of the natural and the physical, in their comings and goings they are, with rare exceptions, unseen and unheard by man.

While this is true of the supernatural forces of God, it is equally true of the supernatural forces of evil. Both are invisible and both affect events on earth to a degree unsuspected by most men.

Once, when King David was tempted in a certain matter and disobeyed the will of God, the Bible says that "God sent the angel to Jerusalem to destroy it, but when he was about to destroy it, the Lord saw, and He repented of the evil, and He said to the destroying angel, 'It is enough; now stay your hand.'

"And the angel of the Lord was standing by the threshing floor of Ornan the Jebusite"—notice that it was a very specific angel standing at a very specific place. "And David lifted his eyes and *saw the angel of the Lord* standing between earth and heaven, and in his hand a drawn sword stretched out over Jerusalem. . . .

"Now Ornan was threshing wheat; he turned and *saw the angel,* and his four sons who were with him hid themselves" (1 Chronicles 21:15-16, 20, RSV).

It was given to David and to Ornan to see beyond the natural into the supernatural and to see, taking place in the supernatural, an event that had the most immediate and momentous bearing on the safety of the city of Jerusalem.

There are events occurring on the earth in our time that are affected not only by what men do and say in the natural realm but by invisible forces operating in the supernatural realm. The Bible reveals that the primary initiative in certain events of history does not proceed from the will of man but from the will of powers beyond man in the supernatural. Since some of the powers are evil, and since their desire is to increase the sum of strife and suffering and death among mankind, it is urgent for Christians to know something about them.

## The Door That Can Never Be Opened Again

Supernaturalism in many forms has come flooding in upon the American and Canadian culture in our time, creating a widespread interest in clairvoyance, psychicism, occultism, witchcraft, out-of-body travel, transcendental meditation, extrasensory perception, precognition, and various forms of mysticism or spiritism. New as they may seem, they are ancient supernatural practices that have found expressions in many cultures at various times in history.

For many people they have, it must be acknowledged, the magnetism of fascination, but these things should not be entered into out of uninformed curiosity, without some knowledge of the possible consequences of even a limited amount of experimentation with them or exposure to them.

If you would not thrust your hand into a snake pit, you should not permit yourself to be drawn into an involvement with one or another form of occultism, even in a tentative and purely experimental way, without knowing that it is possible for you to step over a threshold and past a door that may slam shut behind you as soon as you stand on the far side of it—slam shut so tight that nothing you can do can pry that door open again so that you can get back out.

That does happen. I have seen it happen. Young people have told me that something like this was happening to them but that before the door completely closed somehow they got out of it in time. I have heard from the lips of still others that they wish that they had never become involved in what they are in, but they say that they are helpless to do anything about it now. For them there seems to be *no exit.*

There is no knowing how quickly entrapment in the supernatural may occur. For some the process is slow. They can go for months, perhaps for years, without feeling or observing effects which they regard as damaging. For others a single experiment, entered into even in a casual or ignorant way, may carry them past a point of no return.

The supernatural is a tremendously potent realm. A person may pull what looks to be a small trigger and find that he has set off what for him proves to be a kind of nuclear fission of the human psyche. The powers are far, far beyond the capacity of man to handle. Yet, within clear biblical guidelines, born-again believers in Christ have no cause for unreasoning fear of the supernatural at all. Knowing what to avoid confers safety; and supernatural realities that have their source in God, in the Lord Jesus, and in the Holy Spirit, can be for them a source of joy, comfort, protection, godly power, liberation, perhaps at times even healing.

The author was initially moved to investigate the supernatural and to write about it after a series of encounters with individuals who had been terribly damaged by their involvement in it. (My work as a newspaper reporter in New York City constantly threw me into contact with a great variety of people in many dissimilar circumstances of life.)

Quite a few of these victimized individuals were Jewish, and that is a biblically significant fact. The Old Testament warnings against certain supernatural practices strongly forbid Jews to have anything to do with them. Such practices are a direct traffic with the spiritual enemies of the living God—the God who revealed Himself first to Abraham and the Jews. Ignorance of this fact supplies no exemption from the effects of going against it—any more than a person who idly picks up a live wire is protected by ignorance of the laws of electricity.

Though there is plenty about it on the wrong side that is weird, the supernatural realm is not at all something merely vague or ethereal, as fleeting as an airplane's shadow on the terrain. It is reality, and its effects are often startlingly real.

I watched in close-up the disintegration of a young Jew who went out of his mind as the direct and traceable result of having watched an Indian yogi on television. That gave him a mild taste of the occult. He took a deep dive into it, read widely in some of its literature, and began doing and saying strangely irrational things. He smoked marijuana. He lost his hold on reality, and the unreality that seized his mind was of an especially preposterous kind.

In six months he was changed from a rational, effective human being of more than ordinary capacity and initiative to a futile and oddly warped individual. When he spoke, half the time he sounded about 80 percent rational, the rest of the time he sounded 100 percent out of his mind. He was taken unawares. I knew another young Jew, twenty-four years old, who believed that a certain notorious, self-proclaimed Christ-figure in India was the Messiah, and who became absorbed in that conviction to the exclusion of almost everything else. He got into it to the point of mental aberration. He frankly said that when the idea concerning the Indian came over him, he knew it was wrong and he tried to resist, but he could not. In both of these cases, drugs taken in small amounts served as avenues into the supernatural for these young men and helped undermine their self-control and loose them from their senses.

I knew a man who, at age forty-five, had spent four wasted years in a mental institution, away from his family and away from the good job he had ably held for twenty years, because he dipped into supernaturalism, out of fascination, and got in over his head. Most of his trouble came because he met an elderly "prophetess" whose words and visions got hold of him. He went to her for advice on several occasions and submitted to her magic religious formulas for sickness. Some of it came through reading about the supernatural exploits of medieval so-called saints and some of it came through the use of religious medals. At one key point he had a "sign" that he took as evidence of God's favor on his course. It was a sign all right—a sweet yet perverse small miracle—but it was *not* from God. I warned him repeatedly and strongly against these things—until the time when his wife had him committed to a mental hospital, and he was put through a series of electroshock treatments, which did not help him. The last time I saw him he appeared to be hopelessly insane.

These things do not happen merely by chance. There are active, intelligent, invisible spiritual forces at work today that select particular or susceptible individuals and seek to get them interested in, and then into, the supernatural. These forces have an entire program or path of spiritual ruination laid out for an individual, including events that seem to be "providential," and if the individual chooses that path, step by step, he cooperates in a program that will destroy him. If he knew what those forces are, and what they design to do, he would not allow them to make him their victim.

These powers of evil are skilled at planting events, coincidences, and signs in the lives of those they are after. They present themselves as good, and they offer what they do as the acts of a benign providence. The Bible exposes them for exactly what they are.

These spiritual forces are massively at work in North America, multiplying and spreading the means that are useful to them in hooking individuals on supernaturalism. In doing that, they are also working to subvert parts of our culture by thoroughly infiltrating it with a broad variety of corrupt and dangerous occult practices.

It is no accident—it is a program—that the motion pictures, national magazines, bookstores, and book stands are heavily freighted with graphic accounts of various adventures in supernaturalism. These accounts succeed in introducing supernaturalism into the consciousness of millions of people. For some it is only a brush, a matter of passing curiosity. Upon others it exerts the almost irresistible magnetism of a deep fascination. They feel themselves being drawn into new levels of experience. They are aware that a force is moving upon their souls to draw them into places where they have not been before. The line of least resistance is to go right along as one feels oneself being drawn or "led."

In my work I met a young Jew, a college sophomore, who almost immediately impressed me as having a beautifully balanced combination of good attributes. He was bright, alert, quick of mind and quick of step, naturally and easily personable, just a bit dapper, genuinely willing to be helpful, and he had plenty of well-directed initiative.

One afternoon it seemed to me important that I take a few minutes to talk with him about what he believed. I am glad that I did. He was interested in talking on the subject and, in the course of a ten-minute conversation, he told me that his college-age brother had died recently in an automobile accident. The conversation opened up an area of discussion that proved critically important to him a short time later.

He had switched from a Midwest college to one in New York City and found lodging on Manhattan's upper West Side. About three weeks after our talk, he came to me and said, with a kind of taut urgency, "I've *got* to talk to you." He said that he had "just happened" to see a copy of a magazine lying on the desk near him, that he picked it up and read an account by Episcopal Bishop James A. Pike of his conversational exchanges, through a medium, with what the bishop took to be his late son. That night, he said, he took a walk around his new neighborhood "to see where the good pizza is, the good hamburgers," and he "just happened" to look up and spot the upstairs shop of a spiritual reader and adviser.

"I just felt drawn," he said, "strongly drawn to go up there" to ask her if she could put him into contact with his dead brother.

"Yes," she told him, "but not now. You'll have to come back."

There it was—two coincidences and a strangely compelling urge, and this fellow was on the verge of getting involved in things against which the Bible gives the most clear-cut warnings.

Without knowing it in any way, this young man was beginning to fall into a carefully arranged trap, designed to give evil supernatural powers an access to his soul, his inner being, that they had not previously had.

The next day I opened up the Bible and showed him several passages directly bearing on the things he was dipping into. After he had seen them he said, "I won't go near that place again." By sticking to that decision, made in the light of what the Bible says about the matter, he will keep out of a danger zone in the supernatural.

For this young man, a magazine article that he chanced to read triggered a desire to probe into the supernatural. For another young man, mentioned earlier, a television broadcast sent him on a quest through the pages of books on psychicism. For another man, a chance meeting with a woman who claimed certain prophetic powers set him on the course that led to his confinement in a mental institution.

This book by no means is a condemnation of the supernatural. There is a hunger and a longing in man for contact with something above him that is eternal and sure. There is a human need for supernatural experience, a deep and legitimate need. Others, out of ignorance or prejudice, may deny the supernatural and scoff at it. I do not. I know that it is real. I have had experience with the supernatural. I have seen some of its most warping and destructive effects, and I have known some of its pure, edifying blessings.

You can, thank God, have one without the other, the good experience without the evil kind.


Everyone knows that there are fakers and gyp artists and charlatans among those who deal in the supernatural realm, but there are also individuals who do in fact possess certain powers and who are able to exercise them and to produce results by them, if not always, sometimes. The fakers can do you no good; the others may do you great harm.

For those who do exercise supernatural powers, the right question is not whether their powers are real. The right question is: Where—exactly where—do they obtain those powers?

Too many American churches are stone dead to the supernatural or even stoutly and rigidly antagonistic to it. The Bible, of course, is certainly not an anti-supernatural book. It is just the opposite. It is a book filled from beginning to end with accounts of that which is supernatural. The Bible is not only a book *about* the supernatural. The Bible is a supernatural book. It is alive, and it has a message that God uses to impart spiritual life.

Synagogues and countless churches, by denying and cutting out or shutting out genuine supernatural experiences that the Bible says human beings ought to have, have created a tremendous void that is being filled in the most destructive way by books that anyone can pick from a drugstore rack, or by movies, or gurus.

When churches won't lead them to what God wants the people to have, traffickers in the supernatural offer them substitutes, in what is becoming a wide-open market in black magic.

The Bible recognizes this human desire to know more than may be known by natural means of cognition. It would be correct to say that the Bible is an antimaterialistic (though not an ascetic) book with a very strong emphasis on, and an invitation to, the supernatural. It promises that "your old men will dream dreams and your young men will see visions" (Joel 2:28).

Some people have a kind of thirst for the supernatural. It makes a difference whether they seek to quench that thirst at a well whose waters are poisoned, or at a well whose waters run pure.

Supernaturalism has come to us in a rush and it is here to stay, whether we like it or not. Wearing blinders will not help. Christians need desperately to know what the Bible says about it, before tragedy strikes homes and families who don't know what is happening to their young members, or why.

It is important for everyone to know of this, but it is especially important for young or new believers to know, living as they so often must in the sub-Christian, or even anti-godly, atmosphere of our society.

The Bible is the one safe, sure guide to the supernatural. It distinguishes sharply and adamantly between two enormously potent supernatural realms, as between two irreconcilable forces. These two are in conflict, in the earth and in the heavens. As to their effect upon the earth, which of them shall prevail in this generation, individuals must choose between them.

To make that choice, we need accurate information. The following chapters will lay down the biblical guidelines on the supernatural, exposing that which is harmful or destructive, and illuminating, on the basis of the biblical accounts, that which is full of power and blessing for mankind.

Looking into the supernatural with the Bible as our guide, we will go on a fascinating journey of discovery. It will enrich us—and equip us to be good soldiers of Jesus Christ in a time of rampant spiritual confusion. Remember always that "if a man strives for masteries, yet he is not crowned, except he strives *lawfully*" (2 Timothy 2:5, KJV).

## The Impenetrable Order

In the creation there is a physical order and a spiritual order, both of which are real. The physical universe is natural. The spiritual order is supernatural. There are facts that may be known about both, but not by the same means.

The human body, and the five senses that go with it, is a part of the physical creation. Those senses are able to observe and to take in information and facts about the natural universe—and that is all. They cannot observe the supernatural order. Your senses give you your relationship to the whole physical universe. They are the mediators and sentinels between you and all the rest of the physical creation. You know of it and learn of it by using them.

There it ends. They provide you with no information about the supernatural order. Your ears are deaf to it; your eyes are blind to it. The Bible says: "The things which are seen are temporal, but the things which are not seen are eternal" (2 Corinthians 4:18, KJV).

We know the first part of that statement to be true. The earth, the sun, the moon, the stars, the whole physical creation will wear out.

Psalm 102 says: "In the beginning You laid the foundations of the earth, and the heavens are the work of Your hands. They will perish, but You remain; they will all wear out like a garment. Like clothing You will change them and they will be discarded. But You remain the same, and Your years will never end" (vv. 25-27).

The earth and everything that is in the physical realm "will wear out like a garment" and "they will perish."

We give ready assent to the statement that "the things which are seen are temporal." We know that to be the fact. We are much less sure that "the things which are not seen are eternal."

Notice that the verse does not refer only to ideas, to values and concepts; it refers to *things*. It speaks of temporal things and it speaks of eternal *things*. The contrast is not just between natural stuff and spiritual values, as though a man could read the verse and say, "Sure, money and clothes wear out, but love goes on forever." It will, of course, since "God is love," yet He is also the creator of a vast array of living beings and things. Every saved person will have a new *body* in which to live forever, one that will never wear out or know illness or pain—different from the mortal body, yes, but a body nonetheless. Hear Paul:

But someone may ask, "How are the dead raised? With what kind of body will they come?" [They doubted that the dead could have bodies, but Paul says:] How foolish! What you sow does not come to life unless it dies. . . . There are also heavenly bodies and there are earthly bodies; but the splendor of the heavenly bodies is one kind, and the splendor of the earthly bodies is another. . . . So will it be with the resurrection of the dead. The body that is sown is perishable; it is raised imperishable . . . it is sown in weakness, it is raised in power; it is sown a natural body, it is raised a spiritual body. If there is a natural body, there is also a spiritual body. . . . And just as we have borne the likeness of the earthly man, so shall we bear the likeness of the man from heaven" (1 Corinthians 15:35-49).

Jesus promised His apostles that they would "eat and drink at My table in My kingdom, and sit on thrones" (Luke 22:30). Real people with real bodies sitting at real tables eating and drinking real heavenly cuisine. It is all too easy to spiritualize the promises concerning the unseen and the eternal unduly.

The unseen things the Scripture says are eternal are things that have objective existence. They have that existence not on the natural and physical plane but on the spiritual and supernatural plane.

The natural man, in full possession of his physical faculties and senses, is constitutionally incapable of discovering anything on the spiritual plane. That is as true as that a standard band radio does not receive short-wave signals. The atmosphere may be charged with such signals, but the standard band radio is as dead to them as the leg of a table is.

The Bible declares that the natural man does not receive spiritual truths. "They are folly to him, and he is *not able* to understand them because they are spiritually discerned" (1 Corinthians 2:14, RSV).

Since he cannot, it is an easy thing for him to assert that if something can't be seen it is not real, does not exist. Yet visibility is not the test of existence.

Science, the investigative exercise of the natural senses, is defined as "systematic knowledge of the physical and material world" gained by skilled observation, by measurement. The human baby is an infant scientist as he discovers the uses and proportions of things and his own proportions in respect to them. He does this by watching them, handling and feeling them, by tugging at them.

On a far more sophisticated level, the scientist learns the size and shape and the weight and motion of things by careful observation with his senses. Man has devised numberless tools and instruments that help him observe things more exactly. These tools are really extensions of his senses. They enable man to use his senses to search out finer data and to make far more precise measurements than could be made by the unaided senses.

Science is able also to use methods of observation to determine certain laws that apply in the natural realm, including the laws of mathematics.

Yet there are limits upon what man can discover by the scientific method. The whole physical universe is unlimitedly open to man to explore by the exercise of his senses, directed by his intelligence, as far as his ingenuity will allow him. Matter and energy, substance and structure, in all of their manifold forms may be explored endlessly by the intelligent use of the physical senses—for that is the realm of which they are a part and in which they may freely and effectively operate.

Man may unlock secret after secret in chemistry, in biology, in nuclear physics, in geology, in astronomy by the rigorous application of the scientific method. The natural realm is vast, and man is free to search it to the utmost of his capacity. But beyond it he cannot go by any scientific method. Man's senses reach an end of what they can discover when they reach the end of the physical creation.

Yet there is one great truth that *is* freely given to men through their senses—that God is the Creator and that He is all-powerful. What He has created gives testimony to Him. His immortal hand is seen in His handiwork.

The Scripture that tells of this begins by saying that God is angry at "the godlessness . . . of men who suppress the truth by their wickedness."

Why? Because "what may be known about God is plain to them, because God has made it plain to them."

How? "For since the creation of the world God's invisible qualities—His eternal power and divine nature—have been *clearly seen*, being understood from what has been made, so that men are without excuse" (Romans 1:18-20).

The next verse says that "although they knew God" such men would not give thanks to Him, so "their foolish hearts were darkened" and "they became fools." Such men are doubly blind because they willfully blind themselves. Having eyes, they do not see.

The beauty and the grandeur of God's creation, its dazzling variety, and the many good provisions that He has made for us in nature—think of the delicious foods that no man ever invented that grow abundantly on trees or out of the ground, meeting our daily need for taste and sustenance—all tell of His power and fatherly love.

There are some who assert that God does not exist because He cannot be observed by man. Some scientists and some university professors are especially prone to this point of view. Their eminence in one realm tends to blind men to their incompetence in another.

When a scientist, however brilliant and accomplished in his field, steps out of it and seeks to use the authority obtained in his discipline as a warrant to make pronouncements in an entirely unrelated area, it is an act of sheer arrogance. He leaves the bank in which he has huge deposits and walks into another, in which he has none, and swaggers as importantly there as in the place where his capital actually is. He is entitled to be hustled out as a pauper.

This is particularly so with regard to any attempt to apply credentials earned in the natural realm to the spiritual and supernatural realm.

We know it is possible for a man to be an intellectual genius and a moral idiot; it is equally possible for a man of the highest attainment in the arts, letters, or science to be entirely ignorant regarding the spiritual and supernatural (see 1 Corinthians 1:27-29).

Speculation, of course, and intuition may range beyond the physical universe, and they can construct any system men may fancy, but nothing of what they suppose is subject to any verification. All of it may be the sheerest fiction.

The natural man, whatever his gifts, remains fixedly inexpert in comprehending that which is beyond the physical creation. He may posit anything he wishes, but he cannot prove any of it.

My concern is not with what may be thought to be or with what may be imagined to be, but only with what may be *known* to be.

The senses of man, expert as they are in their physical realm, are deaf and dumb and blind in the realm of the spiritual and supernatural. Beyond that, speculation adduces exactly nothing. Yet man is entitled to know of those unseen things which are supernatural and eternal, and he is *invited* to inquire. "Seek and you will find," said Jesus. "Knock and the door will be opened to you" (Luke 11:9).

## He Comes as Wind

Since nothing beyond the vast physical creation, consisting of matter and energy and all their interactions and relations, can be scientifically proven, we must seek another method.

The natural man is limited to the natural realm, where he has his existence. But that which has its existence in the spiritual realm is not limited to the spiritual realm. It may enter into the natural realm and do so with very pronounced effects upon it.

The chariots and the horsemen of Israel that Elisha's servant was permitted to see were supernatural and normally unseen, but they had taken their stations *in* the natural order and they were there to take effective action to protect the Prophet Elisha and the nation Israel.

There are spiritual forces at work today causing changes of astonishing magnitude in human affairs. If we fail to recognize them we shall continue to be utterly helpless in dealing with their effects.

The dwelling place of God is entirely outside of the capacity of science and the physical senses to discover by any method whatever. God is not found in the realm of the natural but in the realm of the spiritual. Ecclesiastes 11:5 says, "As you do not know the path of the wind . . . so you cannot understand the work of God, the Maker of all things."

If that were the last word on the matter, we would be blind and unknowing forever. But it is not the last word. The Bible says:

> *Eye* has not seen, *ear* has not heard, neither have entered into the heart of man, the things which God has prepared for them who love Him. But *God has revealed them to us by His Spirit,* for the Spirit searches all things, yes, the deep things of God. . . . The things of God *no man knows,* but the Spirit of God [knows them and reveals them to man] (1 Corinthians 2:9-12, kjv).

There it is. If man is to know anything at all about the realm of the spiritual and the supernatural, it must be given to him by revelation. Revelation is a one-way avenue. It comes from the spiritual plane to the natural plane. It never runs the other way.

Until the young man's eyes were opened by God, in response to the prayer of Elisha, he saw nothing, knew nothing, suspected nothing of the chariots and the horsemen of Israel that were camped in that place.

The initiative in scientific discovery lies wholly with man. The initiative in spiritual revelation lies wholly with God. Men can know only what God elects to reveal to them about the spiritual and the supernatural.

If we are truthful, we are obliged to admit that we can know nothing whatever of life after death apart from revelation. We can know nothing whatever about heaven or hell apart from revelation. We can know nothing about angels or demons apart from revelation or by direct, authentic experience.

God has chosen to make an extensive revelation to man regarding these things. He has chosen to do so in a way that makes them readily intelligible to human beings. There is a line of communication from God's supernatural realm into the natural order. The personal agent of this communication is the Spirit of God, the Holy Spirit.

The Holy Spirit—He is a living person—dwells in the spiritual order and He enters the natural order unseen. There are absolutely no limits on where He may go. In the Bible He is likened, in His comings and goings, to the wind: "The wind blows wherever it pleases. You hear its sound, but you cannot tell where it comes from or where it is going" (John 3:8). Unseen the Holy Spirit comes, unseen He goes, yet there are the effects of His wonderful presence among men.

There are no limits whatever on what the Holy Spirit may know, "for the Spirit searches all things, even the deep things of God" (1 Corinthians 2:11). This passage also declares that "*no one* knows the thoughts of God except the Spirit of God."

The Holy Spirit takes the truths of God, and of the spiritual realm, and conveys them according to the will of God, to men. In this He uses words primarily but occasionally also visions (pictures) and dreams as means of communication, so that what is revealed is made plainly intelligible to man.

Prophecy is an aspect of this revelation. True prophecy comes from God. Prophecy comes initially in the form of the spoken word through the lips of a prophet. It is imparted to a man or a woman by the Holy Spirit, and then, as the prophet speaks it out, men hear it and receive the prophecy.

True prophecy does not come because man wills it, but because God gives it.

Speaking of the Hebrew prophets, the New Testament contains this word:

First of all you must understand this, that no prophecy of Scripture is a matter of one's own interpretation, because no prophecy ever came by the impulse of man, but *men moved by the Holy Spirit spoke from God* (2 Peter 1:20-21, RSV).

A true prophecy originates with God. It is given to a selected individual by the inspiration of the Holy Spirit. As that individual speaks it out spontaneously, without premeditation, men hear a message borne from heaven to earth by the Spirit of God. The words of prophecy spoken in this way are pure. They do not fail because they express the intention of God in regard to the matter of which they speak.

With few exceptions, a prophecy exists first in the form of the spoken word. It is often also transcribed in some way and so exists in the permanent form of the written word. That is why we have today many of the words spoken by the ancient prophets of Israel recorded in the pages of the Bible.

God has sent His revelations to the human race through men who are holy and chosen by Him to declare that which He gives to them—such men as Moses, David, Joshua, Isaiah, Daniel, Joel, Micah, and many other inspired prophets of Israel. If given chiefly to men, it was not only to men, for Exodus 15:20 speaks of "Miriam, the prophetess, the sister of Aaron," and we read of "Deborah, a prophetess, the wife of Lappidoth," who led Israel for a time (Judges 4:4), and of "Huldah the prophetess" (2 Kings 22:14, RSV) who spoke the word of the Lord to Judah at a critical time.

The prophets of Israel spoke publicly that which the Holy Spirit imparted to them from God. You can get some idea of the mode of prophecy and of what is accurately claimed for it from the following declarations:

"The Lord called Moses, and spoke to him . . . saying, 'Speak to the people of Israel and say to them'" (Leviticus 1:1-2, RSV).

"And the Lord said to Moses, 'Speak . . . '" (Leviticus 21:1).

"And the Lord said to Moses, 'Tell . . . '" (Leviticus 22:1).

"The Lord said to Moses, 'Say to the people of Israel . . . '" (Leviticus 23:1).

"The Lord said to Moses, 'Command . . . '" (Leviticus 24:1-2).

All of these are instances of revelation to Moses by God.

"*The Spirit of God came upon Azariah* the son of Oded, and he went out to meet King Asa, and said to him, 'Hear me, Asa, and all Judah and

Benjamin: the Lord is with you, while you are with Him. If you seek Him, He will be found by you, but if you forsake Him, He will forsake you. . . . But you, take courage! Do not let your hands be weak, for your work shall be rewarded'" (2 Chronicles 15:1-2, 7, RSV).

Ezekiel says: "In the eleventh year, in the third month, on the first day of the month, the word of the Lord came to me. 'Son of man, say . . . '" (Ezekiel 31:1-2, RSV). The prophet could speak prophetically only by direct, immediate revelation, and only at the specific time it was given him from heaven.

Jeremiah says: "Now the word of the Lord came to me saying, 'Before I formed you in the womb I knew you, and before you were born I consecrated you; I appointed you a prophet to the nations'" (Jeremiah 1:4-5, RSV).

"The word that came to Jeremiah from the Lord, 'Thus says the Lord, the God of Israel: Write in a book all the words that I have spoken to you'" (Jeremiah 30:1-2).

Isaiah prophesied to the *nation:* "Therefore thus says the Lord, the Lord of hosts, 'O My people, who dwell in Zion, be not afraid of the Assyrians when they smite. . . . For in a very little while My indignation will come to an end, and My anger will be directed to their destruction. And the Lord of hosts will wield against them a scourge . . . '" (Isaiah 10:24-26, RSV).

Isaiah prophesied to an *individual:* "Then the word of the Lord came to Isaiah, 'Go and say to Hezekiah, Thus says the Lord, the God of David your father: I have heard your prayer, I have seen your tears; behold, I will add fifteen years to your life. I will deliver you and this city out of the hand of the king of Assyria, and defend this city'" (Isaiah 38:4-6, RSV).

"And the word of the Lord came to Zechariah, saying, 'Thus says the Lord of hosts: Render true judgments, show kindness and mercy. . . .' But they refused to hearken. . . . They made their hearts like adamant lest they should hear the law and the *words which the Lord of hosts had sent by His Spirit through the prophets*" (Zechariah 7:8-12, RSV).

These examples could be multiplied more than a hundredfold from the Old Testament. The prophets received the Word of God directly from God by the activity of the Holy Spirit, and they spoke it and wrote it.

Some of them also received revelation by visions, and they spoke and wrote what they saw. Genesis 15:1 says, "After these things the *word of the Lord* came to Abram in a vision. . . ."

Dreams are another means by which God sometimes conveys His truth to men. Jacob's son Joseph received revelation from God by dreams. The Prophet Daniel interpreted prophetic dreams. God declared through the Prophet Joel, "I will pour out My Spirit on all flesh; your sons and your daughters shall *prophesy,* your old men shall dream *dreams,* and your young men shall see *visions"* (Joel 2:28, RSV).

The active personal agent in communicating God's truth to man is the Spirit of the Lord. The direct result of the activity of the Holy Spirit upon men and women is sometimes seen in inspired prophecies . . . dreams . . . visions.

## Testing Prophets and Dreamers of Dreams

Though they are means God uses to convey His revelations to men, prophecy, dreams, or visions do not in themselves have any claim whatever to expressing truth. More false prophecy is uttered in the world than true prophecy, and by no close margin. Dreams flicker through our sleep like surrealist films in montage. Visions may, and often do, come from mental derangement or from evil spirits. It is only when the Holy Spirit uses these means that the content of the prophecy, the dream, or the vision is truth.

"For a dream comes with much business, and a fool's voice with many words," the Bible says, comparing the sometimes haphazard, fast-changing nature of dreams to the chaotic utterances of a fool. "For when dreams increase, empty words grow many; but do you fear God?" (Ecclesiastes 5:3, 7, RSV) There is nothing here to encourage delving into dreams for their "meaning."

It is especially important to understand that factual accuracy does not constitute evidence that a prophecy or a dream or a vision is from God. Factual accuracy is not an adequate test of the divine inspiration of any prophecy.

The Law of Moses speaks this word regarding prophecy: "If a prophet arises among you, or a dreamer of dreams, and gives you a sign or a wonder, and the sign or the wonder which he tells you *comes to pass,* and if he says, 'Let us go after other gods,' which you have not known . . . *you shall not listen to the words of that prophet* or that dreamer of dreams; for the Lord your God is testing you to know whether you love the Lord your God with all your heart and with all your soul . . . [and] that prophet or that dreamer of dreams shall be put to death" (Deuteronomy 13:1-5, RSV).

True prophecy is, of course, always factually accurate, but the acid test of all prophecy is whether it is in or out of accord with the Scriptures. A prophecy may be factually accurate and spiritually wrong. In that case it is a counterfeit of divinely inspired prophecy designed to impress men mentally but deceive them spiritually.

Such prophecy can be supremely deceiving precisely because it *is* factually accurate. In the Mosaic warning just cited, a prophet gives out a distinct sign or portent. That sign comes to pass exactly as he said it would. The human instinct is to proclaim the man a true prophet, to listen to him with close attention and respect, and perhaps give roughly equal weight to the rest of what he says.

Having accredited himself in the popular imagination as a true prophet, he then gives a piece of spiritual counsel. That counsel is false and stands in direct contradiction to the first commandment. The prophet is therefore a false prophet. Under the law of Moses, he was put to death so as to cleanse the land of an individual of evil religious bent. It was deemed a better thing for such a man to die than for the chosen land to become populated with false prophets speaking words contrary to the word of God and leading many people astray.

Israel was a nation placed under the law of God, not under a human law, and that law required the penalty of death in this and certain other cases (just as our law does for certain types of crimes). It would not do in our diverse and pluralistic society for there to be any supreme religious authority empowered to declare what is and what is not spiritually genuine and to enforce that judgment. But we do not have on that score to be made into the victims of false doctrine or prophecy.

A prophecy can be supernatural and factually accurate but false!

There are many false prophets and there is much false prophecy circulating in North America today. We can accurately define a false prophet as an individual who is spiritually connected to the supernatural, who speaks at times under the influence of supernatural powers, but whose authority as a prophet does not proceed from God and whose words and counsel are not in accord with the Word of God. In God's eyes, such a person is a great offender, because he deals in the supernatural—but not by God's commission!—and he dispenses spiritual counsel—in contradiction to God's Word!

At a time when the Lord had led the great Prophet Jeremiah to prophesy to the people certain important but unpleasant truths that they did not want to hear, other "prophets" were telling the people what they wanted to hear. That made it all the harder for Jeremiah to speak—in the face of sharp contradiction—and he asked the Lord about it. The Lord answered:

The prophets are prophesying lies in My name. I have not sent them or appointed them or spoken to them. They are prophesying to you false visions, divinations, idolatries and the delusions of their own minds. . . . I did not send them, yet they are saying, "No sword or famine will touch this land." Those same prophets will perish by sword and famine (Jeremiah 14:14-15).

Note that the lying prophets were boldly speaking *in God's name*, as His messengers, but without God's authority. What they gave out were "false visions" and "divinations" and their own mental "delusions." The term *divination* is quite accurately defined as "the art or practice that seeks to foresee or foretell future events or discover hidden knowledge, usually by the interpretation of omens or *by the aid of supernatural powers.*"

False prophecy is never any good, but it is doubly dangerous when it is spoken in some part by the inspiration, or prompting, of evil spirits. It is entirely possible for a false prophecy to be in part merely delusional, a product of the mind, while also being spiritually deceitful, a product of demonic inspiration.

A false prophet must be distinguished from a phony prophet. A false prophet has certain supernatural powers that he uses. A phony prophet is an outright fake.

A false prophet may be utterly sincere and unaware of his falsity. A phony prophet knows he is a fake.

A false prophet may practice gross spiritual deception without knowing it, because he himself is thoroughly deceived. A phony prophet knows exactly the deceptions he practices and how he practices them. He does not believe in what he is doing.

A phony can be discovered in his *methods,* if they are inspected closely enough. A false prophet can be clearly identified by his or her disagreement with the Word of God.

God wants man to know of, and to experience, that which is supernatural. But He speaks in the Scriptures to keep man entirely away from that which is bad for him and to lead him to that which will do him good.

It is as though a table were spread with mushrooms, half of them tender, succulent, and fully edible, and half of them deadly, all looking much alike. Your friend will tell you which are which. He will say, "Eat all you can of that, but keep away from all of that." He will identify them with precision for your benefit.

Then along comes your enemy, who wants you to be destroyed, and he says, "Look, dig in! Eat anything that looks good and tastes good to you!

If you listen to that narrow-minded maker of distinctions, you'll starve. Your so-called friend doesn't want you to have any mushrooms." The truth is he does. Your friend just doesn't want you to get any that will kill you.

Because there is a supernatural realm and because that realm impinges on human affairs, God has deliberately chosen to make a revelation to man regarding the supernatural that is fully adequate to keep any man who will pay it heed out of trouble. The Scriptures of the Old and New Testaments are the written Word of God, committed by the Holy Spirit to certain chosen men. They constitute a full and reliable declaration of what is true on the spiritual plane.

Whether by word or by vision, any revelation of which the Holy Spirit is the communicator from God to man is the truth about the facts of which it speaks.

The passage, quoted partially earlier on page 23, on the role of the Holy Spirit in revealing truths of the spiritual realm to man reads in full as follows:

As it is written, "Eye has not seen, nor ear heard, neither have entered into the heart of man the things which God has prepared for them that love Him." But God has revealed them to us by His Spirit, for the Spirit searches all things, even the deep things of God. For what man knows the thoughts of a man except by the spirit of man which is in him? So also *no one comprehends the thoughts of God except the Spirit of God.*

Now we [who are believers] have received not the spirit of the world, but the Spirit which is of God, that we might understand the gifts bestowed on us by God. And we impart this in words not taught by human wisdom but taught by the Spirit, interpreting spiritual truths to those who possess the Spirit (1 Corinthians 2:9-13, COM).

The passage declares that the Word of God is given to men by the Holy Spirit so "that we might understand" what is true and know what spiritual and supernatural gifts belong to men and women who truly believe in God and in the Lord Jesus Christ.

When I speak of the spiritual and the supernatural realm, I speak of that which lies beyond the physical and natural realm, beyond the reach of man's mind and senses, where God reigns, undiscoverable by man except by revelation.

# Journey into the Supernatural: Knowing What Is

There are in the creation orders of living beings who are intelligently active but unseen by man. They are capable of thought, of speech, of volition, of worship, of love, or of hate. Angels constitute one of these invisible orders of beings. They are servants of God, active on behalf of His will in the universe.

To reject this thought too quickly, to insist that all intelligent beings or that all beings whatever must be corporeal (physical), and therefore visible to human sight when in range of it, is to be materialistic to the point of moral blindness.

For a long time in the United States and Canada, the concept prevailed that it was impossible to be sensible and to believe in the supernatural. Rationalism ruled the day across some of the early decades of the twentieth century. It had no room for the supernatural and held it to be imaginary. That mindset also tended to push faith in God to the side.

This view strongly directed attention away from that which is spiritual to that which is natural and material.

While millions were thus self-blinded by a false rationalism, leaving them defenseless against the strategic workings of evil spiritual powers, those powers went relentlessly about their works of moral destruction under the convenient cover of that blindness, ruining lives, harming or tearing apart many families, and distressing the nation by it—all unseen.

By the time we finally began to wake up to the supernatural, this whole process was so far advanced that the popular consciousness was often made more aware of the evil supernatural realm than of the godly.

The idea that what you can't see or feel isn't real has, at last, been given some important setbacks. Science has discovered, for instance, that there is matter and also *antimatter.* "Research in physics has revealed the existence of mirror-image counterparts to all the particles composing matter on this planet," a news report said.

Physicists say there may be worlds, that there may be galaxies made up of antimatter. Some go farther. Isaac Asimov suggested that "somewhere, entirely beyond our reach or observation, there may be an antiuniverse made up almost entirely of antimatter." The universe that we know may be a kind of obverse of another universe, coexistent and concurrent, that we do not know.

The structure of reality as it is revealed in the Bible is not the same as that commonly conceived by man. God has not limited Himself to flesh and blood in creating orders of intelligent beings.

Most people would likely say that they inhabit a universe in which men are intelligent beings, a universe in which there probably are but possibly are not other highly intelligent beings dwelling elsewhere in space, and in which there is, somewhere, a supreme being, God.

Some men inhabit a universe, as they suppose, in which there is no God. The Bible says of them, "The fool has said in his heart, 'There is no God'" (Psalm 53:1, KJV).

The Bible presents a distinctly different picture of reality.

It declares that the God who revealed Himself to Israel is the creator and ruler of the universe.

It reveals that there is an order of intelligent created beings who are the servants of God, called angels.

It reveals man as a created order of intelligent beings made in the likeness of God. Man stands a little lower on the scale of creation than the angels (see Hebrews 2:7).

The Bible reveals an order of intelligent beings who are in active rebellion against God, called evil spirits or demons.

The Bible declares that they are led by an intelligent personality called Satan.

What is set forth here is what the Bible affirms to be the case, from Genesis to Revelation, the first and the last books of the Bible. If a person fails to grasp this, he cannot understand much of the Bible, because that is the structure of reality in which all the earthly events of the Bible—past and future—are set.

They are set in that structure because *that is what is.*

This can be ignored, but it cannot be escaped. Saying that demons do not exist in no way prevents them from intruding into the lives and the affairs of your family. The tragic fact today is that families whose members ignore large segments of this reality are becoming the victims of intelligent forces of evil whose activity they do not even vaguely suspect. This is especially true among young people, and parents are too often unprepared to cope with that which has come to harm or destroy their young.

Ignorance of these things is not God's program for man; it is the program of evil forces whose interest it is to conceal their activities from their intended victims. The Bible focuses the floodlight of revelation upon these forces, so that men may know of them and how to deal effectively with them.

What we need to know about is reality, spiritual reality as well as physical reality. What is important is reality, not fantasy.

I make this point because the assertion that there are invisible orders of beings is no license for creative acts of the mind. If we go out on a tangent of our imagination, or of someone else's possibly more fruitful imagination, we can people a universe full of noncorporeal, invisible, but *wholly imaginary* beings: hobgoblins, and elves, and ghosts and anything else that may strike our fancy or haunt our superstition.

I do not want any part of any system of thought that populates men's minds with phantoms that do not, in fact, exist. On the other hand I want to know, exactly, the orders of beings that *do*, in fact, exist and that operate intelligently and purposefully in the creation.

I want to know the whole extent of reality, as far as it may be known, visible and invisible, but I do not want to go one step beyond reality into fantasy and superstition. And, since neither the investigations of science nor the speculations of my mind can tell me anything about this that is in any degree reliable, I am dependent on revelation.

The biblical revelation—properly understood and not distorted or extended in any way—offers us a reliable, and in some respects a distinctly verifiable, guide to reality. It tells us of the existence and the activities of one order of invisible beings, having two categories: angels and demons. That is not revealed as a matter of curiosity, but because we need to know it.

The rational person ought to agree that if God declares by revelation that there is a being called Satan who actively and radically opposes all the purposes of God among mankind and who works with skill and inexhaustible energy against the best interests of men, it is a good thing for man to know it. In the biblical revelation, Satan is clearly exposed as the enemy of God and man.

By the same token Satan seeks desperately to conceal the fact of his existence. His methods depend for their effectiveness on the concealment both of their source and their purpose. Satan does not want you to believe that he exists. He wants you to believe positively that he does *not* exist. Then he may go about his business against you and against your family unsuspected and undetected.

If you, as a Christian, cannot be deceived about his existence, an effort will almost surely be made to conceal from you his works. The suggestion may be presented to your mind that to know much about him is dangerous, or may somehow detract from the attention you are to give to God, or that such knowledge somehow "glorifies" Satan.

Since the holy Bible is the one and only primary source by which a real knowledge of Satan is to be gained, and since God has, by direct inspiration of the biblical authors, seen to it that this knowledge is available to us, to shun it is thoroughly unwise. This does not mean that we have to concentrate on it unduly, but enough to gain a truly useful understanding of this master worker of evil.

I knew a young Christian who clearly loved the Lord and who at times suffered from what can best be called interferences with his life and soul. When I provided him with some scriptural material that I believed might give him key clues to what was going on, he drew back from them in fear. He expressed this verbally in a way that very nearly suggested a doctrine: that one should not look into such things but just keep one's eyes on the Lord.

No one kept his eyes on the Lord more steadfastly than the great Apostle Paul, but you could never have sold *him* that idea. He knew the Lord as few men—knew Him through "the fellowship of His sufferings" (Philippians 3:10, KJV), through so full a putting away of the self-life that the life of Christ was marvelously manifest in his body and being (2 Corinthians 4:10-11), through revelations exceeding those given to other servants of Christ (2 Corinthians 12:7). But Paul also knew the power and workings of the enemy and taught of them openly. He was both highly intelligent spiritually and keenly aware.

Nearly twenty years after the young Christian so flatly rejected a basic knowledge of certain biblically revealed facts about spiritual opposition and interference, though he had been blessed by the Lord in evident ways, he continued to suffer limitations. They restricted his field of action in life and prevented him from working on a full normal schedule, because he had at times to take weeks off for rest or special treatment. We are not forced to be wise to our enemy, but thank God we can be.

A man or a woman cannot really be well-poised (speaking figuratively here) between heaven and hell—between the blessings and power and love of the Lord and the craftiness and thievery of Satan—unless he or she knows and loves God *and* has an adequate, accurate working knowledge of the powers of evil.

Rational men, accustomed as they are to equating the name of Satan with a variety of purely fantastic caricatures, are a little too quick to smile knowingly when his name is mentioned. One of Satan's devices has been to promote ridiculous caricatures of himself that are so evidently *not* of reality that rational men associate his name with that which is mythical, or grotesque and absurd, and therefore intellectually contemptible.

The Bible does not speak of that kind of figure at all. Satan bears about as much resemblance to the figures in these myths as the God of the Bible does to Santa Claus. Satan is not a folk tale, nor is it at all likely that his body is as red as a boiled lobster.

Dismiss your familiar sharp-eared Mephistopheles entirely when considering Satan as revealed in the Bible. Associating the two confounds reality with mythic unreality.

That will make you do one of two things, neither of which is right. If you are superstitious, or irrational, you may adopt myths or fables for reality.

But if you are intelligent and rational, you are more likely to dismiss spiritual reality solely on the ground of the evident untenability of the mythic unreality with which you are so familiar.

Either way, you get a badly distorted picture of reality. The Bible will give you a balanced, factual, and demonstrably useful picture of reality regarding the things which are supernatural.

I say "useful" and "verifiable" because what the Bible says can be checked against human experience. If you match actual human experience with the revelation, you find that the experience confirms the revelation, and the revelation explains the experience—and tells you what to do about it. There are events and experiences occurring today that are not intelligible in any terms but those of the biblical revelation.

Without the Bible's light upon these events and experiences, we are helpless and bewildered by them. With that light, we not only can understand them, but we can take effective action concerning them.

The chapters that follow set forth what the Bible teaches to be the case about the unseen activity of spiritual beings and spiritual forces that affect men, nations, and history.

**2**

# THE
# BIBLICAL
# STRUCTURE
# OF REALITY

# The Invisible God: "I AM"

The central declaration of the Scriptures is that God *is*. The constant affirmation of the Scriptures is that God *acts*.

It has always been a wonder to me that some men can read the Bible right through and leave God out of it. That is a tremendous feat of intellectual excision. Everything is attributed to nature and man; nothing is attributed to God. The presupposition behind it is that there is no God. It requires a deliberate and selective blindness that screens out much of what the Bible is about.

If a man reads the Bible this way, he fails completely to understand it. As a record of events, the Bible goes beyond the telling of the event to reveal what lies behind the event. More precisely, it goes beyond the event to tell who—whose intelligence and will—lies unseen behind the event.

The Bible asserts, uniformly and from beginning to end, that there are different levels of intelligent and active life: beasts, man, angels, demons, Satan, God. More are unseen than are seen. All but the beasts are intelligent agents whose actions profoundly affect human history. To smash them all down to a single level of existence—the natural—is to read the Bible with resolute unintelligence.

The intelligent way to read the Bible is not to lump everything together without discrimination, assigning to man or to nature the acts of God. The intelligent and discriminate way to read the Bible is to assign the acts of man to man, the acts of Satan to Satan, the acts of God to God, the acts of angels to angels, and the acts of demons to demons. There are events today that are not intelligible apart from the biblical structure of reality.

The central declaration of the Scriptures is that God is. When God commissioned Moses to lead the people of Israel, Moses wondered if the people would recognize his commission as genuinely divine. God said to Moses, "Say this to the people of Israel: 'I AM has sent me to you'" (Exodus 3:14, RSV).

Through the Prophet Isaiah God said, "For I am God, and there is no other; I am God, and there is none like Me, declaring the end from the beginning, and from ancient times things not yet done" (Isaiah 46:9-10, RSV).

"In the beginning God . . . " are the first words of the Bible. Look at the first chapter of Genesis: "And God said. . . ." "And God saw. . . ." "And God made. . . ." "And God called. . . ." "And God set. . . ." "So God created. . . ." "And God blessed them. . . ." "So God created man. . . ." "And God saw everything that He had made, and behold, it was very good." The Bible is in large part an account of God in action.

The God of the Scriptures is a God of intelligent, purposeful, and efficient activity. He is the God who acts—who acts in human history. He is the God who speaks, and the signature of His divinity is that what He speaks far in advance is fully acted out in history.

In Genesis, and throughout the Bible, we see God exercising attributes of volition and intelligence and personality and speech of which man is capable on a diminished scale, because man is made in the image of God.

There are scholars who scoff at this as "an anthropomorphic God," perversely implying that man has simply imagined a god in man's own image. That is a great lie. They fail to grasp that God deliberately speaks to man about Himself in terms understandable to man. When the infinite God speaks to finite man, He speaks in terms measured to the mind and experience of man, just as a parent in speaking to a child brings his words and illustrations within the range of a child's comprehension. If God is like man it is because the faculties with which man is endowed are in major respects Godlike.

Genesis declares that "God said, 'Let Us make man in Our image, after Our likeness, and let them have dominion. . . .' So God created man in His own image, in the image of God He created him; male and female He created them. And God blessed them . . ." (Genesis 1:26-28, RSV). God endowed the first man Adam with attributes of will and intelligence and speech, so that man was like his Creator.

Man was made in the image of God, but sin entered the human race and man is now a badly marred image of God. Psalm 82:6 says, *"You are gods, and all of you are children of the Most High. But you shall die like men . . ."* (KJV).

## The Invisible God

The Bible says that "God is a spirit" (John 4:24, KJV). He is invisible and He is immortal (1 Timothy 1:17).

The invisible God has expressed Himself in the physical creation. His creative hand is seen in the natural order. Romans 1:20 says, "Ever since the creation of the world His invisible nature, namely, His eternal power and deity, have been clearly seen in the things that have been made" (COM).

God is a spirit, invisible to the eye of man, and He dwells on the spiritual plane. He is supernatural—that is, above nature. All that we see in the natural realm, from the intricate design of the atom to the great balanced wheels of the stars and galaxies, is the product of God's creative genius and His infinite power. Nature is His handiwork. The Milky Way alone is a system of over a hundred billion—yes, billion—stars!

"No one has ever seen God" (John 1:18). He cannot be discovered in any way other than by His own self-revelation made to man at times and by the means of His own choosing. The Scriptures—the sum of revelation after revelation given to Hebrew men over many centuries—are the appointed means that God uses to convey to mankind the truth about who He is, what His purposes are, and about the intelligent forces that operate in the supernatural realm.

God commenced His public revelation of Himself with Abraham and continued and expanded it through Isaac, Jacob, Joseph, Moses, David, the prophets, the apostles and other New Testament writers.

A man may learn something *about* God through teaching, but he only comes to *know* God by a direct, personal revelation to himself.

Jacob had learned about God and about the acts of God from his fathers, but he did not know God until God revealed Himself to Jacob. That is the difference between head knowledge and heart knowledge. A man may be told all about a certain young woman—her birthplace, her background, her schooling, her character, her activities—and he may have a very complete and accurate *concept* of what she is like, but it is not until he meets her that he begins to know her as she really is.

Jacob made a long journey from his father's house to his uncle's house. Chapter 28 of Genesis says, "Jacob left Beersheba, and went toward Haran. And he came to a certain place, and stayed there that night, because the sun had set. Taking one of the stones of the place, he put it under his head and lay down in that place to sleep. And he dreamed that there was a ladder set up on the earth, and the top of it reached to heaven; and behold, the angels of God were ascending and descending upon it! And behold, the Lord stood above it and said, 'I am the Lord, the God of Abraham your father, and the God of Isaac; the land on which you lie I will give to you and to your descendants. . . . Behold I am with you and will keep you wherever you go, and will bring you back to this land. . . .'

"Then Jacob awoke from his sleep and said, 'Surely the Lord is in this place, and *I did not know it.*' And he was afraid and said, 'How awesome is this place! This is none other than the house of God and this is the gate of heaven'" (RSV). Jacob named that place Bethel, "the house of God."

It was, by all appearances, an entirely ordinary place when Jacob stopped there to rest on his journey. The sun had set, darkness had settled over the land, and Jacob could find no shelter or comfort except a stone for his pillow. God was invisible to Jacob's eye there. The place did not impress him. He took a stone, lay down, and went to sleep. Bethel was different only because God chose at that place, on that night, to reveal Himself to Jacob.

Jacob sensed nothing of the presence of God by his own faculties at that place—"the Lord is in this place, and *I did not know it*"—until God deliberately broke through the unseen veil that divides the natural from the supernatural and revealed Himself to Jacob there. Then that ordinary place seemed "awesome . . . the house of God . . . the gate of heaven."

Jacob could have strained his natural faculties to their utmost and not have discerned anything more about that place than its physical attributes. The natural senses cannot penetrate into the supernatural at any time. They are stone dumb to the presence of God, or angels, or evil spirits, in any place.

Jacob received the revelation of God by three means: in a dream, by a vision, and by words—the words that God spoke to him that night.

God had spoken previously to Abraham: "To your descendants I give this land, from the river of Egypt to the great river, the river Euphrates . . ." (Genesis 15:18, RSV). The subsequent revelation spoken to Jacob was in strict accord with the revelation previously received by Abraham. That was an evidence of its validity. Supernatural revelations that contradict the Word of God—and they regularly occur—are not of God. They are borne in upon men by evil spirits, and they are meant to deceive. An account I read told of one such revelation that occurred in the Middle East, when a virgin figure appeared as by a vision in a church and promised the enemies of Israel success in eradicating her.

There at Bethel, God spoke to Jacob: "I am the Lord, the God of Abraham your father and the God of Isaac; the land on which you lie I will give to you and to your descendants. . . . Behold, I am with you and will keep you wherever you go, and will bring you back to this land; for I will not leave you until I have done that of which I have spoken to you" (Genesis 28:13-15, RSV).

Bethel was the beginning of Jacob's personal knowledge of God. No longer was it by family tradition and teaching alone that he knew of God. Now he knew God for himself.

Later, at Peniel, Jacob was to experience a greater and more thoroughly transforming revelation of God that would alter his character permanently and cause his name to be changed, from Jacob (which means a supplanter, one who pushes somebody else aside), to Israel (which means prince with God).

This God who revealed Himself to Jacob at Bethel is the God who is. He identified Himself to Jacob as the God of Abraham, because that is exactly who He is. This was not because Abraham had been a religious genius or a masterful theologian, but because God had deliberately revealed Himself to Abraham, had made certain promises to him, and because Abraham had believed God and obeyed Him. The God of Abraham is the God who makes promises and keeps them.

This God of the Hebrews is the only true God. He is a living being, supreme above all others in the universe, Creator of all that is, the Author of life. All others who are worshiped by men as gods are either creatures of imagination or evil spirits seeking to usurp God's place among mankind.

"No man has seen God at any time," the Apostle John writes in 1 John 4:12 (KJV).

The Scriptures speak of God:

—as "the invisible God" in Colossians 1:15.

—as "the King eternal, immortal, invisible, the only God" in 1 Timothy 1:17.

—as "Him who is invisible" in Hebrews 11:27.

This passage in Hebrews says that "by faith Moses left Egypt, not being afraid of the anger of the king [Pharaoh]; for he endured as *seeing Him who is invisible*" (RSV).

God is "the blessed and only Sovereign, the King of kings and Lord of lords, who alone has immortality and *dwells in unapproachable light, whom no man has ever seen or can see*," 1 Timothy 6:15-16 (RSV).

Psalm 104:2 says that God covers Himself "in light as with a garment."

The Scriptures admonish men, "Let us offer to God acceptable worship, with reverence and awe, *for our God is a consuming fire*" (Hebrews 12:28-29, RSV).

"God is light and in Him there is no darkness at all," the Bible says in 1 John 1:5. It says also that "the fear of the Lord is the beginning of wisdom" (Proverbs 9:10).

## The Personal God

The God revealed by the Bible is a personal God, who reveals Himself to individual men. He deals directly and personally with women and men. He seeks them out to belong to Him. The Prophet Hanani told Asa king of Judah, "The eyes of the Lord run to and fro throughout the whole earth, to show Himself strong in behalf of them whose heart is perfect toward Him" (2 Chronicles 16:9, KJV).

Adam, when he had sinned, tried to hide from God in Eden, but God found him there. Men, in their sin, seek to hide themselves morally from God. Some say that there is no God, and that gives them a temporary and delusive relief from concern over the consequences of their sins. Others tell themselves that God is very remote and unconcerned with man; that God set the universe in motion and then went off to some distant eyrie in the heavens to attend to matters far more important than the little affairs of men.

Scholars especially are prone to regard it as vanity that God would take any particular notice of men. Their supposition is that the God of the cosmos could not be a God interested in fine details. All of these are ways of declaring that man is free to sin and go his own way because God is blind to sin or so withdrawn from humanity as to be indifferent to individual acts.

The Bible gives the flattest possible contradiction to this. It states that "even the hairs of your head are all numbered" (Luke 12:7, RSV). The God who knows the number of the hairs of your head surely knows the number of the sins of your heart.

And the God who knows the number of your hairs also knows the number of the stars. "He tells the number of the stars; He calls them all by their names" (Psalm 147:4, KJV). Or, as Isaiah puts it, in majestic poetry: " 'To whom then will you liken Me, or shall I be equal?' says the Holy One. Lift up your eyes on high, and see: Who created these? He brings out their host by number; He calls them all by name. . . . Why do you say, O Jacob, and speak, O Israel, 'My way is hid from the Lord, and my right is disregarded by my God'?" (Isaiah 40:25-27, COM).

Here the Lord refutes the idea that His power over the creation takes His attention away from people on the earth.

When God revealed Himself to Hagar, Abraham's servant, she called Him "the God who sees me" (Genesis 16:13). In warning against a certain sin, the Scripture adds, "For a man's ways are in full view of the Lord, and He examines all his paths." And later, "The eyes of the Lord are everywhere, keeping watch on the wicked and the good" (Proverbs 5:21; 15:3).

Man has devised telescopes to probe outward into the creation, and with them and by radio search he has discovered some corners of the universe. Only lately has man begun to know something of the vastness of the creation. When a photographic atlas of the universe in 200 sky maps was published at the Palomar Observatory, it was reported that "far beyond in outer space there are galaxies similar to the Milky Way. Sometimes these galaxies group into clusters. Whereas only a scant three dozen such clusters were known before the sky survey, now more than a thousand have been found"—1,000 clusters of galaxies.

Congregated in *one* such system, called the Coma Cluster, are about 11,000 galaxies.

If the Milky Way were observed from an immense distance away, it would be seen as a crowd of billions of suns (some estimate as many as 200 billion), arranged in a flat spiral structure. Its density would be so great as to suggest, to the untutored eye, that they are jammed together, with very little space between them. But we know how perfectly the solar system is arranged around our sun as just one tiny wheel within this massive swarm of suns.

Our solar system is a beautifully ordered mote in a single galaxy—having something less than the prominence of the dot over one *i* in an unabridged dictionary. (Actually, some scratch-pad figures by a scientist show the solar system is as prominent in the Milky Way as one dot over an *i* would be on a shelf of 2,850 unabridged dictionaries.)

There are times when the galaxies "collide." One galaxy meets another head-on and they pass through each other and eventually come out on the other side, with no star having brushed another.

"The galaxies within reach of telescopes like that on Mount Palomar probably number in the billions," it was reported in the atlas after the sky survey. The atlas of the universe mapped the sky out to a depth in space of 600 million light-years. (A light-year is about six trillion miles.) Isaac Asimov wrote that "the 200-inch telescope can make out objects up to an estimated two billion light-years away, and there is no sign of an end of the Universe—yet."

The galaxies *within reach* appear to number in the billions. If each galaxy is a family of billions of stars, we begin to get a notion of the extent of it—billions of billions—yet God knows the number of the stars and He "calls them all by their names."


The God of Creation is the God of the cosmos to be sure. He is also the God of the most minute details.

Man has devised microscopes and particle accelerators that enable him to look inward upon the creation, and by them he has sliced matter down to fractions so fine as to make a billionth of an inch sound like an exceedingly crude measurement, but he has not yet managed to pierce to that which is so fine that it does not have clear structure and intelligent design.

An uncle of mine, Dr. Robert H. Phillips, is a nuclear physicist who worked for 25 years at the Brookhaven National Laboratory on Long Island. He has occasionally given me an evening-long talk on the sub-atomic world (remember when we used to think of an atom as something terribly small?) and has told me of the precision of nuclear measurement.

Nuclear measurements carried out with a particle accelerator deal in "such sizes as 10 to the minus 25th square centimeters," Dr. Phillips told me. "That means that if you put one over one and add twenty-five zeroes—

$$\frac{1}{10,000,000,000,000,000,000,000,000}$$

—then you have written in ordinary decimal system the fraction of a square centimeter that a nucleon occupies in space." That is *one ten-septillionth of a square centimeter.*

"That isn't the very smallest thing that we look in on by any means," he said. "The subdivision of matter certainly reaches to smaller objects than that."

Nucleons are protons or neutrons. "Nobody really believes that a nucleon is the last subdivision of matter," Dr. Phillips said. Physicists have found that nucleons are composed of still more elementary particles—quarks.

If man looks outward he sees the creative hand of God, and he cannot search to the end of it; and if man looks inward he sees the creative hand of God, and he has not yet come to the end of it.

Study everything between quarks and quasars and you find structure, motion, order, a lawful stability, arrangement, and design.

Whenever man seems to be near the inner or outer limits of the creation, another layer unfolds to his astonished gaze. The God who made the planets also designed the molecule. He who formed man also formed the living cells. The God of the whole is also the God of the parts. And He cares particularly for man.

Hear David, the poet-king of Israel: "When I consider the heavens, the work of Your fingers, the moon and the stars which You have ordained; What is man, that You are mindful of him? and the son of man, that You visit him?

"For You have made him a little lower than the angels, and have crowned him with glory and honor. You made him to have dominion over the works of Your hands; You have put all things under his feet. . . . O Lord our Lord, how excellent is Your name in all the earth!" (Psalm 8:3-6, 9, KJV)

There is nothing hidden from God. There is no refuge a man can find in which he can hide from the searching eyes of God. "Nothing in all creation is hidden from God's sight. Everything is uncovered and laid bare before the eyes of Him to whom we must give account" (Hebrews 4:13).

"Nothing is hid that shall not be made manifest, nor anything secret that shall not be known and come to light. . . . Whatever you have said in the dark shall be heard in the light, and what you have whispered in secret shall be proclaimed upon the housetops" (Luke 8:17; 12:3, RSV).

"His eyes are upon the ways of a man, and He sees all his steps. There is no gloom or deep darkness where evildoers may hide themselves" (Job 34:21-22, RSV). Death will not remove sinners from the face of God; it will bring them to the judgment.

At a time of great decline of faith, even the elders of Israel said, "The Lord does not see us; the Lord has forsaken the land" (Ezekiel 8:12).

The *King James Version* rendering of Genesis 16:13 is, "Thou God seest me."

To the saying of certain evil men, "The Lord does not see; the God of Jacob does not perceive," the psalmist delivers this sharp rebuke:

"Understand, O dullest of the people! Fools, when will you be wise? He who planted the ear, does He not hear? He who formed the eye, does He not see? . . . The Lord knows the thoughts of man, that they are but a breath" (Psalm 94:7-11, RSV).

Also, "Woe to those who seek deep to hide their counsel from the Lord, and their works are in the dark, and they say 'Who sees us?' and 'Who knows us?' Surely your turning of things upside down shall be esteemed as the potter's clay: for shall the work say of him who made it, 'He made me not?' Or shall the thing framed say of him who framed it, 'He had no understanding?' " (Isaiah 29:15-16, KJV)

"O Lord, You have searched me and known me!" David says in Psalm 139. "You know when I sit down and when I stand up. You discern my thoughts from afar. You search my path out before me and know all my ways. Even before a word is on my tongue, You, O Lord, know it fully. . . . Where can I go from Your Spirit? Or where shall I flee from Your presence?

"If I ascend to heaven, You are there! If I make my bed in Sheol [where the dead lie], You are there! Wherever I go Your hand will lead me, and Your right hand will hold me. If I say, 'Let darkness cover me . . . ,' even the darkness is not dark to You, the night is bright as the day; for darkness is as light with You.

"You formed all my inward parts and knit me together in my mother's womb. . . . Your eyes beheld my unformed substance" (COM). Here *The Living Bible* seems to capture David's exuberant love for God: "Thank You for making me so wonderfully complex! It is amazing to think about. Your workmanship is marvelous—and how well I know it. . . . Search me, O God, and know my heart. . . . Point out anything You find in me that makes You sad, and lead me along the path of everlasting life."

## The Invisible God Made Visible

There is no more awesome and wonderful fact than that God, the Creator, in making Himself known to man, has come to man as man.

Of the several means of revelation God uses to reveal the truth about Himself, the chief one is the incarnation: God coming as a man.

We are living on a visited planet. That is far more than a New Testament idea. That God Himself—the Creator—would come to Israel as a man is prophesied in the most explicit terms in the Old Testament. Isaiah 9:6 says, "For unto us a child is born, unto us a Son is given; and the government shall be upon His shoulder; and His name shall be called Wonderful, Counselor, The mighty God, The everlasting Father, The Prince of Peace" (KJV).

Think of that: A man born a Jew—nothing less than Emmanuel, a word that means *God with us.*

Never has the natural and the supernatural, the human and the divine, come together so absolutely as in the incarnation. It is the crux, the decisive center, of human history.

Yet it is more: it is the means by which the final conquest of all spiritual opposition—of Satan and evil—is to be enforced and fulfilled.

The very first prophecy of the Bible told of a spiritual conflict and revealed its outcome. God said that the seed of the serpent, Satan, would bruise the heel of a promised Deliverer, but that the seed of the woman (a man to be born of a woman, yet divine) would bruise the serpent's head—a fatal wound (see Genesis 3:15).

The whole vast warfare of evil with good, of angels with demons, of Satan against God, would come to its climax, and be perfectly resolved, as the outcome of the incarnation.

The scale of this is staggering, and, since our redemption is all bound up in the incarnation, it touches us profoundly. We who believe, dwelling on this little planet Earth, will live for tens of millions of years, on into hundreds of millions of years, stretching on and out into endless eternity. Though not without origin at a point in time, we who are saved by the act of incarnational redemption will be as immortal as God!

Glance again at Isaiah 9:6. In fewer than forty words, the mystery of divinity inseparably conjoined to humanity is crucially revealed in a bit of Hebrew Scripture: A child was to be born to the people of Israel by a Hebrew woman. This child would be a son. He would be very like other infants, yet unlike any other ever born.

Of that human baby it would be said with utter accuracy that He *is* "The mighty God, The everlasting Father, The Prince of Peace." What a leap that is—from heaven to earth, from birthplace to eternity! A round trip from the throne to the womb to a throne—for "The government will be upon His shoulders . . . and of the increase of His government and peace there will be no end" (Isaiah 9:6-7).

The Hebrew Prophet Micah, speaking for the living God, tells where the birth of this child was to take place:

> But you, O Bethlehem Ephrathah,
> who are little to be among the clans
>     of Judah,
> from *you* shall come forth for *Me*
>     One who is to be ruler in Israel,
> whose origin is from of old,
>     even from everlasting (Micah 5:2, com).

The incarnation must take place at Bethlehem and, of course, it did.

Jesus was born there to a young woman, a virgin—a baby formed in her womb, as Luke 1:35 tells, by the Holy Spirit. By that exception to male generation, one man would come into the world with no inheritance of sin.

These remarkable prophecies of Isaiah and Micah reach from eternity past to eternity future—this child's origin is "even from everlasting," and His government will have "no end."

In no sense is the incarnation a Gentile notion, as some ignorantly say. It is all right there, in sublime simplicity, in the words of the Hebrew prophets. They were given inspired boldness to speak of this ultimate convergence, and union, of the human and the divine—"God with us"—or, as John expressed it, "the Word made flesh."

"In the beginning was the Word," John's Gospel starts, "and the Word was with God, and the Word was God. . . . He was in the world, and the world was made through Him, yet the world knew Him not. He came to His own and His own people received Him not. But to all who received Him, who believed in His name, He gave power to become the sons of God" (John 1:1, 10-12, com).

God thus made His most complete revelation of Himself to mankind in a Jew named Jesus. Jesus perfectly showed forth the character of God in His person. He, alone among all men, had no part in sin from birth to death.

His rightful claim to earthly and universal preeminence includes the awesome fact that this man is the Co-creator: "All things were made by Him, and without Him [nothing] was made that was made," John 1:3 declares (kjv).

The man Jesus "is *the image of the invisible God,* the first-born of all creation; for in Him all things were created, in heaven and on earth, visible and invisible, whether thrones or dominions or principalities or authorities—all things were created through Him and for Him. . . . For in Him all the fullness of God was pleased to dwell, and through Him to reconcile to Himself all things, whether on earth or in heaven, making peace by the blood of His cross" (Colossians 1:15-16, 19-20, rsv).

Jesus made the invisible God visible to man in His own person. He claimed, in absolute harmony with the Old Testament prophecies of the Messiah, to have lived before His birth at Bethlehem. Jesus said, "I came from the Father and have come into the world; again, I am leaving the world and going to the Father" (John 16:28, rsv).

"Before Abraham was born, I am," Jesus said (John 8:58). In that, He declared Himself to be God.

He knew this to be true of Himself and proclaimed it openly, a fact that renders the opinion that Jesus was merely "a good man" untenable.

**48**

If the things He said were not true, Jesus was no "good man."

Jesus said, "Truly, truly I say to you, the hour is coming, and now is, when the dead will hear the voice of the Son of God, and those who hear will live."

And, "I seek not My own will but the will of Him who sent Me . . . the works which the Father has granted Me to accomplish . . . bear Me witness that the Father has sent Me. . . . *His voice you have never heard, His form you have never seen;* and you do not have His word abiding in you, for you do not believe Him whom He has sent" (John 5:25, 30b; 36-38, RSV).

He said to the disciples: "If you had known Me, you would have known My Father also. . . .' Philip said to Him, "Lord show us the Father, and we shall be satisfied.' Jesus said to him, 'Have I been with you so long, and yet you do not know Me, Philip? *He who has seen Me has seen the Father'*" (John 14:7-9, RSV).

"I will not leave you desolate; I will come to you," Jesus told His disciples shortly before His death. "Yet a little while, and the world will see Me no more, but you will see Me; because I live, you will live also. . . . He who loves Me will be loved by My Father . . . and We will come to him and make Our home with him" (John 14:18-23, RSV).

The Book of Hebrews begins with these words: "God, who at sundry times and in diverse manners spoke in former times to the fathers by the prophets, has in these days spoken to us by His Son, whom He has appointed heir of all things, by whom also He made the worlds; who being the brightness of His glory, and *the express image of His person,* and, upholding all things by the word of His power, when He had by Himself purged our sins, sat down on the right hand of the Majesty on high" (Hebrews 1:1-3, KJV).

The Old Testament is explicit on the humanity and the divinity of the Messiah. The New Testament, in the declarations of Jesus as well as those of the apostles and writers, is unequivocal on the divinity of the man Jesus.

The scope of all this is nothing if not magnificent, having the sweep of eternity in it. Yet ponder the *humility*—the willingness of God to put aside the grandeur of His all-embracing authority and power in His created universe and be born as a man, to walk among us, to speak with us, to die *for* us! The love that went that far is unsearchably deep.

I am grateful to Major Ian Thomas, the superb British Bible teacher, for the persuasive talk I once heard him give from the Scriptures pointing out that Jesus, divine and absolutely human, lived and walked and spoke and did miracles, not as someone who was half-God/half-man. Jesus, Major Thomas said, did what He did by faith *as a man.*

Jesus walking on the sea, he said, was not a demonstration of divinity—levitating, so to speak, or suspending the law of gravity. Jesus walked on the water by faith that His Father would hold Him up. With every step, Major Thomas said, Jesus in effect "heard" His father say, "*I am.*" And with every other step, Jesus affirmed, "*Thou art.*" And so it was, step by step atop the sea, "*I am*" "*Thou art*" "*I am*" "*Thou art*" "*I am*" . . . all by faith.

When Peter, seeing Jesus walking in this way, said, "Lord, . . . bid me to come to You on the water," Jesus did not say, "It is too much for you. You are just a man. I am the Son of God." Jesus said, "Come."

Peter did, and not for just a step or two, for we read, "So Peter got out of the boat and walked on the water and came to Jesus." Having done that, he then took notice of the stormy water, was afraid and "began to sink." When Jesus reached out His hand to catch him, He asked Peter just one thing, "Why did you doubt?"

What Jesus did as a man by absolute faith in His Father, Peter had also done by faith, up to the point where doubt swept in (Matthew 14:28-33, RSV).

If it were otherwise, then Jesus could not truly have said to His disciples, "He who believes in Me will also do the works that I do, and greater works than these he will do, because I go to the Father" (John 14:12, RSV).

Had Jesus acted in and by His divinity, rather than as a man, His works would be a demonstration, not of what men can do by faith in God, but of what a divine man alone can do. An invitation to other men to follow in such works would be a mocking tantalizing of feeble mortals.

How could sinful men reproduce the works of a sinless, divine man? That gap would be too wide for us to cross. In fact, God closed the gap by crossing it Himself and living as a man!

Paul wrote of Jesus "who, though He was in the form of God, did not count equality with God a thing to be grasped, but *emptied Himself,* taking the form of a servant, being born in the likeness of men. And being found in human form He humbled Himself and became obedient unto death, even death" on a bloody and painful cross (Philippians 2:6-8, RSV).

Jesus "emptied Himself" and further "humbled Himself." Born as a man, He walked as a man. He did not do His own works. "The Son can do nothing of Himself," Jesus told the people, "but only what He sees the Father doing. Whatever the Father does, the Son does likewise" (John 5:19, COM).

"I can do nothing on My own authority; as I hear, I judge," Jesus said (John 5:30, RSV).

Jesus walked and worked, not as God but as an *empowered man,* ever looking by faith to His Father in heaven for what He did and what He said: "I have not spoken on My own authority," Jesus declared; "the Father who sent Me has Himself given Me commandment what to say and what to speak. . . . I speak what the Father has told Me" (John 12:49-50, COM).

At another time, He said, "The words that I say to you I do not speak on My own authority, but the Father who dwells in Me does His works" (John 14:10, RSV).

What was true of Jesus is true of us. We can do nothing for God on our own authority.

Jesus spoke of "the works that I do *in My Father's name"* and said that "they bear witness to Me" (John 10:25). He then told *us* to do His works in His name, by faith, saying, "If you shall ask any thing in My name, I will do it" (John 14:14, KJV).

Jesus, who could do nothing without His Father, told us, "apart from Me you can do nothing" (John 15:5). For Jesus as for us, the works of God are done exclusively by faith. The degree of dependency on God for all such works is necessarily total, and that is conducive to close fellowship with God. The open secret of Jesus' power and authority was His close, daily, intimate walk with His Father, often refreshed and kept alive by special times of prayer apart. "The One who sent Me is with Me," Jesus said. "I always do what pleases Him" (John 8:29).

Fellowship with man, restored by atonement, is what the coming of Jesus Christ to this earth 2,000 years ago was about. An intimate faith relationship to Himself, through Jesus, is what God supremely wants for man.

You can learn about God by reading the Bible, but God wants more than that for you. He wants you to know Him personally, if you don't already. God specifically offers to come into your life in so definite a way that you will know He has come in; you will know He is there, with you and in you. It doesn't make any difference who you are. "God is no respecter of persons" (Acts 10:34, KJV). The social and class distinctions of the world count nothing with Him. After He had risen from the grave, Jesus said, "Behold, I stand at the door and knock; if any one hears My voice and opens the door, *I will come in to him* and eat with him and he with Me" (Revelation 3:20, RSV).

I remember the morning many years ago when I asked Him to come into my life on the basis of His promise. He came in that day, and my life was immediately and wonderfully changed—far beyond my own capacity to alter it—and that change has never lost its freshness or its power.

## God's Love and His Fury

Most men have heard that "God is love." The passage that declares this says: "He who loves is born of God and knows God. He who does not love does not know God, for God is love. In this the love of God was made manifest among us, that God sent His only Son into the world, so that we might live through Him. In this is love—not that we loved God but that He loved us and sent His Son to be the expiation for our sins" (1 John 4:7-10, RSV).

God created the world and man, and everything else that He created, as the expression of His generosity and love. "God saw that everything He had made . . . was very good." God intends that His creation be joyously perfect. There is a glimpse of this primeval state of things in the Bible. God spoke these words to Job:

"Where were you when I laid the foundation of the earth? Tell Me, if you have understanding. Who determined its measurements—surely you know! Or who stretched the line upon it? On what were its bases sunk, or who laid its cornerstone, when the morning stars sang together and all the sons of God shouted for joy?" (Job 38:4-7, RSV)

That is the way it was, and that is the way it ceased to be when Satan brought sin and hatred and rebellion into God's creation, and later persuaded man to turn his back on God.

The beauty, the symmetry, the order, the sheer loveliness of what God made was all designed to serve the best interests of man and to afford him scope for achievement and discovery, endless provisions, pleasure and joy. It has been terribly impaired by the introduction into its affairs of the active principles of sin and self-will, whose effect is to spread blight and ruin in many different forms over the landscape of God's creation.

Contrary to a common notion of it, the quality of God's love is not bland. The love of God is strong. The love of God is discriminate, and it is purposeful. The perfect complement to the love of God—that which throws it into strong relief and shows its purity—is the hatred that God expresses toward that which is evil. God hates sin. He hates evil.

The greater an individual's sensitivity to that which violates what he truly prizes, the less patience he has with it. A love of purity requires by its nature a coequal abhorrence of filth. A symphony orchestra conductor will not rest until he drives everything that mars the symmetry, beauty, and perfection of the music out of the performance. He is intolerant of that which disfigures it musically, and the greater his love of the score the more absolute his intolerance becomes.

Because He is love, God is consistently intolerant of everything that violates His own intention in creation. God hates evil with pure and furious hatred because He sees that it is constantly at work to destroy what He has made—at work to destroy man, to destroy families, to destroy nature, to destroy civilization, to destroy harmony, to destroy joy. He does not look upon it as man does, that is, relatively, because He sees it not limitedly but in the whole path of its effective ruination.

The intention of Satan is to make moral, spiritual, and even physical chaos and wreckage out of as much of God's creation as he possibly can. Satan enlists man in that attempt, by appealing to his lawless lusts and passions. We can see the effects of that all around us, in our cities, in the nation, in the world.

Man is infected with the moral disease that God calls sin. God is not tolerant of human sin because He knows that if it were allowed to go unarrested it would ultimately corrupt and destroy everything in its reach.

It is God's will to separate man from sin, but if any person refuses to be separated from his sin, if he exhibits a resolute preference for it, then he must bear the full penalty for it, death. God will put such a person in quarantine forever in a place of fire prepared for the devil.

God seeks to separate the sinner from the sin, so that He may express His pure love to the sinner and His pure wrath against the sin. That is what He did in sending Jesus to die on the cross for sin. God placed man's sin upon Jesus at Calvary and judged it there with the penalty of death. "He Himself bore our sins in His body on the tree" (1 Peter 2:24). The love of God is strong. Strong enough to send His Son to die for sin.

God has spoken and demonstrated His love for man and His abhorrence of sin in this one act—Christ's voluntary death on the cross.

> Surely He has borne our griefs, and carried our sorrows; yet we esteemed Him stricken, smitten by God and afflicted. But *He was wounded for our transgressions,* He was bruised for our iniquities; upon Him was the chastisement that made us whole, and with His stripes we are healed. . . . The Lord has laid on Him the iniquity of us all (Isaiah 53:4-6, rsv).

That is why Jesus could cry, "It is finished!" (John 19:30) The work that He came to do was done. The penalty of sin was fully paid. Death and evil lost their power to take men captive and hold them tight. "Since the children have flesh and blood, He too shared in their humanity so that by His death He might destroy him who holds the power of death—that is, the devil—and free" mankind (Hebrews 2:14).

God's love is expressed in the creation, but it is supremely expressed in the act of redemption.

God cannot go farther in loving man and in dealing with sin than to die for sin. To go another step would be to tolerate sin. Every person who accepts the blood atonement is cleansed of sin and escapes the wrath that God must, by the deepest necessity of His holy nature, express against sin. The person who rejects the full atonement God has provided for sin, by the blood of Jesus Christ, leaves God with no option but to bar him from His presence and to confine him forever to what the Bible calls "the lake of fire."

The love of God, as well as the wrath of God, is shown throughout the pages of the Bible. It is sheer ignorance to state, as some do, that the God of the Old Testament is a God of wrath, while the God of the New Testament is a God of love.

The anger of God against evil is shown not less in the New Testament than in the Old. The New Testament is full of the expressed fury of God at evil.

The scope of the outpouring of God's wrath against sin is shown in several chapters of the Book of Revelation, and its magnitude is as great as any judgment of God recorded in the Old Testament, including the destruction of Sodom and Gomorrah.

"For the wrath of God is revealed from heaven against all ungodliness and wickedness of men," declares Romans 1:18 (rsv).

In the Old Testament, Moses declared, "The Lord your God is a consuming fire" (Deuteronomy 4:24).

The New Testament also declares, "Our God is a consuming fire" (Hebrews 12:29).

"Hate evil, and love good," the Old Testament enjoins (Amos 5:15). It is not possible to love the good without hating the evil, because the evil actively antagonizes and runs against the good.

Jesus perfectly mirrored His Father in this respect too. In Hebrews, the Father says of the Son, "You have *loved righteousness* and *hated iniquity*; therefore God, even Your God, has anointed You with the oil of gladness above Thy fellows" (1:9, kjv).

Jesus' love is seen in the Gospels, and so is His fury at sin and dissimulation. Matthew, chapter 23, records Jesus' address to the self-righteous religious leaders: "Woe to you, hypocrites...." "Woe to you, blind guides...." "You blind fools ... hypocrites!" "You serpents, you brood of vipers, how are you to escape being sentenced to hell?"

In the Old Testament Jeremiah prophesied, " 'Woe to the shepherds who destroy and scatter the sheep of My pasture!' says the Lord.... 'I will attend to you for your evil doings,' says the Lord.... Behold, the storm of the Lord! Wrath has gone forth, a whirling tempest; it will burst upon the head of the wicked" (Jer. 23:1, 19, rsv).

Jesus repeatedly warned men that if they continued in sin they would at last "be thrown into hell, where their worm does not die, and the fire is not quenched." He spoke of men who will "go to hell, to the un-quenchable fire" (Mark 9:43, 48). He said, "The Son of man"—speaking of Himself—"will send His angels, and they will gather out of His kingdom all causes of sin and all evildoers, and throw them into the furnace of fire; there men will weep and gnash their teeth. Then the righteous will shine like the sun in the kingdom of their Father. He who has ears, let him hear" (Matthew 13:41-43, RSV).

When there is a fire, true love warns of the fire; love will not say there is no fire. God's love seeks to keep men from a destiny of fire.

The New Testament speaks of a day "when the Lord Jesus is [to be] revealed from heaven with His mighty angels in flaming fire, inflicting vengeance upon those who do not know God. . . . They shall suffer the punishment of eternal destruction and exclusion from the presence of the Lord and from the glory of His might" (2 Thessalonians 1:7-9, RSV).

Isaiah prophesied, "For behold, the Lord will come in fire, and His chariots like the stormwind, to render His anger in fury, and His rebuke with flames of fire. For by fire will the Lord execute judgment . . . upon all flesh" (Isaiah 66:15-16, RSV).

When it falls upon men, the judgment of God is always the last resort of His faithful dealing with them. He calls to them first in love. He invites them to come to Himself to receive the restoration guaranteed by the sacrificial blood. He has made every provision for their full liberation from sin.

God will not depart by so much as a shade from His original plan for a perfect and joyous creation. At judgment there will be a complete separation of the just from the unjust and a complete, eternal exclusion of the unjust from any participation in the future. There will then ensue the most wonderful effects.

> "In that day the deaf shall hear
>    the words of a book,
> And out of their gloom and darkness
>    the eyes of the blind shall see.
> The meek shall obtain fresh joy in the Lord
> . . . the ruthless shall come to nought
>    and the scoffer cease,
>    and all who watch to do evil shall be cut off . . ."
>                           (Isaiah 29:18-20, RSV).

"The wolf shall dwell with the lamb, and the leopard shall lie down with the kid, and the calf and the lion and the fatling together, and a little child shall lead them ... for the earth shall be full of the knowledge of the Lord as the waters cover the sea" (Isaiah 11:6, 9, RSV).

Both testaments promise a new heaven and a new earth in which no sickness or sorrow or evil will dwell.

The Old Testament says: "For behold, I create new heavens and a new earth, and the former things shall not be remembered or come into mind. But be glad and rejoice for ever in that which I create..." (Isaiah 65:17-18, RSV).

The New Testament says: "Then I saw a new heaven and a new earth; for the first heaven and the first earth had passed away.... And I saw the holy city, New Jerusalem, coming down out of heaven as a bride adorned for her husband; and I heard a great voice from the throne saying, 'Behold, the dwelling of God is with men. He will dwell with them, and they shall be His people, and God Himself will be with them; He will wipe away every tear from their eyes, and death shall be no more, neither shall there be mourning nor crying nor pain any more, for the former things have passed away'" (Revelation 21:1-4, RSV).

No honest man can drive a wedge between the Old Testament and the New as to the love of God, the wrath of God, atonement by blood, salvation, judgment, and the future renewing of the creation to an unblemished, sinless, wholly joyous state.

All of these, including the act of Creation itself, conduct—as the rivers run to the sea—straight to the person and work of our Lord Jesus Christ. He is the "Alpha and the Omega, the beginning and the ending" (Revelation 1:8, KJV).

Much more could be said about the nature and character and purposes of God as shown in the Bible. In summary, these primary truths are noted:

God is a living being, a Person. God is a spirit. He is immortal and invisible. God is love. He hates evil. Nothing can be hid from Him.

The God who revealed Himself to Israel is the Creator. Jesus Christ, who "brought life and immortality to light through the Gospel" (2 Timothy 1:10) by tasting "death for every one" (Hebrews 2:9), is the express image of the Father:

"He who sees Me sees Him who sent Me" (John 12:45, RSV). This Man showed us by His life and words and acts exactly who God is.

The supernatural and the natural, the human and the divine, found their ultimate conjunction in the birth, the person, the life, the death, the bodily resurrection and ascension into heaven of Jesus Christ. The godly preacher Paris Reidhead used to raise his hand, point his index finger skyward and say, "There's a *Man* in glory!" In some absolutely real sense the God who became a man will be a glorified Man forever.

## Angels

The intelligent order of created beings who serve God is called angels. They have to do with God, and they also have to do with man. Angels are in many ways very much like men. They possess attributes of intellect and personality and will similar to those of man. Angels can speak. So like men are the angels that it is possible to sit and talk with one and not to know that he is an angel, but to take him for a man. The New Testament says, "Do not neglect to show hospitality to strangers, for thereby some have entertained angels unawares" (Hebrews 13:2, RSV).

Angels are spiritual beings. They dwell on the spiritual plane, above nature. They are normally invisible to man. They enter the natural order, visibly and invisibly, but it is not their primary abode. They stand a step higher on the ladder of creation than man.

Man, who is set at the summit of the natural order, was made "a little lower than the angels" in the scale of creation. David wrote, "What is man that You are mindful of him . . . ? For You have made him a little lower than the angels, and crowned him with glory and honor" (Psalm 8:4-5, KJV).

The whole natural order, including man's physical body, is mortal. The angels are immortal. They are not subject to disease or death.

Quite a lot of eye-popping material concerning angels has been presented to the Christian public in books or by tape-recorded teaching. The reliability of some of it is shaky. I knew a successful Christian businessman whose demeanor was characteristically modest and sensible. He believed that the Lord wanted him to uncover new sources of wealth for use in advancing the Gospel overseas. Under the influence of a very peculiar teaching, he believed that he could "order" angels to take a part in this effort by commanding them to do certain things in Jesus' name.

Such a belief, which in Scripture has no leg to stand on, seems a quite dangerous invitation to spiritual presumption. The truth about angels is, all in itself, quite sensational enough; we do not need to reach to sensationalize the truth.

A major difference between angels and men is their mobility. The soul and the spirit of man are perfectly united to his body, and his body is primarily bound to the earth. Thus, as a being, man is limited in his mobility (though he can increase it immensely by inventions that cooperate with the laws of nature).

Angels are in no way bound by the laws of the natural realm. They can travel immense distances very swiftly. A physical object must move at a stated rate from one point in the natural creation to another. There is no shortcut; the whole distance must be physically traversed.

A spiritual being is subject to no such necessity. Angels can enter the natural realm. They can submit to and obey its laws, but they can, at will, leave it and ignore its laws and limitations. Far more significantly, angels can inhabit the natural realm without being observed and without obeying its laws. They rove, unseen, among men accomplishing their appointed work.

Angels can, if they wish, make themselves visible to men, but they almost never do. When they do, they often look very much like men. So much so that it is sometimes difficult, or impossible, to tell them apart. At times the Bible uses the term man interchangeably with the term angel.

God can open a man's eyes so that he may see angels, but He rarely does. In such a case, the eye is allowed to observe beings and objects which exist on the spiritual plane. That is entirely different from an angel coming into the natural order and becoming visible there. When a person's eyes are opened to see the angels, he sees them in the spiritual realm as they are: though the angels have the form of men, they are seen in their splendor and full beauty, and they would not then be mistaken for men.

When angels visit men visibly, they come into the natural realm and show themselves in the physical similitude of men. That which is invisible becomes visible in the natural realm and the angels move among men as men.

In chapter 19 of Genesis, there is an account of a visit by angels to Abraham's nephew Lot:

"The two angels came to Sodom in the evening, and Lot was sitting in the gate of Sodom. When Lot saw them, he rose to meet them, and bowed himself with his face to the earth, and said, 'My lords, turn aside, I pray you, to your servant's house and spend the night, and wash your feet; then you may rise up early and go your way.' ... So they turned aside to him and entered his house, and he made them a feast, and baked unleavened bread, and they ate" (19:1-3, RSV).

These were not men; they were angels. Yet they had feet and they needed to wash them after their walk, and Lot prepared a feast for them "and they ate."

There is no indication at this point that Lot knew that these visiting strangers were angels. He treated them like wayfarers, with the best hospitality of the East. He was entertaining angels unawares.

If angels eat of man's food, as they sometimes do, men have also eaten of angels' food, according to Psalm 78:25. We read that God "rained down upon [Israel] manna to eat, and gave them the grain of heaven. Man ate of *the bread of angels;* He sent them food in abundance" (RSV).

In their unseen ministry, angels do things that have very practical consequences in human lives. When the Prophet Elijah, exhausted with the relentless persecution he suffered from an evil government, "lay down and slept under a broom tree," the Scripture says that "an angel touched him, and said to him, 'Arise and eat.' And he looked, and behold, there was at his head a cake baked on hot stones and a jar of water. And he ate and drank . . . and went in the strength of that food forty days and forty nights to Horeb the mount of God" (1 Kings 19:5-6, 8, RSV).

When Abraham sent his servant out to seek a wife for his son, Isaac, from among his kinsmen, Abraham told him, "The Lord, before whom I walk, will send His angel with you, and prosper your way" (Genesis 24:40, RSV).

The angels' purpose is to serve God and carry out His orders concerning men. The angels protect and assist humans who serve God. Sometimes they hinder and oppose men who directly defy God's purposes. Sometimes they destroy men. God has a plan in history, and the angels have an active role in advancing that plan.

I heard Charles E. Fuller, founder of the Fuller Theological Seminary, tell of a highway accident in which the car he was driving went off the roadbed and turned over. He said that as the car turned over, he momentarily saw angelic protectors that completely surrounded him, and he received not a scratch in an extremely dangerous accident. He said that while he was turning upside down he saw himself fully enveloped in light.

The psalmist says that God "makes His angels spirits; His ministers a flaming fire" (Psalm 104:4, KJV).

There are three key words in that Old Testament verse—"angels" . . . "spirits" . . . "ministers." This accords perfectly with Hebrews 1:14 in the New Testament, which says the angels are "*all ministering spirits*, sent forth to minister to men who are the heirs of salvation." The angels are spirits and they are ministers of God to men.

The word *angel* literally means messenger. The angels are messengers of God sent to men. As ministers and messengers, angels are active in spiritually important or critical work, not in trivial errands. Again and again in the biblical accounts, angels are seen acting in interventions of great spiritual significance.

After Adam followed his wife in disobeying God in Eden, it became urgent that man "not be allowed to reach out his hand and take also from the tree of life and eat, and live forever," as Genesis 3:22-24 recounts. So God sent members of a certain class of angels called cherubim "and a flaming sword flashing back and forth" to keep fallen man from the tree of life.

In the Old Testament, the Prophet Zechariah talked repeatedly with angels who brought him messages from God: "And the angel who talked with me came again, and waked me. . . ." "Then the angel who talked with me came forward and said to me. . . ." "Then I said to the angel who talked with me, 'What are these, my Lord?' And the angel answered me . . ." (Zechariah 4:1; 5:5; 6:4-5, RSV).

In the New Testament, a priest named Zechariah talked with an angel: "Now while he was serving as priest before God . . . it fell to him by lot to enter the temple of the Lord and burn incense. . . . And there appeared to him an angel standing on the right side of the altar of incense. And Zechariah was troubled when he saw him, and fear fell upon him. But the angel said to him, 'Do not be afraid, Zechariah, for your prayer is heard, and your wife Elizabeth will bear you a son, and you shall call his name John. And you will have joy and gladness, and many will rejoice at his birth; . . . he will be filled with the Holy Spirit, even from his mother's womb. And he will turn many of the sons of Israel to the Lord their God. . . .' And Zechariah said to the angel, 'How shall I know this? For I am an old man . . .'" (Luke 1:8-18, RSV).

A man who is far more diligent than I at tabulation informs me that angels are referred to 172 times in the Old Testament and 108 times in the New Testament, and there is a consistency of description throughout.

Angels work actively in protecting the people, whether individuals or groups of people who belong to God. Psalm 91 is the great psalm of divine protection ("A thousand may fall at your side, ten thousand at your right hand, but it will not come near you"), and it says: "He will give His angels charge over you, to guard you in all your ways. On their hands they will bear you up, lest you dash your foot against a stone. . . .

Because he cleaves to Me in love, I will deliver him; I will protect him because he knows My name" (Psalm 91:11-12, 14, RSV). The protection of God is for those who love Him and trust Him and worship and serve Him.

"The angel of the Lord encamps round about them that fear Him, and delivers them" (Psalm 34:7, KJV). In His charge to Moses, God said, "Depart, go up hence, you and the people whom you have brought up out of the land of Egypt, to the land of which I swore to Abraham, Isaac, and Jacob, saying, 'To your descendants I will give it.' And *I will send an angel before you,* and I will drive out the Canaanites, the Amorites, the Hittites, the Perizzites, the Hivites, and the Jebusites" (Exodus 33:1-2, RSV).

## Warriors from Heaven

The victories of Israel against foes and invaders often came by the active intervention of unseen forces. When the huge army of Assyria, which had easily overrun a series of nations, came to take Jerusalem and the inhabitants had no military power to repel them, God intervened: "And that night the angel of the Lord went forth, and slew a hundred and eighty-five thousand in the camp of the Assyrians; and when the men arose early in the morning, behold, these were all dead bodies" (2 Kings 19:35, RSV). "So the Lord saved Hezekiah and the people of Jerusalem from the hand of Sennacherib, king of Assyria . . ." (2 Chronicles 32:22).

The great English poet, Lord Byron, celebrated this event in lines that began:

*The Assyrian came down like the wolf on the fold.*
   *And his cohorts were gleaming in purple and gold;*
*And the sheen of their spears was like stars*
      *on the sea . . .*
[and ending with this phrasing:]
*And the might of the Gentile, unsmote by the sword,*
   *Hath melted like snow in the glance of the Lord.*

The Apostle Peter was thrown into prison. His friends prayed for him. "Peter was sleeping between two soldiers, bound with two chains, and sentries before the door were guarding the prison; and behold, an angel of the Lord appeared, and a light shone in the cell; and he struck Peter on the side and woke him up, saying, 'Get up quickly.' And the chains fell off his hands. . . . And he went out. . . .

"He did not know that what was done by the angel was real, but thought he was seeing a vision. When they had passed the first and the second guard, they came to the iron gate leading into the city. It opened to them of its own accord, and they went out and passed on through one street, and immediately the angel left him" (Acts 12:6-10, RSV).

In his discourse on God's love for children, Jesus said: "See that you do not despise one of these little ones; for I tell you that in heaven their angels always behold the face of My Father who is in heaven" (Matthew 18:10, RSV).

When I was a boy, a relative on my father's side had a large family. One day, a four-year-old child caught fire at the stove and was badly burned. Just before death, the child became radiant and said to his parents, "Oh, don't you see all the angels here!" They saw only the dying child, but they saw that their child was dying in evident joy. Those angels had come as a guardian escort to take the living soul of the dying child from earth to heaven and into the presence of God.

Jesus told of a rich man and a poor man, both of whom died. The rich man went to Hades and was in torment. "The poor man died and was carried by the angels to Abraham's side," Jesus said (Luke 16:22, COM).

John Wesley, the English evangelist who rode through England alone on horseback for more than forty years, once met a man who told him that he had been hiding beside the road and would have come out to rob Wesley. When Wesley asked him why he had not, the man said it was because of the men riding beside Wesley. But the evangelist had been riding alone. What the man had seen, Wesley thought, was an escort of angels.

Horses are mentioned in the Scriptures in immediate association with angels. The Prophet Elisha saw "the horsemen" of Israel. Later, Elisha's servant's eyes were opened and he saw that "the mountain was full of horses and chariots of fire round about Elisha" (2 Kings 6:17). Revelation 19:14 says, "And the armies of heaven, arrayed in fine linen, white and pure, followed Him on white horses" (RSV).

Angels are not all equal in occupation or power. Some angels are set as rulers and leaders over other angels in the work of God. The Bible speaks of angels and archangels. Two of the latter, who occupy very elevated places in the plan of God, are named. They are Michael and Gabriel.

God described Michael to the Hebrew Prophet Daniel as "the great prince who has charge of your people" (Daniel 12:1, RSV). He would appear to be the leader of the angelic forces assigned to protect the nation Israel.

Because of a burst of anger in front of the people of Israel, God forbade Moses to enter the Promised Land. Instead he died in Moab. Deuteronomy 34:1-5 says: "So Moses the servant of God died there in the land of Moab, according to the word of the Lord, and *He buried him* in the valley in the land of Moab opposite Bethpeor; but *no man knows the place of his burial* to this day" (RSV). Undoubtedly because of Moses' sin of anger, Satan came to make some claim regarding the body of Moses, but Michael intervened. Verse 9 of Jude says that "the archangel Michael, contending with the devil, disputed about the body of Moses" (RSV).

The Angel Gabriel appears twice by name in the Old Testament and twice in the New Testament, each time on errands of the highest consequence to the plan of God.

The Prophet Daniel received a vision setting forth future world history in broad outline. "When I, Daniel, had seen the vision, I sought to understand it; and behold, there stood before me *one having the appearance of a man.* And I heard a man's voice . . . and it called, 'Gabriel, make this man understand the vision.' So he came near where I stood, and when he came I was frightened and fell on my face. . . . He said, 'Behold, I will make known to you what shall be . . .' " (Daniel 8:15-17, 19, RSV).

At another time Daniel fasted and prayed. "While I was speaking in prayer, the man Gabriel, whom I had seen in the vision at the first, came to me in swift flight at the time of the evening sacrifice. He came and said to me, 'O Daniel, I have now come out to give you wisdom and understanding' " (Daniel 9:21-22, RSV).

It is this same angel, Gabriel, who appeared to Zechariah the priest in the temple and told him he would have a son. When Zechariah said to the angel, " 'How shall I know this?' . . . the angel answered him, 'I am Gabriel: I stand in the presence of God; and *I was sent* to speak to you, and to bring you this good news' " (Luke 1:18-19, COM).

It is interesting that the reactions of Daniel and of Zechariah to the appearances of the Angel Gabriel were virtually identical. Daniel says, "When he came, I was frightened and fell on my face." "And Zechariah was troubled when he saw him, and fear fell upon him."

The young woman, Mary, had the same reaction. "In the sixth month the Angel Gabriel was sent from God to a city of Galilee named Nazareth, to a virgin betrothed to a man whose name was Joseph. . . . And he came to her and said, 'Hail, O favored one, the Lord is with you!' But she was greatly troubled at the saying. . . . And the angel said to her, 'Do not be afraid, Mary, for you have found favor with God. And behold, you will conceive in your womb and bear a son, and you shall call His name Jesus. He will be great, and will be called the Son of the Most High, and the Lord God will give to Him the throne of His father David . . .' " (Luke 1:26-32, RSV).

The birth of Jesus was announced by angels: "In that region there were shepherds out in the field, keeping watch over their flock by night. And an angel of the Lord appeared to them, and the glory of the Lord shone around them, and they were filled with fear. And the angel said to them, 'Be not afraid, for behold, I bring you good tidings of great joy, which shall come to all the people; for to you is born this day in the city of David a Saviour, who is Christ the Lord.' . . . And suddenly there was with the angel a multitude of the heavenly host praising God and saying, 'Glory to God in the highest, and on earth peace, good will toward men'" (Luke 2:8-14, COM).

Though they are normally invisible, that does not mean that angels are weak or powerless. They are extremely powerful, and their power can be applied with force in the physical realm. In terms of what he can accomplish physically, an angel is stronger than a man. Over and over again, the Scriptures emphasize the power of the angels.

"Bless the Lord, O you His angels, you mighty ones who do His word, hearkening to the voice of His word! Bless the Lord, all His hosts, His ministers that do His will!" (Psalm 103:20-21, RSV)

Peter says that angels are "greater in might and power" than men (2 Peter 2:11).

The resurrection of Jesus from the dead was attended by angels. A man named Joseph of Arimathea took the body of Jesus and laid Him "in a tomb which had been hewn out of the rock; and he rolled a stone against the door of the tomb" (Mark 15:46, RSV).

A guard of Roman soldiers was sent to the tomb with orders to make it secure, so the body of Jesus could not be stolen. "So they went and made the tomb secure by sealing the stone and setting a guard. . . .

"And behold, there was a great earthquake; for an angel of the Lord descended from heaven and came and rolled back the stone, and sat upon it. His appearance was like lightning, and his clothing white as snow. And for fear of him the guards trembled and became like dead men" (Matthew 27:66; 28:2-4, COM).

"And when the Sabbath was past, Mary Magdalene and Mary the mother of James, and Salome brought spices, so that they might go and anoint Him. And very early on the first day of the week they went to the tomb when the sun had risen. And they were saying to one another, 'Who will roll away the stone for us from the door of the tomb?' And looking up they saw that the stone was rolled back, for it was very large.

"And entering the tomb, they saw a young man sitting on the right side, dressed in a white robe; and they were amazed. And he said to them, 'Do not be amazed; you seek Jesus of Nazareth, who was crucified. He is risen, He is not here; see the place where they laid Him. But go, tell His disciples and Peter that He is going before you to Galilee; there you will see Him'" (Mark 16:1-6, RSV).

That "young man" seated in the tomb on the right side was an angel (see John 20:12-13).

The Prophet Daniel was thrown into a pit of lions for defying an edict against praying to God. King Darius, under whom Daniel served, respected and valued him. The king had not intended to cause Daniel harm, but he had been tricked by a conspiracy of officials into signing the edict that Daniel broke. The officials, jealous of Daniel, wanted to do away with him.

"At break of day, the king arose and went in haste to the den of lions. When he came near to the den where Daniel was, he cried out in anguish and said to Daniel, 'O Daniel, servant of the living God, has your God, whom you serve continually, been able to deliver you from the lions?' Then Daniel said to the king, 'O king, live for ever! *My God sent His angel* and shut the lions' mouths, and they have not hurt me, because I was found blameless before Him...'" (Daniel 6:19-22, RSV).

On the night of Jesus' betrayal, the Apostle Peter, in typical haste, "drew his sword, and struck the slave of the high priest, and cut off his ear. Then Jesus said to him, 'Put your sword back into its place; for all who take the sword will perish by the sword. Do you think that I cannot appeal to My Father, and He will *at once send Me more than twelve legions of angels?* But how then should the Scriptures be fulfilled, that it must be so?'" (Matthew 26:51-54, RSV)

Once Jesus fasted for forty days. At length it was over, "and behold, angels came and ministered to Him," according to Matthew 4:11 (RSV).

Some clergymen asked Jesus a long and complicated question about a woman married many times. They wanted to know whose wife she would be in heaven. Jesus replied, "Is not this why you are wrong—because you do not know the Scriptures nor the power of God? For when they rise from the dead, they neither marry nor are given in marriage, but are like angels in heaven" (Mark 12:24-25, COM). Angels are not male and female; they do not have offspring. They do not die.

"The sons of this age marry and are given in marriage," Jesus said, "but those who are accounted worthy to attain to the next age and to the resurrection from the dead neither marry nor are given in marriage, for they cannot die any more, because they are *equal to angels* and are sons of God, being sons of the resurrection" (Luke 20:34, COM).

The angels are a numerous company. Psalm 68:17 says, "The chariots of God are twenty thousand, even thousands of angels; the Lord is among them, as in Sinai, in the holy place" (KJV). Jesus said that, at His call, twelve legions would come from heaven—50,000 to 60,000 angels. Hebrews 12:22 speaks of "the city of the living God, the heavenly Jerusalem, and to innumerable angels." The Apostle John writes, "Then I looked, and I heard around the throne . . . the voice of many angels, numbering myriads of myriads and thousands of thousands" (Revelation 5:11, RSV).

Except when they move among men as men, angels are repeatedly spoken of in terms of fire, brightness, white and shining clothing, and in terms of the fear that humans feel when they first see them.

Angels have the power to destroy. The two angels who visited Lot told him to get out of Sodom with his family in the morning, "for we are about to destroy this place . . . and the Lord has sent us to destroy it" (Genesis 19:12-13, RSV).

On another occasion, "God sent the angel to Jerusalem to destroy it; but when he was about to destroy it, the Lord saw, and He repented of the evil, and He said to the destroying angel, 'It is enough, now stay your hand.' And the angel of the Lord was standing by the threshing floor of Ornan the Jebusite"—a specific angel in a specific place—"and in his hand a drawn sword stretched out over Jerusalem. . . . Now Ornan was threshing wheat; he turned and *saw the angel*, and his four sons who were with him hid themselves" (1 Chronicles 21:15-16, 20, RSV).

Angels are seen in the Scriptures executing the judgments of God. In the great judgments that are to fall upon the earth, as detailed in Revelation 8 and 9, angels are centrally involved.

Jesus promised that He would come again to the earth, and angels would come with Him. Exactly when that coming will be is the best kept secret of the universe.

Jesus said the people of the earth "will see the Son of man coming on the clouds of heaven with power and great glory; and He will send out His angels with a loud trumpet call, and they will gather His elect from the four winds, from one end of heaven to the other. . . . But of that day and hour no one knows, not even the angels of heaven, nor the Son, but the Father only" (Matthew 24:30-31, 36). "When the Son of man comes in His glory, and all the angels with Him, then He will sit on His glorious throne. Before Him will be gathered all the nations. . . ." (Matthew 25:31-32, RSV).

The day is coming "when the Lord Jesus is revealed from heaven with His mighty angels, in flaming fire, inflicting vengeance on those who do not know God . . ." (2 Thessalonians 1:7-8, RSV). "So it will be at the close of the age. The angels will come out and separate the evil from the righteous, and throw them into the furnace of fire; there men will weep and gnash their teeth," Jesus declared (Matthew 13:49-50, RSV). "For the Lord Himself will descend from heaven with a shout, with the voice of the archangel, and with the sound of the trumpet of God, and the dead in Christ shall rise first," Paul wrote in 1 Thessalonians 4:16 (COM). Jesus once told the crowd that was following Him that "whoever is ashamed of Me and of My words in this adulterous and sinful generation, of him will the Son of Man also be ashamed, when He comes in the glory of His Father with the holy angels" (Mark 8:38, RSV).

## Satan:
## The Name Means "Adversary"

Though some deny it and few really understand it, no human being escapes evil. "Man is born to trouble as surely as sparks fly upward," an ancient sage remarked (Job 5:7).

Some of the biggest and hardest questions that people face boil down to the single word, "Why?" This was the mystery that the man Job could not fathom while he went through the searing anguish of evidently senseless suffering, though he later understood it very well.

Except to the radically self-blinded, evil in the world is an observable phenomenon. It seems to be a fact of nature, but it is much more than that: evil has a *source*.

As much as evil may seem unorchestrated and general among mankind, a ruling purpose lies behind it. It is part of a much larger scheme than the random aspect of its occurrence normally indicates.

The Bible does not hide—it expressly reveals—the fierce dynamic that lies hidden behind evil. It declares that God has an enemy and adversary: Satan. He is a being of great power, but he is in no sense a kind of dark force equal to the Creator. All of the saved are going to see his power cut short, and they will outlive him by the factor of infinity!

Until that occurs, he is man's enemy too. While we do not need to fear him, it is urgent to know what *can* be known about him—right up to the measure of the biblical revelation as it deals with, and unmasks, this master strategist of evil.

Satan is at work today in the world, and in the United States and Canada, with an intensity unmatched in our experience, and the Scriptures warn that his activity will be stepped up greatly among the nations, both in degree and in velocity, as end-time events accelerate. Unless we are aware of this, we will be caught short and find ourselves unable to cope with the events that descend upon us.

The first rule of intelligent spiritual warfare and resistance to evil is—*know your enemy.* Know who he is, what he intends, what he does, and how he goes about it.

An accurate knowledge of Satan will not harm you in any way, but a lack of such knowledge may allow him to inflict damage upon, or to interfere with, you or your family to your entire bafflement—while he works in the way he so greatly prefers, hidden and unsuspected.

Satan very actively promotes ignorance of himself. He would prefer that you believe that he does not exist. He will go to almost any length to perpetuate and enforce that persuasion in a man's thinking. He can work much more effectively against us if we think he is not working at it.

The Bible pointedly exposes Satan and exposes his tactics for our sake. It gives us all the knowledge we need to resist effectively and to overcome.

What a believer needs first is not the practical particulars of spiritual warfare but an overview, very much as a field general needs to know the whole scope of the military situation—what and where his resources are, and where and what the enemy's resources are. When he knows that, then he can begin to plot a working strategy.

The Scriptures sharply etch for our sake the existence, the person, the character, the purposes, and the tactics of Satan. While this does not fall in the category of pleasant knowledge, it is a thing for which we can give thanks to God. What Satan does, and how he does it, are the concealed factors behind many eruptions of evil in the world.

The Bible alone reveals him initially to the understanding of man, but once that is done, we can apply this knowledge to experience in a way that makes our knowledge of immediate personal value. As crucial as facts and principles are, they come alive and come into far surer and stronger possession, when they are tested in the actual arena.

That is why missionaries to lands of deep darkness are often way ahead of church people on the home front in their working knowledge of the powers of darkness. Wrestling against massive, adamant spiritual opposition on the basis of biblical reality, they have overthrown it in actual fact, gaining openings for the Gospel where none had existed.

Believers have tended to regard such distant lands as places of spiritual conflict while looking upon North America as a scene of spiritual peace. If that was so in earlier days, it has ceased to be the case. Yet believers have often remained in a stance of peace in the face of satanic assault upon our society.

When he can lull believers by it, Satan *speaks* peace while in the act of war, tearing things down. "His speech was smoother than butter, yet war was in his heart," King David wrote of one who had deceitfully turned against him (Psalm 55:21, RSV). "His words were softer than oil, yet they were drawn swords."

Paul wrote that men must "keep Satan from gaining the advantage over us; for we are *not ignorant of his devices*" (2 Corinthians 2:11, COM). The reverse of that is: If we remain ignorant of Satan's devices, he will gain advantage over us. In plain fact, he already has gained such advantage. He has gained such advantage especially over millions of young people.

The Bible is very clear on the point of Satan's origin and person and his domain. Satan is seen at work in Genesis, the first book of the Bible, and in Revelation, the last book, and he is seen at important junctures in between.

There have been many appeals to "tell it like it is," to rip off all the sham and the pretense, to lay matters bare to their roots. That is exactly what the Bible does. It tears away the camouflage, the cover-up, and exposes this architect of evil: who he is and how he works.


Satan is a living creature. He is not corporeal or physical. He is a spiritual being, but that does not make him any less real. The fact that he is invisible and powerful greatly serves him in the pursuit of his cause. The idea that Satan is a term for a generalized influence of evil—instead of the name of a specific living personality—is a strictly antibiblical idea.

The name Satan does not speak of an impersonal influence. It speaks of a single, identifiable, distinct living being with a will, a personality, and a highly directed intelligence.

One thing we have to do to get a clear view of Satan is to divest ourselves of any caricatures of him as a leering boiled-live-lobster-red being with a tail and a pitchfork. There is no such creature. The difference between the Satan revealed in the Scriptures and all such cartoons is vast.

The being now called Satan—the name means "adversary"—was at his creation a very beautiful being. His beauty has been corrupted by evil, but he still disguises and presents himself to much of mankind as god.

The Bible declares that "God is a spirit." It describes angels as "ministering spirits." The Bible calls Satan

> *the prince of the power of the air,*
> *the spirit that is now at work in the*
> *sons of disobedience* (Ephesians 2:2, RSV).

So Satan is a spirit—that is, an intelligent living being who is invisible to the natural eye. This one brief portion tells a great deal about him: First, that he is a prince. Second, that his domain has an important center in the atmosphere of the earth, in the envelope of air in which the earth is enclosed. Third, that Satan is active, or "at work." Fourth, that his activity is carried out through the lives of fallen or sinful men, who are called "the children of disobedience." It is a stark fact that Satan exercises some degree of actual authority and control over all people who have never become worshipers of the living God.

The Bible calls Satan "the god of this world" (2 Corinthians 4:4, RSV). The statement gives us some idea of the tremendous scope of his activity and power on the earth. It is a literal, precisely accurate description of the position that he occupies with respect to mankind, but it requires reflection to grasp the measure of it.

The appalling fact is that God is rejected now, as He has been through nearly all of human history, as the Lord of mankind. God is not the spiritual leader of most people.

Satan has succeeded in usurping the place that belongs only to God among the masses of mankind. He has substituted his will for the will of the living God among multiplied millions. He has taken the central place that God ought to occupy in people's lives and has polluted lives with other things—including false religions.

If the living God were worshiped by mankind, the earth would be "full of the knowledge of the Lord as the waters cover the sea"—as someday it will be (Isaiah 11:9). The earth is now filled with conditions that suit Satan, "the god of this world"—strife, treachery, bloodshed, tyranny, upheavals, crime, suffering, addiction, commotions, wars and rumors of wars, death.

Satan is a ruler, and he is consistently spoken of in terms of royal power. As well as being designated "the god of this world," he is called "the prince of this world" (John 12:31).

As a prince and ruler, Satan has a domain, and he also has subjects. He is seen at times in Bible accounts in heaven or near God's throne, but he has no authority there, only temporary and limited access. His domain, the chief arena of his activity, includes the earth and the atmosphere of the earth. His subjects are sinful people, millions of them, whom he has blinded and led astray from the living God—by false religions, by bald denials of God's existence and love, by cults of state that demand entire devotion contrary to the Word of God (notably communism and fascism), by many lies of philosophy, by every form of idolatry.

Satan, the usurper, is wholly conscious of his position as the god of this world. When Jesus faced and met the temptations of Satan, "The devil took Him to a very high mountain, and showed Him all the kingdoms of the world and the glory of them; and he said to Him, 'All these I will give You, if You will fall down and worship me'" (Matthew 4:8-9, RSV).

This panoramic showing was an extraordinary supernatural event, and there was enough to it to make it a credible, though utterly deadly, offer. The kingdoms of this world and their glory do significantly reflect the sway of Satan. "Jesus said to him, 'Begone, Satan! for it is written, "You shall worship the Lord your God, and Him only shall you serve"'" (Matthew 4:10, RSV).

Like all other created beings, Satan can only be in one place at a time. He is not omnipresent, as God is, but he manages to seem ubiquitous. Because he exists on the spiritual plane, he is probably able to move with almost instantaneous speed. At times he comes directly to an individual on the earth to oppose or to tempt him.

"Resist the devil," the Bible says, "and he will flee from you" (James 4:7). You cannot resist him, of course, if you do not believe he is there.

### Satan's Policy of Secrecy

Satan's purpose is to draw people away from God and to keep people away from Him by every means he can use. In accomplishing this, Satan finds it convenient and strategic to conceal his own identity and his activities as much as possible from human view. He is an enemy, an adversary. Therefore he moves under the cover of secrecy.

Consider the tactics of an enemy in battle. The enemy finds it far easier to send fire upon his target if he conceals and hides his own position, so that he may strike by sudden surprise. Sneak attack, it is called.

To obtain this advantage, the enemy moves in darkness, by stealth, and takes his position over the target in a hidden or camouflaged place. He wants the other side to be as unalert as possible, unguarded, unsuspecting, exposed to attack. The less the intended victims know of his existence, his position, his intention, and his power, the greater the advantage to him in bringing injury or death upon them.

These are among the tactics of Satan toward mankind. The less you know about Satan the better he likes it. Then you will do little or nothing to prepare yourself, or your family, or your children, against his activities, and by that neglect many are made his victims.

There are three ways you can know of Satan and his work: By what the Bible reveals about him. By personal experience (as it may occur while you follow the Lord Jesus—never by seeking it out). By reading of the personal experiences of other believers.

Satan, the active adversary of the purposes of God, is the supreme leader of a rebellion against God.

God is the creator. Satan is the destroyer. The first words of the Scriptures are "In the beginning God created . . . ," and every book of the Bible tells us something about the character and purposes of God. Almost from the very start, Satan worked craftily to introduce sin and destruction and misery into the affairs of mankind.

## The Author of Idolatry

The being the Bible calls Satan is a spiritual leader. As the head of the rebellion against God and against the government of God, he works, using every means he can, to see that God is supplanted as the center of man's desire.

*He does not greatly care to what secondary object or desire or pursuit a man gives his chief loyalty, just so long as it is not to God, the source of life and of truth.* He works constantly to divert man's attention from God, to direct it to something else. It may be to money, property, fame, power, pleasure, success, science, art, a religious idol, a dead saint, a human leader, a false god, a political system, or anything else. Whatever it is that takes first place in a person's life is that person's idol, and Satan is the author of idolatry.

Find out to what a person's ultimate loyalty goes, and that is his god. That idol is Satan's tool to keep him from God and, by it, to claim him as a member of his rebellion against God.

The thing may not be evil in itself, it may be good, but it is accursed when it takes the place of God, and it becomes the destroyer of the soul. A man who refuses to serve God and to love Him on the earth will not be allowed to serve Him in eternity. "What shall it profit a man," Jesus asked, "if he gain the whole world and lose his own soul?" (Mark 8:36, RSV)

By the idol—the chief desire—Satan draws a man away, depriving God of His rightful place in the life of one of His creatures. He counts that a triumph. It is his inflexible purpose to secure the allegiance of as many millions of people as he can to *anything* other than to God. By it, he causes them to break the First Commandment.

"Acknowledge and take it to heart this day," Moses said, "that the Lord is God in heaven above, and on the earth below. There is no other" (Deuteronomy 4:39).

God commanded, "You shall have no other gods before Me" (Deuteronomy 5:7).

If there is anything a person wants more than God, that thing will bar the gates of heaven to him forever. He is an idolater. He has put the creation in the place of the Creator. He is absorbed with a thing, when he ought to be absorbed with a Person.

That is why Jesus said, "No servant can serve two masters; for either he will hate the one and love the other, or he will be devoted to the one and despise the other. *You cannot serve God and mammon [money]*" (Luke 16:13, RSV). The Book of Colossians warns of "covetousness, which is idolatry" (3:5, KJV).

That is not a summons to asceticism or deprivation. When God promised Israel "a land flowing with milk and honey," He meant a place of abundance. Psalm 84 promises, "No good thing will God withhold from those who walk uprightly." First Timothy 6:17 charges men not to "trust in uncertain riches, *but in the living God, who gives us richly all things to enjoy*" (KJV).

God delights to have people enjoy good things. But He abhors it when we take those things and make them gods, wresting them to our own destruction. Matthew 6:32-33 sums it up: "Your Heavenly Father knows that you have need of all these things. But seek *first* the kingdom of God and His righteousness, and all these things shall be *added* to you" (KJV). It is when we seek these things *first,* and they become our chief delight, that we are guilty of idolatry. In doing that we make ends out of what were meant to be means.

If we put God first, if we seek Him first, and if we seek Him as earnestly and wholeheartedly as most people seek sundry things, God will see to it that we have everything we need. And we shall be saved from ever having made them our idols and goals.

Satan's purpose—on the earth and among mankind and in the heavens—is *to oppose God at every point.*

A chief issue on which Satan opposes God is worship. It is right that people worship God. God calls people to worship Him, and Him only.

Satan does not want men and women to worship God. He desires that they blaspheme Him, using His holy name as an oath and a curse. He has succeeded in getting vast numbers in this way to violate the Third Commandment continually: "You shall not take the name of the Lord your God in vain, for the Lord will not hold him guiltless who takes His name in vain."

One of the great, intended uses of the human tongue is to sound the worship and adoration of God, to sing His glory, to utter thanksgiving to Him. Satan endeavors to pervert that faculty—one that separates man from the beasts—and to cause the human tongue to be occupied in speaking out curses. It is no accident, it is by express design, that so much of swearing consists of the misuse of God's name. Swearing, when it is deliberate as well as when it is automatic and habitual, is a sign of Satan's dominance over the persons who engage in it.

It is interesting, and significant, that while the name of God or Jesus Christ is on the lips of millions as a curse and is spoken countless times daily in the world—in explicit violation of the biblical commandment—the name of Satan is not used that way. That is a sign of his dominion over the minds and tongues of mankind.

Satan lusts for worship. Because it belongs exclusively to God, he desires it for himself. He would rather have worship than anything else, but because he knows he would not succeed in getting great numbers of men to worship him—if they knew that that was what they were doing—he sets up many objects as alternatives to the worship of God. This is idolatry in its crudest form, and the world is full of it.

It makes little difference whether it is someone coming before a Buddah-figure in the Orient or another weeping at the figure of a saint in New York, it is idolatry in God's eyes, all of it, and He despises it. It is the breaking of the Second Commandment, the words of which are clear beyond mistaking: "You shall not make for yourself a graven image, or any likeness of anything that is in heaven above, or that is on the earth beneath, or that is in the water under the earth; you shall not bow down to them or serve them; for I the Lord your God am a jealous God" (Deuteronomy 5:8-9, RSV).

Idols are not to be made, much less to be bowed before. They are an offense to God. All religions that foster images and idols, wherever they may be—in Tibet, India, Europe, in the jungles of New Guinea or Brazil or Africa or anywhere else—whatever the rationale that may go with them, are under the active sway of Satan to a significant degree.

Satan stands, so to speak, behind every image and every idol, receiving as to himself the worship, the respect, and adoration that is directed to them, which belongs only to the living God. "Do not be idolaters," Paul the Apostle warned believers, ". . . flee from idolatry. . . . Do I mean that an idol is anything? No, but the sacrifices of pagans are offered to demons, not to God, and I do not want you to be participants with demons. You cannot drink the cup of the Lord and the cup of demons too" (1 Corinthians 10:7, 14, 19-21).

Satan promotes the use and worship of idols wherever he can. They are useful to him in one of his chief desires—to rob God of worship.

The use of idols cheats men. It is grotesque for a living being to use his breath to pray to a dead object. The Scripture says of idols, "It is not in them to do good" (Jeremiah 10:5).

The biblical revelation is at constant war with the worship of idols. Scalding denunciations of every deviation into idolatry are one of the main themes of the Old Testament prophets. Wherever the Bible is truly influential, wherever the Word of God is proclaimed and honored, there the idolatry of religious statues and objects is minimized. This form of idolatry has certainly been far less prevalent in North America than in most civilizations, but there is a considerable push to bring religious statues and objects here, especially from the East.

Some people are dabbling in religious idolatry, using Tibetan and Chinese and other images and idols. A friend told me of a young man who married a Jewish girl who had impressed him in part because she exhibited a sincere interest in her religion. They separated after she brought a Buddah into their house and set it up and started burning candles in front of it.

The enemy adapts his tactics to fit circumstances and human tolerances. In North America we have been used mostly to the tamer forms of idolatry, with occasional exceptions, such as sensations stirred up over weeping statues or visions seen in connection with idols, or so-called "miraculous medals."

I was a bit surprised to find that, in its short article on idols, *The Columbia Encyclopedia* cut to the heart of idolatry. It reads in part:

Idol, an object, frequently an image, which is worshiped as a deity. The object may become a deity through magic or through the will of a supernatural power to manifest itself through that object. . . . Idols are usually found in human and animal form and may be treated as though alive; they are fed, bathed, anointed, crowned, and sometimes even provided with a consort.

There is a key here to why some idols acquire special reputations. A particular idol will be said to bestow a special benefit on those who venerate it, such as the healing of a certain kind of ailment. People seek idols for fertility, money, marriage, and a whole range of things desired. Because certain events have attended veneration of an idol, people are drawn from many distant places to seek similar help from that idol, while bypassing more readily accessible idols. All of this is part of "the mystery of iniquity."

A supernatural power that manifests itself through an idol is always and only satanic. Some statues will seem at times to "come alive" to those who most raptly devote themselves to them. Near the culmination of his worldwide program of idolatry Satan will cause a great idol to breathe and to speak. (See Revelation 13:14-15)

From our perspective on a sin-filled earth, idolatry does not always appear as the starkly awful thing that it is, but from the perspective of heaven and God's throne it is an utter abomination. Worship is the most holy of acts and it belongs solely to the Creator. Idolatry perverts and twists the impulse to worship, tearing it away from God and directing it to dead things, to nature or to evil supernatural powers.

One of the charges of heaven against mankind at the end-time is to be that, "The rest of mankind, who were not killed by these plagues, did not repent of the works of their hands nor give up worshiping demons and idols" nor repent of their murders and sorceries (Revelation 9:20-21, RSV). Nearly all worship of demons is carried out through idol worship.

In the sight of God, a land is "polluted" by its idols, as the Bible puts it. In every place in which an idol is set up, Satan enjoys the presence of a symbol of the dominance of his religious policy in that place. The cumulative effect of idols and images is finally to bring a curse upon a land.

It is bad enough for Gentiles to engage in religious idolatry. For a Jew to use a statue or a charm in religious practices is to fly in the face of the lessons of the whole history of the Jews.

Moses spoke for God in commanding: "Turn not to idols, nor make yourself molten gods: I am the Lord your God. . . . You shall make for yourselves no idols and erect no graven image or pillar, and you shall not set any image of stone in your land, to bow down to it; for I am the Lord your God" (Leviticus 19:4; 26:1, COM).

The young man Gideon wrote a brilliant chapter in the history of the chosen people, delivering Israel from a grinding foreign oppressor (Judges 6–8). His daring faith on the field was attested by God's intervention. Thereafter "the land enjoyed peace forty years."

This made Gideon a national hero: "The Israelites said to Gideon, 'Rule over us—you, your son, and your grandson—because you have saved us out of the hand of Midian.'"

Gideon's response was godly and true: "I will not rule over you, nor will my son rule over you. The Lord will rule over you." In the next breath, he made one modest request, asking each man to give him a gold earring from the spoil seized. "So they spread out a garment" and gladly threw about 43 pounds of gold earrings into it. Gideon then had a beautiful religious vestment made, probably as a kind of memorial to the Lord's victory. The next note is a sad one:

"All Israel prostituted themselves by worshiping it . . . and *it became a snare to Gideon and his family*" (Judges 8:22-27).

God told the Jews through Moses that if they walked contrary to Him, "Then I will walk contrary unto you also in fury; and I, even I, will chastise you seven times for your sins. . . . And I will destroy your high places, and cut down your images, and cast your own dead bodies upon the dead bodies of your idols, and My soul shall abhor you. . . . And I will scatter you among the heathen, and will draw out a sword after you, and your land shall be desolate, and your cities waste. Then shall the land rest and enjoy her sabbaths (Leviticus 26:28-34, COM).

God never intended, anywhere in all the universe, idols to be set up as objects of veneration. So profound is the effect of religious idols and images upon a land that the land of Israel could not "rest and enjoy her sabbaths" while the people of Israel disobeyed God and practiced idolatry in it. It was better in God's sight for the land to be emptied of its population than for it to continue to be defiled. (See 2 Kings 17:9-18.)

Isaiah speaks of a better time: "In that day men will regard their Maker, and their eyes will look to the Holy One of Israel; they will not have regard for the altars, the work of their hands, and they will not look to what their own fingers have made, either the idols or the altars of incense" (Isaiah 17:7-8, RSV).

An individual gives Satan a claim on his soul and a basis for activity in his life by using idols or religious charms of any kind.

### The Father of Lies

There is no realm in which Satan is more active than religion. As a spiritual leader, Satan has devised many forms of religion, none of which can bring a man into relationship with the living God or release him from the grip of sin. Satan's *systems* of religion are always non-redemptive. They are unable to furnish what they seemingly promise, usually either an illusory "oneness with God" or some way of man making himself acceptable to God by religious self-effort. In primitive regions he often promotes religious practices for the placating of various demon "gods" and forces.

His systems of religion tend to have certain similarities over the world. They are marked by rote and ritual; repetitions and incantations; idols, images, and protecting charms.

It is striking, a sign of their supernatural inspiration, that the primitive facial masks carved in Africa, in India, in South America, in Borneo, and other places among which there was no possibility of natural communication whatever, are often nearly identical in their design and use in tribal religions. In most cases the ugly, contorted masks were designed to represent invisible supernatural beings in visible form.

Look at an ancient temple in Tibet or in Egypt, and you see them similarly figured with stone carvings and reliefs of gods and animals. Religious rituals and customs and dress in highly divergent cultures separated by oceans are often strikingly alike. That so many of them, so remote from one another in place and in time, look so very much alike is an index to the source of their inspiration.

There are those among mankind who worship spirits or who directly worship the devil. In this nation some openly or secretly worship the devil, in such religions as satanism. From those who delve deeply into that dark evil, Satan does not hide himself. Satan worshipers know exactly who they are worshiping and know beyond doubt that he is real.

But usually Satan finds it more useful in drawing people astray to hide behind an object or a living person, and to let the worship he is stealing from God be directed to an idol or a person. But Satan prefers *man* worship to idol worship. For that reason he will cause a system of idol worship to be overthrown when he can successfully replace it with a system of *man worship*. That came about in China, especially under the rule of Mao from 1949 to 1976, a Communist who systematically put religion down and whose bulky form was displayed in statues and huge photographs all over China. Mao admitted that 800,000 people had been put to death under his bloody regime. (Western experts set the figure far higher.) He permitted a "little red book" of his sayings to be distributed massively to the population for daily readings, and it was also widely used for the public singing and chanting of his words. An evil man is a more useful tool for Satan to set up as an object of worship than an idol, because the man who is worshiped is able to galvanize his followers to Satan's purposes of widespread terror and destruction.

Contradiction of the Word of God is another means by which Satan opposes God among men. His policy is to suppress the Scriptures wherever he can—that is, wherever he can get people to cooperate with him in that purpose.

There have been in the past, and there are today, nations in which the possession and reading of the Scriptures is forbidden or restricted by every means available. Such nations are carrying out the policy of Satan against the dissemination of the knowledge of God. Satan hates the Scriptures because they reveal God and because they expose him.

Where he cannot suppress the Scriptures, he contradicts them, distorts them, heaps scorn upon them, causes them to be misapplied, and seeks by every possible means to nullify or severely limit their actual influence. "The god of this world" has turned the universities, which once were centers for the study and promulgation of the truths of the Scriptures, into centers where they are often mocked and repudiated, with guile, with enmity, with sophistication, and with a false show of scholarly objectivity. Much of the contradiction of the Scriptures in university classrooms is purely gratuitous—dragged in by the preceptor with no relevance to anything but his own arrogant bias—and part of it is a matter of scruple by deceived men. The effect is, as it long has been, profoundly to subvert the Bible's influence among the young, leaving them ultimately without defense against the undermining of their character and morals.

Steal the influence of the Bible, once so great, away from the German youth and you have, at the end, a generation of storm troopers and goose-steppers—a youth mobilized by Satan for great, profane destruction. Steal the influence of the Bible, once so great, away from American young people and you have what we are now beginning to have, a generation drawn toward moral anarchy.

Men live either in liberty or in tyranny. By far the majority of men in history have had tyranny for their portion. Satan wills it for them. It matches his nature well, which is to rule by fear or by force. It has been accurately said that "Satan has slaves or subjects, God has sons."

"Where the Spirit of the Lord is, there is liberty," the Scriptures affirm in 2 Corinthians 3:17. God is the author of liberty, and He wills liberty for man. Where men honor God and hold His Word in respect, liberty flows to them. The Holy Scriptures have been a beacon of liberty wherever they have had real influence with men in the world.

That is one reason why Satan seeks either to keep the Scriptures from men or, failing that, to hold them up to contempt. The American society was, from colonial days, a Bible-influenced society. The public standard was, to a remarkable degree, a biblical standard for quite a long time. The churches, by and large, vigorously upheld the Scriptures and proclaimed their truths.

The effective attack on the Bible as the public standard in the nation began late in the last century, and it gathered great momentum after World War I. The consequences have been piling up on the nation heavily since.

The public standard of morality in the nation—at least as it is reflected in literature, motion pictures, advertising, and the arts—is beginning to approximate that of Sodom. Crime, addiction, violence, occultism, perversion, adultery, family instability, and social instability have all been steeply on the rise. Those who rebel against truth and sow the wind shall "reap the whirlwind," the Bible warns in Hosea 8:7.

The United States and Canada have afforded liberty and abundance and safety to millions of men in proportions far above what had ever been known in the world. Satan's long-term strategy for taking these things away has been the continual diminishing of the influence of the Scriptures among the people.

The Scriptures have both a restrictive and a liberating effect. Where they are honored, they restrict sin and misery and evil to a pronounced degree, and they check religious and political tyranny to a pronounced degree. People are thus made free to expand along lines that are most beneficial to themselves and to society.

Where it is not imposed by force, tyranny always comes in under the banner of lies. It is devilish in its nature and its works. It is the nature of God to speak truth. "God is not a man, that He should lie," Numbers 23:19 asserts. "Has He said, and will He not do it? Or has He spoken, and will He not make it good?" Titus says that *"God, who cannot lie,"* has promised certain things to man. Jesus said, "Man shall not live by bread alone, but *by every word that proceeds out of the mouth of God"* (Matthew 4:4, KJV). Jesus was directly quoting Moses (see Deuteronomy 8:3b).

"Every word of God is pure," says Proverbs 30:5.

"Thy word is very pure," Psalm 119:140 affirms.

"The words of the Lord are pure words: as silver tried in a furnace of earth, purified seven times," David wrote in Psalm 12:6 (KJV).

In contrast to this, the Bible says of Satan, "When he lies, he speaks his native language, for *he is a liar and the father of lies"* (John 8:44).

It is the nature of Satan to speak lies. He is a liar, but more than that, he is "the father of lies." Satan is the one who introduced lying into the relationships between intelligent beings in the universe, and he still promotes lying today—the breaking of the ninth commandment, which forbids bearing false witness.

A lie is designed to deceive. Satan does not present his lies as lies; he presents them as truth. Satan's lies are designed to deceive men about the most important things: about God and the nature of God; about sin and evil; about redemption and salvation; about death; about judgment and hell. He is the father of the religious lie, which contradicts the Word of God and betrays men's souls forever if they believe it. He is the father of the political lie, the big lie, which, when men accept it, leads them to national enslavement or destruction.

In every case where God says something is true and Satan says it is not true or that the opposite is true, what Satan says is a *lie*. Every man who speaks a word contrary to the truth of the Scriptures is a liar. Wittingly or unwittingly, he has lent his tongue to the father of lies. That is why the Scripture says, "What if some did not believe? Shall their unbelief make the faith of God without effect? God forbid! Let God be true, but every man a liar; as it is written, 'That You [God] may be justified in Your words, and prevail when You are judged' " (Romans 3:3-4, COM).

Because God is active in promulgating truth and Satan is active in promoting lies, every man stands between the truth of God and the lies of Satan, and he must decide which to believe.

"Jesus Christ, the Son of God," the Apostle Paul wrote, "isn't one to say 'yes' when He means 'no.' He always does exactly what He says. He carries out and fulfills all of God's promises . . ." (2 Corinthians 1:19-20, TLB).

For every promise, the prince of darkness has a *doubt.* For every truth, he has a *but.*

Satan began his policy of lies in Eden. God told Adam, "You may freely eat of every tree of the garden, but of the tree of the knowledge of good and evil you shall not eat, for in the day that you eat of it you shall die" (Genesis 2:16-17, RSV).

Satan, whose desire for man is death, told Eve, "You will *not* die. For God knows that when you eat of it your eyes will be opened, and you will be like God, knowing good and evil" (Genesis 3:4-5, RSV).

Satan's purpose was death for the human race. His method was flat contradiction of what God had said. His promise to Eve that she, by disobeying God, could be "like God" was his first huge religious-spiritual lie.

Satan sought to make his lie more acceptable to Eve by adding a promise of knowledge to it. He often tries to sweeten his lies by promising that something good is to be gained by believing them. His method is rather like that of the fisherman who baits the hook with something delightful and apparently much to be desired. That is his *offer* to the fish. But it is not his purpose. His purpose is death.

"The wages of sin is death," the Bible declares (Romans 6:23). God goes all the way to the end of sin and shows it to be death so that men, by seeing the last result of it, may avoid it and be saved. Satan says another thing entirely. "The wages of sin is" ... pleasure, he says ... or gain, or security, or wealth, or station, or power, or some other desirable thing. He is careful not to show the end of it—death.

What is the offer of a narcotics experiment? Pleasure, relaxation, escape, transcendent experience—one or more of these. But it often brings addiction, enslavement, death.

A sixteen-year-old boy in Brooklyn walked over to a woman getting off a bus, snatched her pocketbook, and ran off. A policeman happened to be walking nearby. He chased the boy, shouted at him to stop, fired a warning shot, and then, as the boy continued to flee, shot at him. The aim was high and the boy sprawled on the sidewalk—dead. The pocketbook slipped from his hand and its contents scattered on the pavement. "Be sure your sin will find you out," the Bible warns. "The wages of sin is death."

In this case, the payoff came pitifully soon. If the boy had resisted the temptation to attempt theft, on the hint of quick or easy gain, he would no doubt be alive today. Obedience to a lawless impulse brought sudden, unexpected death. We could shout, "It wasn't worth it. It wasn't worth it." Whatever sin promises, at the end it isn't worth it.

## A Dealer in Sin

Satan is a dealer in sin. He tempts men and women, teenagers, children to sin because it suits his purposes to do so. He knows that if he can get the consent of an individual to sin he has a claim upon that man's soul. He hopes that sooner or later he can destroy that person through his sin, and in the process afflict, torment, twist, or destroy others by it.

Garbage is the rightful domain of the garbageman. Where there is garbage, the garbageman must come—to the wealthiest house in town or to the alley of some slum. As garbage is the rightful province of the garbageman—so sin is the rightful province of Satan. It is something he can make a claim upon.

A person's sin, whatever it is, is Satan's stake in him. He wants to hold that claim and, if possible, to expand it. What pleases him keenly is that it reflects in the life of man Satan's own defiance of God.

A person in sin devotes some or all of his faculties, his time, his energy, his money, and his bodily members to the works of sin. He may lend his mouth to blasphemies, his influence to injustice, his hands to theft or violence, his mind to impure thoughts, his money to perversion, gambling or organized crime, his will to purposes of greed. Whether he does so in greater or smaller measure, he has consecrated himself and his faculties to that extent to sins that grieve a loving Creator.

Some individuals give themselves over quite fully to sin. Satan uses them to inflict much harm on others, some of it seen, much of it not easily traceable.

A writer allows lust to rise up and occupy his mind and his spirit. As it does so, he transmits it to words on paper. He allows his thoughts, stirred and fire-fed by Satan, to go to excesses of filthy imagination. He does so because he wants the money and because he enjoys the inward motions of lust. Someone else paints a cover for the book that has a pointed sexual appeal. That book goes into a drugstore rack. A high school kid browses among the books, finds a fascination in the cover, buys it and reads it and is led through detailed descriptions of things of which he had not heard or thought. Excitement may lead on to some damaging adventure in a new form of sin, and it may involve another person, or several others. It may even lead to the disaster of a sexually twisted life.

Through the services of a publisher, the writer is brought into contact with thousands of people he does not know, into whose minds he deposits a load of filth. It will be shown to him at the Judgment how many of them were unable to bear it and turned his words into acts of sin.

Satan loves to incite the widespread communication of sin, particularly in the realms of immorality and evil supernaturalism, and there are writers and publishers and filmmakers today who serve him abundantly in sowing sin over the nation. Segments of the film-video-television-records and publishing media are engaged in a continual assault on, and push against, biblical moral standards. The immediate harvest of it may be money, but behind it there is a harvest of shame, misery, perversion, even mental derangement, and, ultimately, grievous social stress.

The Apostle John writes, "He who commits sin is of the devil" (1 John 3:8, RSV). That is why Satan is a dealer of sin.

One of his tactics is to tempt and urge people to give reign and expression to bodily lusts, because he knows the harm that can be done by it.

The tempter knows that if he can get young people to give themselves over for a few minutes to the electric pleasure of an illicit act of fornication, he has a chance of producing a harvest of suffering out of it—a time of shame and fear for a pregnant girl and years of unshared burden in rearing a not-really-wanted child; a sense of guilt and shame for the young man; an abortion perhaps; a suicide possibly; above all, a chance at bringing misery or unwantedness into the life of the child. The consequences, which run on for years, sometimes for generations, are not in any way worth the flashing pleasures of a moment.

Even in those cases where there are no manifest physical or social consequences, *there are spiritual consequences to such an act.* The Bible distinguishes clearly between an act of fornication, which God abhors, and the physical love of the marriage bed set within the larger context of a complete and continuing union. That love is the most intimate privilege of the full union God has ordained for one man with one woman. It is holy enough, in His eyes, for Him to use human marriage as a figure for the relationship which Christ has to the church (which is called His bride in John 3:28-29 and Revelation 21:9). Ephesians 5:25-32 speaks of human marriage as it typifies "a profound mystery . . . Christ and the church."

"Flee fornication," the Bible says. "Every sin that a man does is without the body, but he that commits fornication sins against his own body" (1 Corinthians 6:18, KJV).

If God's blessing rests upon true marriage, His curse falls upon fornication. Because He loves man, God shows the thing in its true light. Satan always puts *all* the emphasis on the short-term pleasures. He seeks always to publicize and glamorize and emphasize the pleasure, and to deny or conceal or mock the payoff. "It will not be so in your case," he suggests. "You will escape." But there is no guarantee of that.

I was being driven through a pleasant, wealthy town in Connecticut one evening by a newspaper reporter, and I remember the sadness with which I heard him tell of a young woman, the daughter of a prominent executive, who was found dead in a motel a few miles from her home in that town, the consequence of a brief adventure in premarital sex. The unlawful pleasure of that "romantic" interlude proved to be one short deadly fling.

"Be sure your sin will find you out." Her sin found that young lady out so very soon. His sin will find that young man out at some future, inconvenient time. It waits for him at the last great Judgment, where every hidden or secret thing shall be brought to light.

Tens of thousands of young women have gone through long, drab years of loneliness or suffering because on one evening years before they agreed to break a law of God.

It is wise never to underestimate the effect of sin. At the Judgment, millions of human souls will be caught short, found out and cut off forever, wasted trophies of Satan's merciless thievery.

Those who have been born again have a radically different relationship to sin than do the unsaved. We do not automatically escape temptation (we must be careful never to court it or to be "lured and enticed" by its appeal to our fleshly nature, as James 1:12-15 warns), and the world around us solicits us to sin continually. But we escape the compelling power of sin.

That is not to say that we live sinlessly (sin may take us unawares along life's path), but that we are free from sinning habitually or by compulsion. If we sin, the assurance is given that when "we confess our sins, He is faithful and just and will forgive us our sins and purify us from all unrighteousness" (1 John 1:7-9).

The truth that resonates in the Word for us is this: "Sin shall not have dominion over you" (Romans 6:12-14, KJV). The *power* of sin is broken in the lives of the redeemed.

## Taking Sober Measure

In the desire not to overestimate Satan, there is a tendency among some believers to underestimate him and his works, to belittle or mock him, or rather lightly to understand overcoming him. Some seem almost to think that he can be routed by a slogan.

Such attitudes are shallow and thoroughly unscriptural. They are, taken together, a travesty on the depth and sweep of satanic activity in human history. In the present century, by wars and vast annihilations and purges, the toll in human lives soars above 100 million victims of every age. The totality of the sufferings and grief and loss and dislocations, stemming from the dynamic interaction of human sinfulness and satanic provocation, goes far beyond our capacity to comprehend.

Believers are by no means to be awed by him—in Christ we have the power and authority to overcome him, sometimes by a single act, sometimes at high cost, and we are commanded to do so. The Book of Revelation promises specific, wonderful rewards to those who do.

Further, since Satan is, to use a rough figure of speech, playing on God's chessboard, he is both consigned to, and promised, ultimate futility in all his strategies. God, of course, always has the upper hand, and He always has the last move!

The curse pronounced by God upon the serpent-being who deceived Eve in Eden is: "Dust you shall eat all the days of your life." In all his workings, Satan rarely if ever tastes anything like victory. Let him, in his rage against the biblical promises to the Jews, instigate the fury of the holocaust and take six million Jews to their deaths, and out of it comes the very thing he so desperately sought to obliterate—the beginning of the restoration of the nation Israel. How quickly, how surely his vast seeming victory turned to dust!

No, Satan cannot win, not really ever, but he can act and he does, with appalling effect.

Have you, as I have, heard believers and even ministers mock Satan or belittle him with ridicule? As though he could be dealt with by a wave of the hand or a slighting phrase from the lips! The Bible does not sanction this.

Those who most loudly and assertively boast against him often are trifling with things they know little about.

The Apostle Peter warned of certain "bold and arrogant" men. He says that "these men are not afraid to slander celestial beings, yet even angels, although they are stronger and more powerful, do not bring slanderous accusations against such beings in the presence of the Lord" (2 Peter 2:10-12). Men may wrongly estimate satanic powers; angels do not.

Jude also reproves individuals who "slander celestial beings" informing us that "even the archangel Michael, when he was disputing with the devil about the body of Moses, did not dare to bring a slanderous accusation against him, but said, 'The Lord rebuke you!'" (Jude 8-9)

What that mighty angel of God "did not dare" to do, we would be thoroughly unwise to venture.

No being who has stood at the head of so great a rebellion and conspiracy to overthrow God's rule among intelligent beings should be casually or indifferently measured. The very fact that God has reserved a place called "the lake of fire" specifically for Satan and his followers, and that smoke shall ascend from that place of punishment forever, gives some concept of how God looks upon him.

At earth level, "Be watchful, be sober," the Scripture says, "for your adversary, the devil, goes about as a roaring lion seeking whom he may *devour*" (1 Peter 5:8, com).

Whose adversary is he? Is he God's and the world's adversary only? The Bible says that he is *your* adversary and mine, one who has no intention of leaving us alone but who will at some point test us, perhaps severely. We have in 2 Timothy 3:12 what might be called a written guarantee that "everyone who wants to live a godly life in Christ Jesus will be persecuted." That does not mean constantly but somewhere along life's way.

Do not cringe at this, and do not borrow trouble, thinking that some unseen force is soon to descend upon you just because you are reading of these spiritual realities. In Christ, we have more power standing for us than can ever work against us.

There is no lifelong "PRIVATE PROPERTY—DO NOT TOUCH" or "DO NOT TEST" sign on a believer. But there is a mighty assurance: "Greater is He who is in you than he who is in the world" (1 John 4:4, KJV). This does not suggest a state of nonconflict, but one of victory in conflict. It is not a promise of automatic exemption, but of actual overcoming. Such experiences will make us strong in Christ.

With it there is another *guarantee:* God will allow you to be tested and tried at times—it proves to the powers of darkness that you and He together are invincible in the face of evil attack—but He will not allow you to be tested beyond your endurance, and He will *make a way of escape* for you (1 Corinthians 10:13).

Our adversary is a wily strategist. In going about his earthly work, Satan will initially settle for almost anything, even seemingly small advantages and inroads. They are all he needs to stake a soul to death by sin, but sometimes he can later magnify the results remarkably.

His cunning temptation to Eve took the form of enticing her to do an apparently small thing—just to eat something pleasant looking that grew right there in the garden. All he showed her was a lie—that it would make her "wise"—but out of that one act he fully intended a calamity—the fall of mankind.

That was all he needed, with Adam's equal cooperation, to steal people away from God and to put them under his banner and the power of sin, with vast and cataclysmic consequences all through human history. The Scripture says that "sin entered the world through one man, and death through sin, and in this way *death came to all men*" (Romans 5:12). Just one act, but what a harvest!

So it is that, even when his results may finally be spectacular, his immediate working may be in seemingly small ways. He knows, for instance, that just a little wandering of the eye and mind, just a start of giving way to temptation, may lead a man to infidelity and adultery, a wife to divorce, a family to a split, several children to perplexity, uncertainty and the shadow of a sorrow they cannot escape, sometimes becoming warped because of it. Just one act—what a harvest!

We should never underestimate what a little sin will do. The Scripture warns of the "deceiving power of unrighteousness in them that perish." All alcoholism, with the grief, loss, suffering, stupor that it brings, starts with just one drink. All drug addiction stems from just *one* dose.

Always remember this: when the devil puts one card of sin down on the table, he is always ready to raise the stakes, just as high as he can finally raise them. If we don't take that card, we never have to see what he's got in his full hand for us.

The wise Christian does not underestimate Satan, but in taking sober measure of him, he also does not underestimate the resources, and the readiness to act, of God on high.

This vital, necessary balance is found in the Apostle Paul, a man who stood at the very forefront of the advance of the Gospel in much of the civilized world.

"We know that as you share in our sufferings, you will also share in our comfort. For we do not want you to be ignorant, brethren, of the affliction we experienced in Asia; for we were so utterly, unbearably crushed that we despaired of life itself. Why, we felt that we had received the sentence of death...."

What a test! Yet it was not more than Paul was able to bear, and he tells what he learned and experienced by it: "... but that was to make us rely not on ourselves but on God who raises the dead. *He delivered us* from so deadly a peril, and He will deliver us; on Him we have set our hope" (2 Corinthians 1:7-11, RSV).

No easy believism here. No top-of-the-head, tip-of-the-tongue faith. No sense at all that the way would be easy, but that it would be triumphant. Invulnerability and invincibility are not the same thing. Paul was vulnerable and he knew it, but in Christ he found he was invincible. When he speaks of overcoming, he speaks with the authority of pit-deep experience.

Paul and Barnabas visited several young churches to strengthen and encourage the believers. "We must go through many hardships to enter the kingdom of God," the missionary apostles frankly told them (Acts 14:22).

"In this world you will have trouble," Jesus forewarned His disciples. "But take heart! I have overcome the world" (John 16:33).

The notion that the Lord has the believers and the devil goes after the unbelievers, or that the Lord wraps believers in devil-proof goose down, does not come from the Scriptures. It verges on the error of Mary Baker Eddy, the founder of Christian Science. She went through the Bible and emphasized all the nice and pleasant and God-affirming things and cut out all the evil and unpleasant and Satan-revealing things, and said that evil and sickness were mere illusions, "errors of mortal mind," and called that lie the truth.

The danger of a soft-life Christianity, so readily available in our society, is that it sets up nonbiblical expectations. Those who follow it may, if they later face hardship and persecution for the faith, be offended and fall away.

How real is the devil in his actual effects on believers who are serving the Lord? Here is some plain talk from the Bible about that. Again it is the voice of Paul writing to the Thessalonian church, saying, "Out of our intense longing we made every effort to see you. For we wanted to come to you—certainly I, Paul, did, again and again—but Satan stopped us" (1 Thessalonians 2:17-18).

Certain of the overly specialized Bible teachers of our day, who much more emphasize the believer's victory than they do the believer's overcoming, might portray this as the testimony of a defeated Christian, deficient in his use of the promise box after his morning coffee.

How many times have you heard the magnificent Scripture quoted that "all things work together for good to them who love God and who are called according to His purpose"? In all those times, how often has the *purpose* of that promise been quoted with it—that we be "conformed to the image of His Son"? (Romans 8:28-29, KJV) I have heard the first part quoted hundreds of times, and I do not recall the second part ever being quoted with it.

The Apostle Peter, writing to "God's elect," told them to "be truly glad! There is wonderful joy ahead, even though the going is rough for a while down here." Why so? "These trials are only to test your faith, to see whether or not it is strong and pure. It is being tested as fire tests gold and purifies it ... so if your faith remains strong after being tried ... it will bring you much praise and glory and honor on the day of His return" (1 Peter 1:6-7, TLB).

Man is by nature almost always *goal-oriented,* what we can do for the Lord. We emphasize our work.

God is far more *gold-oriented,* what He can make us to be in Christ. His own likeness in us is what pleases Him most.

The trials that we sometimes go through are to have the same good effect on us that fire has on gold—refining, clarifying, purifying, and making stronger. That wonderful and godly man Job said, "He knows the way that I take; when He has tested me, I will come forth as gold" (Job 23:10-12).

After they had "received the light" of Christ, some of the early Jewish believers were mistreated. Yet they took it joyfully, the writer of the Book of Hebrews says. "You stood your ground in a great contest in the face of suffering ... publicly exposed to insult and persecution ... the confiscation of your property" (10:32-39).

Later, when certain troubles continued, they were told to go right on.

"Your confidence . . . will be richly rewarded. You need to persevere," and they were warned that if a believer "shrinks back," God will have no pleasure in him.

The risen Lord Jesus, in His message through John to the church at Smyrna, said: "Do not fear what you are about to suffer. Behold, the devil is about to throw some of you into prison, that you may be tested, and for ten days you will have tribulation. Be faithful to death, and I will give you the crown of life. . . . He who conquers shall not be hurt by the second death" (Revelation 2:10-11, rsv).

It was going to happen—not to all but to some—and it was the devil's direct working against them, and it would not be prevented. They were not to fear; they were to endure it in faith, even to the point of death.

This is in accord with the classic statement of the Scriptures regarding the stance of believers toward Satan, which says: "They *overcame him*" by three things:

"By the blood of the Lamb and by the word of their testimony [and] they did not love their lives so much as to shrink from death" (Revelation 12:11). That is what real overcoming is made of.

John, the man who received the Book of Revelation for us, was shown a glimpse of a special company of overcomers: "I saw under the altar the souls of those who had been slain because of the Word of God and the testimony they had maintained" (6:9).

Were they defeated? No, there are victorious overcomers who kept their testimony to Jesus even in the face of death. They could not be cowed into submission by *any* earthly authority or any demon.

The believers at Smyrna who were going to be thrown into jail were about to go through a severe test, of which they had gracious warning beforehand. Why a test? In part, because what was to happen would seem to mock their faith, and, in part, because the devil would tempt them toward unbelief, hopelessness, even accusation against God in the vile prison.

We believers have a shield of faith that we can raise against "the fiery darts of the wicked one" so that his flaming lies and attacks upon our inner emotions may be turned aside in every case, but it is extremely important to know that we are not always *circumstantially shielded* from direct enemy attacks.

The "fiery darts" aimed at believers going through such troubles would have included the fear of which the Lord spoke and the thought that God had abandoned them and did not love them. All such false interpretations of their tribulation they had the absolute power to overcome.

You are almost certainly aware that it is the Christian believer who must "put on the whole armor of God," as Ephesians 6:10-13 (rsv) instructs. But do you remember *why?* To be able to "stand against" something very specific—"the wiles of the devil." Wiles means deceitful strategies and carefully devised lies aimed directly at believers from time to time—to delude us in some way if possible, confuse us, mislead us, weaken or overthrow our precious faith, distress us, or discourage us.

We do not escape those wiles by exemption; we overcome them by the intelligent use of the armor available to us. We must, of course, recognize them first for what they are to be able to overcome them.

When a lie is slung at us that goes against truth or our faith, we can let it land and do its work in us, or we can immediately raise the shield of faith, invisible but powerful, and turn it back. Ephesians 4:27 warns us not to "give place to the devil" (kjv).

Believers in Christ have the authority, the spiritual weapons, and the power to overcome Satan. Sometimes that is by a word or an act, and sometimes it is by being willing even to die for Him who loved us and gave Himself for us (Galatians 2:20).

## Battle for Allegiance

The earth we live on is the chief locale, the theater in the universe, of a challenge to the supremacy of God over a portion of His creation. Its inhabitants are the objects of what may accurately be called a dispute between Satan and God for their obedience and worship. This conflict is so severe that the Bible calls it "warfare," and men are very much at its center.

Satan hates it that any person—that even one person—should worship God and love Him supremely. One of his desires is to show, if he can, that every person has his price, that no one loves God so well that he will allow nothing to stop him from worshiping and trusting God. That is why, at one point in history, God allowed a man named Job to stand a severe test of affliction. God loved Job and believed that he would not fail or fall.

Job was the best of men—yet for a time all sense of God's love, protection, and provision was taken from him.

Though a primary scene of Satan's activity is the earth and the atmosphere of the earth, Satan also has access to God: "Now there was a day when the sons of God came to present themselves before the Lord, and Satan also came among them. The Lord said to Satan, 'Whence have you come?' Satan answered the Lord, 'From going to and fro on the earth, and from walking up and down on it.'

"And the Lord said to Satan, 'Have you considered My servant Job, that there is none like him on the earth, a blameless and upright man, who fears God and turns away from evil?'" (Job 1:6-8, RSV)

The reply of Satan affords a glimpse of his character. "Then Satan answered the Lord, 'Does Job fear God for nothing? Have You not put a hedge about him and his house and all that he has, on every side? You have blessed the work of his hands, and his possessions have increased in the land. But put forth Your hand now and touch all that he has, and he will curse You to Your face.'" What a combination of cynicism, skepticism, accusation, and hatred breathes in that speech!

We are here shown a restriction that was upon the activity of Satan toward the man Job, a restriction that Satan found extremely frustrating. He could not get at Job because God had "put a hedge about him and his house and all that he has, on every side." It was an invisible barrier, set up by the decree of God, and Satan could not get past it.

Satan therefore accused Job of worshiping God for gain. He asked God to wipe Job out—"touch all that he has, and he will curse You to Your face."

"And the Lord said to Satan, 'Behold all that he has is in your power; only upon himself do not put forth your hand.' So Satan went forth from the presence of the Lord" (Job 1:9-12, COM).

Satan now had what he wanted, access to Job, and he was sure he could prove that Job was not a selfless worshiper of God.

A series of calamities fell upon Job in a single day. These came by the direct activity of Satan, but it is interesting to see their immediate sources. From one side, a party of the Sabeans invaded his property. They stole his animals and slew the servants. From another side, the Chaldeans formed three companies and swept suddenly down upon Job's property in a devastating raid. Men in action, yes, *but Satan in action behind them!* At almost the same time, a fire broke out in the property and shortly thereafter "a great wind came across the wilderness and struck the house," and it collapsed, killing his sons and daughters. Natural forces, yes, but Satan in action behind them!

A key fact here is that the enemy used many instruments in his attack on Job, but he showed his hand in none of them. Job did not know the who or the why, only the what, of these losses.

"Then Job arose, and rent his robe, and shaved his head, and fell

**92**

upon the ground and worshiped. And he said, 'Naked I came from my mother's womb, and naked shall I return; the Lord gave, and the Lord has taken away; blessed be the name of the Lord'" (Job 1:20-21).

His words gave the lie to Satan's accusations! Job stood the test. God told Satan that Job had "held fast his integrity." But Satan was not satisfied.

"Then Satan answered the Lord, 'Skin for skin! All that a man has he will give for his life. But put forth Your hand now, and touch his bone and his flesh, and he will curse You to Your face.' And the Lord said to Satan, 'Behold, he is in your power; only spare his life.'"

Once more a restriction that was on Satan in the case of Job was removed, but his life was to be spared. Satan filled Job's body with pain and running sores "from the sole of his foot to the crown of his head," and Job went "and sat among the ashes."

At this point Job's wife looked at him and said, "Do you still hold fast your integrity? Curse God, and die" (Job 2:4-9, RSV).

It was the counsel of Satan from the lips of his wife! Seemingly natural speech is sometimes directly prompted by a supernatural source, for a spiritual purpose. When Peter assured Jesus that He would never be killed, Jesus said, "Get behind Me, Satan!" (Matthew 16:21-23, RSV)

Notice especially that every word that Job's wife spoke on earth had already been spoken in heaven! Her words cut to the heart of what was going on, but on the wrong side. Satan had said that the result of severe loss and affliction would be that Job would "curse God."

Now here—at a critical juncture in Job's trial, and also at the critical juncture in Satan's dispute with God concerning Job—comes Job's wife, standing over him and telling him to do that very thing. All Satan wanted was for Job to curse God. If Job had sunk under his wife's counsel and done that, Satan would have been proved right: Job worshiped God for what he got out of it.

All of her words—"Do you still hold fast your integrity? Curse God, and die"—were put into her mind and into her mouth by an evil prompting. This must have hit Job hard, yet he did not sin with his lips. By faith he resisted every temptation. The end of it was complete vindication for God, complete vindication for Job, and complete defeat for Satan. Satan understood now that there was a man upon the earth who loved God *solely for Himself.*


Having a realistic sense, then, of Satan's intentions toward mankind, and of our eternally secure position in Christ toward him, we understand

**93**

that it is our distinct *privilege* to be the human overcomers in actual fact of this one preeminent foe—the foe of God, angels, men, and the creation.

Job is one of history's greatest overcomers. Yet see *how* he overcame. Job did not overcome by mighty deeds of daring or outwardly heroic acts (though all that he withstood was the essence of heroism).

Job overcame in great personal weakness. Hear a little of what he said about himself:

> "My body is clothed with worms and scabs,
>     my skin is broken and festering . . .
> I wish I had died before any eye saw me . . .
> Men open their mouths to jeer at me;
>     they strike my cheek in scorn . . .
> God has made me a byword to everyone,
>     a man in whose face people spit"
>             (Job 7:5; 10:18-19; 16:10; 17:6).

There was nothing showy about what Job did, but it registered resoundingly in heaven. Job overcame chiefly by two things—by suffering and faith. In this he was like our Lord Jesus, whose ultimate act of overcoming was to be mocked and spit on and to be nailed in blood to a Roman cross.

Others overcame by their steadfast obedience to the Lord, without regard to personal consequences good or bad.

Though overcoming is sometimes outwardly spectacular, it is far more often quiet, deep, steadfast, obscure, costly. Either way, what is important about it is that it is true and real in fact, not just apparently so. A good many seemingly spectacular "overcomers"—those who boast that they "cast out demons" in Jesus' name and did "many mighty works"— will never spend half a day in heaven! Jesus will say to them, "I never knew you. Depart from Me, you who work iniquity" (Matthew 7:21-23, KJV).

Even though they may have looked like mighty overcomers, these never actually overcame Satan at all. (This is not to denigrate acts of power in ministry; it is to insist that they are valid *only* when they proceed from inward spiritual reality and a heart for God.) The only thing that counts is real overcoming. No shadow boxing, however vigorous or impressive, is of any effect. Paul called it "beating the air" (1 Corinthians 9:26).

Why did Satan strain to be unleashed to go after Job? Why, when he was allowed to do so for a time, did he act with such sudden, total, merciless fury, throwing everything he could against the man and taking everything he could away from him?

The quick answer, and it is fully right, is that he did so because Job was a righteous man, one whose life reflected true godliness, including a great kindliness to the needy. But there is so much more to it than that.

Satan's acts and words are the expression of his *nature*, and his nature is the moral "black hole" of the universe. (A black hole is anything but a hole; astronomers who have spied out such blackness in the very distant heavens believe it to be matter that has collapsed into extreme density, so that a piece of it the size of a marble would weigh many tons.)

There is no understanding what Satan does apart from what he *is*. His inward state and motivations beget all his acts.

The great key to his interior state lies in the fact that, when he turned against God and became his dynamic enemy, God, who alone is the source of light and truth and love, cut him off from His nature forever, leaving Satan in total inward darkness. He is a reprobate being, actually incapable of anything but evil, yet having for a time the use of his darkened faculties—energy, intelligence, and will.

At large in sectors of the creation but utterly frustrated in his desire to overthrow God, Satan hates whatever God loves with a virulent hatred, and he actively promotes what God hates. Because he is cut off in every way from the nature of God, who is love, Satan is an infinitely cruel taskmaster and tyrant, merciless to a degree not suspected by men, bent on moral chaos, devastation, deception, destruction, and death in as profuse a measure as men will allow him to produce in their affairs.

Clearly Satan would have had Job killed if he could have; that is why God expressly told him not to take Job's life. But for what gain? For nothing but to satisfy his own evil nature. For no reason other than hatred—hatred of God and hatred for a man who wholly worshiped God.

He poured everything he could upon Job, yet in sheer and ultimate futility. Job was not overcome. Satan was! Job was not *his* victim finally. Job was Satan's overcomer.

How far will the enemy go? He will never put limits on himself. He will go as far as he possibly can. As far as men will let him, but never any fraction of a millimeter beyond the scope that is allowed to him by God. That limited scope is nevertheless often very wide in earthly terms.

Though he is surely that, Satan is much more than just your enemy or your family's. The Bible reveals him as the destroyer of cities, the corrupter of culture, and the deceiver of nations.

# The Origin of Satan

In an allegorical description, Satan is spoken of in the Book of Job in these terms: "Upon earth there is not his like . . . *he is king over all the children of pride*" (Job 41:33-34, KJV).

Satan, as he is now called, was not evil at his origin. The one who now bears the name Satan and the title of devil was in the beginning good. The living being who became the devil was beautiful in every way, in character and appearance.

The prophets Ezekiel and Isaiah tell of the origin and fall of Satan. They tell of the birth of evil desire in him, some of his activities, and they show his destiny.

The prophets did this, not by reflection or insight, but by pure revelation, given to them in oral prophecy, subsequently written down.

There are times in prayer when an individual will start praying about some local event but will be led by the Holy Spirit to go from that to some far greater theme, entirely to his own surprise, in intercession. There may be an aspect of revelation to such intercession—as when a believer is drawn to pray with great urgency for the safety of a missionary overseas and later learns that the missionary's village was visited by bandits on that day.

Something like that appears to be the case in these prophecies of Ezekiel and Isaiah. Neither man began to speak about Satan. Each prophet begins by speaking of an earthly ruler. In Ezekiel, it is the prince of Tyre. In Isaiah, it is the king of Babylon. But in each case the prophet is led by the Spirit of God to go beyond those men to the wicked one who stood behind them, prompting them to do evil.

"You were the signet of perfection, full of wisdom and perfect in beauty," Ezekiel declares. "You were in Eden, the garden of God. Every precious stone was your covering, carnelian, topaz, and jasper, chrysolite, beryl, and onyx, sapphire, carbuncle, and emerald—all in beautiful settings of finest gold. They were given to you on the day you were created" (Ezekiel 28:11-19, COM).

This passage shows that the being now called Satan was *a created being;* that he was full of wisdom; that he was a being of great beauty; that he was *perfect.*

Ezekiel continues:

"You were the anointed cherub who covers; I set you so. You were on the holy mountain of God, in the midst of the stones of fire you walked. You were blameless in your ways from the day you were created, *until iniquity was found in you.* In the abundance of your trade you were filled with violence, *and you sinned.* So I cast you as a profane thing from the mountain of God, and the guardian cherub drove you out from the midst of the stones of fire."

This portion declares that this perfect and beautiful being occupied, by the express appointment of God, a station in heaven, "on the holy mountain of God."

The word "anoint" in Hebrew usage means to pour oil upon a person to consecrate that person to God or set him apart for a specific office. God had anointed this being for a special office in the highest heaven, near the place where God's throne is.

But Satan sinned. He fell in iniquity. He was driven out of his place of high privilege in heaven because of it.

The next verse tells why:

"*Your heart was proud because of your beauty;* you corrupted your wisdom for the sake of your splendor." Ezekiel thus declares by prophecy that Satan fell because he became proud of his beauty, and that he turned from serving God and began to serve his own vanity and to seek his own glory. He let his magnificence carry him into vanity and self-pride. That turned his wisdom into corruption.

This drove him to extremities of ambition and rebellion against God. In presumption, he is without limits.

Isaiah tells more of how he corrupted his wisdom, set himself in opposition to God, and began to lead a rebellion against God's government—a rebellion that instigated something that had never existed; a conflict for the loyalty of other intelligent created beings. That conflict will reach its earthly climax when Satan foists upon the world a ruler the Bible calls "the man of sin."

Isaiah begins with the fact of Satan's fall, tells why that happened, and details some of its impact upon world history, before telling of Satan's latter end.

"How are you fallen from heaven, O Lucifer, son of the morning!

"How you are cut down to the ground, you who laid the nations low! You said in your heart, '*I will ascend to heaven, above the stars of God, I will set MY THRONE on high.* I will sit on the mount of assembly in the far north. I will ascend above the heights of the clouds, I WILL MAKE MYSELF LIKE THE MOST HIGH.'

"But you are brought down to Sheol, to the depths of the Pit. Those who see you will stare at you, and ponder over you, 'Is this *the man who made the earth tremble, who shook kingdoms, who made the world a desert and overthrew its cities,* who did not let his prisoners go home?' " (Isaiah 14:12-17, com)

Do not read over these terse but meaty declarations too quickly, for in very little space they are packed with information about who our adversary is, what he intends and the effect of his evil power in shaking kingdoms, overthrowing cities and denying his captives a place in God's eternal house.

Lucifer was not an ordinary servant of God, one of the ranks, so to speak. He was an extraordinary servant of God, created for and appointed to a place of leadership. It is probable that he was the messenger of God to other created beings, their angelic leader within the universal government of God. Lucifer was a creature so beautiful that he was called "the son of the morning."

Lucifer decided, on the basis of his beauty, his exalted station, and his perfection, that he would no longer submit to being subordinate to God but that he would make the attempt to set himself above God, to depose God from His throne, to overthrow His authority, and to bring God into subordination to him. That was the astounding iniquity that was found in his heart. Here we glimpse the creature desiring to exalt himself above his Creator.

Supplanting God as the supreme governor and object of worship in the universe is utterly out of his reach. Satan knows that, but it is still his burning and consuming ambition.

He cannot achieve it, so he will seek to wreck as much of the creation as he can, spiritually and physically. He will cause God to be supplanted in the hearts and lives of as *many* human beings as possible.

A man is the spiritual subject of the spirit he obeys—either Satan— "the spirit now at work in the children of disobedience"—or God.

Yet Satan, for all his power on the earth, is not a universal figure. He is not a kind of wicked equal to God. In his preface to *The Screwtape Letters,* C.S. Lewis put the matter well:

The commonest question is whether I really "believe in the Devil." Now, if by "the Devil" you mean a power opposite to God and, like God, self-existent from all eternity, the answer is certainly No. There is no uncreated being except God. God has no opposite. No being could attain a "perfect badness" opposite to the perfect goodness of God. . . . The proper question is whether I believe in devils. I do. . . . Satan, the leader or dictator of devils, is the opposite, not of God, but of Michael [the archangel].

In the Scriptures this deliberate enemy of God and man is called, among many other things, the devil, the adversary, Lucifer, the serpent, the evil one, Satan.

His design is to extend his rebellion against God to as many beings as he can and to reproduce in them aspects of his own nature of sin, thereby claiming them as *his* subjects and servants.

God's design is to enjoy the worship and voluntary obedience of His created beings, to reproduce in them His own character. He invites them to come to Him, but He honors the freedom of their wills and He will never, never oblige them to do so: He desires willing sons, not automatons. If they finally go the way of Satan, they go his way forever.

Self-will and self-exaltation began Lucifer's ruin. Five times he declared "I WILL" in express opposition to God. Each of those five times, he asserted that he would do something to promote his own interests in defiance of the interests of God:

"I will ascend to heaven."

"I will set *my throne* on high."

"I will sit on the mount of assembly in the far north."

"I will ascend above the heights of the clouds."

"*I will make myself like the Most High.*"

That was Satan's program for himself, his incredibly audacious bid to overthrow the supremacy of God and to make himself the center of the creation.

He has not succeeded at that impossible ambition. But he has succeeded in becoming that evil one "who made the earth tremble, who shook kingdoms, who made the world a desert and overthrew its cities," and he is still working at that. He has succeeded also in drawing human beings after him.

God has permitted that, perhaps to prove eternally that the will of every intelligent being is free and that it was open to them to disobey God or to obey Him, perhaps to prove forever that those who serve Him serve Him because they love Him, not because they lack another option.

It is clear that the nature of God is to be the loving Creator (and also the all-sufficient nourisher and sustainer of what He creates). It is probable that His greatest act of creation was to make man in the very image of God. Even though man was made a little lower than the angels, the destiny of redeemed mankind is to become joint heirs with Christ of the entire creation! Coregents over everything that is and ever will be. Ponder that awhile and it may take your breath away, but that is exactly what is promised.

It seems highly unlikely that God will at some point freeze the population of the universe at a fixed and final level, or that the Creator will shut off forever His power to create and go out of the grand business of creating. It is certainly conceivable that creation will be either a continuous or a recurrent process through endless ages. The promised new creation, successor to everything that has been touched by sin, may receive vast new populations fresh, so to speak, from the hand of God.

It is, in one respect, a highly dangerous thing to create intelligent beings in the likeness of God who are fully and continuously capable of unforced devotion to God or of autonomous and selfish action. Yet no lesser being, no matter how devoted, could fully satisfy the desire of God to live in the free and full exchange of love with His creatures. Any lesser arrangement—essentially one of controlled and guaranteed obedience—would populate the creation with beings incapable of any but a programmed response. *Love must have more.* To have more at the ultimate level, it must dare to make beings who are entirely free.

The creation must be clear of sin, so keeping intelligent moral beings in a state of unbroken obedience to God is altogether important, but it is not *the point.* The point is true love in true freedom forever.

We do know that the almighty God deals with moral beings by moral persuasion, not by irresistible constraint, applying discipline where necessary in love, and drawing them more and more by love. He also warns and even chastens—both aimed at obtaining a true moral response—but if these are rejected He almost never does more. He has too much respect for what He has made man to be to do so.

It may be that at this stage, from all eternity past to eternity future, in the grand adventure of creation, God is allowing moral rebellion to run its course, both in the heavens and on this earth, so that the moral force of its ruinous example will be demonstrated beyond all question by what it has cost and what it has ruined. Perhaps "the smoke of their torment rises for ever and ever" from the lake of fire (see Revelation 14:11) as an everlasting signpost to all free moral agents of that cost.

Many of the statements in these last five paragraphs are, of course, reasoned conjecture. Care is taken to name them as such, since they cannot be stated dogmatically from revealed Scripture.

What is not conjecture is that God has deliberately permitted a great rebellion to run on for quite some time toward its absolutely final end for reasons that are, in His sight, both good and necessary. What is not conjecture is that Satan has made himself a little god and that much of mankind is under his sway. The Bible tells us that Satan is "the god of this world [and] has blinded the minds of the unbelievers" (2 Corinthians 4:4, RSV).

Those who live in unforgiven sin, of whatever form, are not the sons of God. They are the subjects of Satan.

The idea that "we are all children of God," that all men are God's children, is not at all a biblical idea. We are not, by birth, the spiritual children of God. We inherit the nature of sin from our first father, Adam. We are "by nature the children of wrath," the Bible says (Ephesians 2:3, RSV).

Since we are not children of God by birth and by nature, we need to become the spiritual children of God. We do not have the power to make ourselves that. We become the children of God only by being "born anew," by spiritual rebirth.

The Scripture says of Jesus, "He was in the world, and the world was made by Him, yet the world knew Him not. . . . But as many as received Him, to them He gave power to *become the sons of God . . .* who were *born,* not of blood nor of the will of the flesh nor of the will of man, but of God" (John 1:10-13).

How does someone become a member of any family? By being born into it. It is the same with the family of God. We must be born into it. It is not by natural birth. It is "not of blood, nor of the will of the flesh, nor of the will of man." A person must be *"born of God."* There is no other way.

Satan, "the god of this world," is the promulgator of the dangerously deceptive religious teaching that "all men are the children of God." That stands in direct contradiction to the declaration of the Scriptures. Those who believe it understand themselves to be what, in fact, they are not.

"By this it may be seen who are *the children of God,* and who are *the children of the devil,*" 1 John 3:10 says, drawing the line of division between the two.

"We have one Father, even God," a religious leader said to Jesus, who replied, "If God were your Father, you would love Me, for I proceeded and came forth from God. I came not of My own accord, but He sent me. Why do you not understand what I say? It is because you cannot bear to hear My word.

*"You are of your father the devil, and your will is to do your father's desires.* He was a murderer from the beginning, and has nothing to do with the truth, because there is no truth in him. . . . He who is of God hears the words of God. The reason why you do not hear them is that *you are not of God"* (John 8:41-46, RSV).

Though it is often not clearly perceived, the stark fact is that Satan is the hidden, actual spiritual head of all men who stand short of the blood atonement that God has provided to make us His twice-born sons and daughters.

In summary, Satan was, at his origin, a being of consummate beauty.

He was created as a prince, a leader of the angels of God, was given a place of high responsibility and privilege, and was endowed with capacities that fully suited him for his work. He may have been the closest to God of all created beings.

When iniquity was found in him, he lost his position in heaven, but he did not lose his immense capacity, his intelligence, his quality of leadership, nor even apparently certain aspects of his appearance that seem Godlike and desirable. What he did was take them out of the service of God and devote them to the leadership of an insurrection against God.

In presenting himself, when he does, Satan does not present himself as he is, but he presents himself in disguise—that is, he presents himself as what he is not. The Bible says that "Satan disguises himself as an angel of light" (2 Corinthians 11:14, RSV).

It is a triumph of Satan's policy that so little is known of him in a world in which he promotes and sponsors so much evil and destruction and death. Concerning the scope of his influence and power, the Bible says quite flatly that *the whole world is in the power of the evil one* (1 John 5:19, RSV).

In the activities of his rebellion against God and his bid for the destruction of man, Satan is not alone.

# 3

# THE
# THIEVES
# OF
# FOREVER

# The Angels of the Dragon

Just as God has angels who do His will, Satan has angels who do his will. The Bible calls them evil spirits. It also calls them demons and devils.

There is no more dire reality confronting human existence than that of evil spirits. They are the unseen enemies of God and of man; they are ceaselessly at work against the will of God and against all the best interests of man. The effects of their activity are all around us today, and the Scriptures inform us that these effects are going to be multiplied many times, and at a very rapid pace, as the prophesied events of the end-time occur—events that precede the era when the returned Lord Jesus will righteously "rule all the nations with an iron scepter" and martyred believers will come to "life and reign with Christ a thousand years" on earth (Revelation 12:5; 20:4).

The fact that the flag of Israel flies over the ancient land, after nearly 2,000 years when Israel had no existence as a nation, is a miracle of history and geography and a major signpost of end-time events, many of which are to center on Israel.

A secular writer wrote a book with the intriguing title *The Rush Hour of the Gods.* Such "gods" are demons and they will, indeed, be in a rush to push their wicked programs before their time is up. Yet, there is no major area of biblical revelation that is more appallingly neglected than that telling of evil spirits.

The term *demons* is foreign to the American consciousness; remote from the common American concepts of the nature of life and being. Yet no living person escapes the attention of demons.

Ignorance of them, just about total in the West, is becoming less and less convenient in our society, because there has been a marked step-up in demonic supernatural activity in North America in recent years. We see its effects on almost every hand, but too often we are blind to its source.

The demons depend for success in their program of disrupting and destroying human life on ignorance of who they are, what they do, and how they do it. The Bible, the accurate guide to the who and what of the supernatural, throws a searchlight of revelation into the darkness in which demons thrive and shows them up.

By the knowledge gained through the Word of God, demons may be exposed, identified, and dispossessed by men. They may also be intelligently and effectively resisted.

As the head of an organized rebellion against the government of God, Satan leads a host of angelic collaborators. It appears that they number in the millions.

The angels are a divided company. The Scriptures speak, in Matthew 25:41, of "the devil and his angels." That description came from the lips of Jesus, and by it we know that there are angels who follow Satan and are under his command.

The demons were not created as such. They had their origin among the angels of God, as Satan had. Demons are reprobate angels who follow Satan and do his will.

Some quite wonderful speculations have circulated among believers that demons are the disembodied wicked spirits of a human race that existed before Adam. The biblical evidence for this seems so thin as to be virtually invisible unless it is energetically whipped up into an imaginative froth. But I will say no more of it because of this more important fact: even if believers have different views of their origin but are agreed that they are wicked and are to be resisted and overcome by the power of the risen Lord, our approach to them and their works will be the same.

All of the angels were servants of God until Lucifer, the "son of the morning," rebelled and caused a great split among them. Most held to their loyalty to God. Others abandoned that loyalty and went after Lucifer, or Satan.

The Scriptures speak of the angels who sinned against God. The Bible says that "God did not spare the angels when they sinned, but cast them down . . . and committed them to pits of nether gloom to be kept until the judgment" (2 Peter 2:4, RSV).

Again, the Epistle of Jude tells of "the angels who did not keep their first estate but left their own habitation" (v. 6). The demons are angels who left their first estate, as Satan left his. It appears that some evil spirits were put away in confinement. Others are scripturally described as working closely with their leader.

The demons are all individual personalities and they have names. Like all spiritual beings, demons are normally invisible to man. They possess the same faculties as angels, but they have put them out to wicked ends. Every evil spirit has a will, intelligence, a personality, and a distinctive character of its own.

When these angels turned away from God and followed Satan, God turned against them. He did so because their misuse of their native capacities began to undermine the safety and tranquility of the universe.

"Evil spirits" is an accurate descriptive term for demons because they are spirits—invisible living beings—wholly devoted to doing evil.

I have quoted the Scripture that declares that "God is a *spirit.*" Angels are described as "ministering *spirits.*" As fallen angels, demons are described as "evil *spirits.*"

We are told that Satan, "the prince of the power of the air," is "the spirit who is at work in the children of disobedience" (Ephesians 2:2, KJV). Notice that term "at work." It speaks of direct, personal satanic activity upon and within individual human beings. Since Satan cannot be everywhere at once, much of his active work is carried out by spirits whose allegiance is to him, to whom he delegates certain assignments.

The men and women who are now engaged in conveying so many evils throughout this society are "children of disobedience" in whom and through whom Satan and his demons are "at work." Such individuals, whether they know it or not, allow demons to use them to carry forward some of Satan's purposes in the earth.

*The work of evil spirits is to do whatever they can to ruin people morally, spiritually, physically, and mentally.*

They seek especially, but not exclusively, to ruin human beings morally in the sexual area of life and to ruin them spiritually in the religious area of life. Both of these are critical areas in which, if a person is affected by evil spirits, the results are particularly destructive.

In either of these areas, human beings, if they turn aside from the will of God and are overcome, can be ruined not only in this life but for eternity. Satan is acutely aware that God has declared that no fornicator or adulterer or homosexual offender, no drunkard or idolater will enter heaven, unless truly and fully repentant, forgiven and cleansed. That is why he specializes in promoting or justifying just such things (1 Corinthians 6:9-11).

The word *angel* literally means "messenger." The angels are messengers of God. The demons are messengers of Satan who engage in tempting people to do what is evil and in encouraging them to believe what is not true.

The Scriptures reveal that demons have "doctrines," or a system of spiritual teachings that they present to mankind, contrary to the truth. Demons have false doctrines of salvation, of eternal destiny, of love, of reincarnation, of self-sacrifice, of asceticism, of the way of access to God, and many others. Each of these doctrines is a lie, presented as truth. That is why the Scriptures warn us not to be "ignorant of the devil's devices" and not to "give heed to deceitful spirits and doctrines of demons" (1 Timothy 4:1, RSV).

The demons—as deliberate, conscious agents of Satan—are occupied in constant, active rebellion against God. They also engage in conflict against men and women who are truly God's servants. They come unseen to do whatever they can to hinder or buffet such individuals, to snare them, to withstand or thwart them in carrying out God's will. They will stoop to any trick or deceit or treachery or lie to prevent God's will from being done on the earth as it is done in heaven.

Their work is not directed solely to men and women who belong to God. They endeavor to get all men and women to violate the will of God. Demons are particularly bent on damaging and destroying human beings—individually, in groups, or, when possible, *en masse*. They use whatever means are convenient to that end.

Taken together, demons constitute the invisible forces of evil assailing mankind today—assailing individual men and women, societies, and nations. Their activities will intensify as the great prophetic events of the end-time occur. Ignorance of who they are and what they do will become more than ever costly.

The American society, once largely free of a good many workings of evil spirits common in areas of the world where the light of God's Word was little known, has come under massive invasion and attack by evil spirits. The attack is especially concentrated on young people, and though people see the results of it, they are often bewildered by the destructive forces now active among us.

Spiritual powers and spiritual forces, of good and evil, are at warfare today, not figuratively but literally, and that fact is reflected in many surprising, untoward, and frequently violent eruptions among men and nations.

This conflict between the will of God and the will of Satan is conducted on several levels. It is conducted on the earth, it is conducted in the atmosphere of the earth, and it is conducted in the lower heavens.

The angels who serve God and the demons who follow Satan engage in conflict. The Book of Revelation gives us a glimpse of this:

*"Now war arose in heaven, Michael and his angels fighting against the dragon, and the dragon and his angels fought"* (12:7, RSV). The dragon is a figurative term for "the devil and Satan," as the next verse states.

Here are seen two companies of angels under different leaders—Michael and his angels, and Satan and his angels. Michael, an archangel, is a leader of the angels of God, while Satan leads the host of angels called demons, devils, or evil spirits.

This conflict bears upon man, for both angels and demons have to do with men and women.

The earth, and particularly the atmosphere of the earth, is under occupation by Satan and his angelic legions. That is why Satan is called "the god of this world" and "the prince of the power of the air." Acting with him, among the demons, are other evil princes subordinate to him. They stand together in unrelenting defiance of God's will.

There is a graphic account of this in the Book of Daniel, which tells the life of that Hebrew prophet in the court of Babylon. To Daniel was entrusted a series of prophecies concerning the whole course of Gentile world kingdoms and concerning the destiny of the Jewish people "in the latter days." These prophecies are of momentous character and they are immensely relevant to world events today and to events that lie ahead. Because they provide a key to these events, the enemy did all that he could to oppose Daniel's receiving God's Word concerning them.

After Babylon fell, Daniel continued as a high government official and a prophet in the court of Persia. Chapter 10 of the Book of Daniel starts: "In the third year of Cyrus king of Persia a word was revealed to Daniel, who was named Belteshazzar. And the word was true and it was a great conflict. And he understood the word and had understanding of the vision."

Because of the gravity of what he was shown, Daniel devoted three full weeks to prayer and partial fasting. In response, a remarkable thing happened. A visitor came to Daniel from heaven.

When this "man clothed in linen" appeared to him, Daniel writes, "I stood up trembling. Then he said to me, 'Fear not, Daniel, for *from the first day* that you set your mind to understand and humbled yourself before your God, your words have been heard, and I have come because of your words. *The prince of the kingdom of Persia withstood me twenty-one days;* but Michael, one of the chief princes, came to help me, so I left him there with the prince of the kingdom of Persia and came to make you understand what is to befall your people in the latter days'" (Daniel 10:11-14, RSV).

The amazing fact is that the visitor from heaven had trouble getting through! He was powerfully withstood.

Daniel's prayer was heard the *first day,* and the visitor was sent on the first day, but when he reached the atmosphere of the earth "the prince of the kingdom of Persia" arose and withstood him for twenty-one days. Victory came, but it was neither easy nor automatic. Daniel engaged in prayer and fasting that entire time.

In this passage God, angels, demons, and men are seen in related action in the conflict.

"The prince of the kingdom of Persia" who withstood the visitor was the demonic leader of the forces of spiritual darkness in Persia—the chief demon appointed by Satan to rule over Persia in the interests of Satan and against the interests of God. (There are, no doubt, prince demons over many regions or peoples in the world, inspiring and seeking to enforce particular forms of darkness designed for and imposed upon these regions—hence the extremely heathen, 10,000-gods religious practices of India, so distinct from the heavy hand of the autocratic Muslim clergy upon much of the Arab world, a religion sometimes characterized by a vengeful extremism.)

Notice that Michael, a chief prince of the angels of God, came to the side of the man from heaven. This visit to the earth created an emergency for "the rulers of the darkness of this world" and aroused them to a mighty effort to prevent the crucial visitation. Michael came and stood against the prince of the kingdom of Persia—a prince angel contending against a prince demon—and occupied him so that the heavenly visitor was free to continue on his way to Daniel. Here, in the Old Testament, we see conflict between the angels under Satan and the angels of God under Michael similar to that shown in the New Testament Book of the Revelation.

The man Daniel had a part in this conflict in his day. It was his wholehearted prayer that caused the visitor to come. "I have come because of your word," he told Daniel. His purpose was to impart vital information about the future of the world and of the Jews.

From this episode it can be seen that there is a definite interrelatedness between the work of God, angels, men, and demons. It was Daniel's prayer from the earth that stirred heaven to respond, and it was the appearing of the heavenly visitor that stirred the prince demon to oppose. This brought Michael to the scene to contend against the prince demon. There was something going on in the earth, something going on in heaven, and something going on in the atmosphere of the earth; and each bore a relation to the other events and to the central conflict.

This episode from Daniel exposes the reality of the intense opposition of evil spirits to the purposes of God. Do not underestimate that conflict, for it is going on today with great ferocity, and some of the very events revealed to Daniel appear to be coming to a head—events connected to the "latter days" of the Jewish people, which could not occur while Israel was only a dream, and a promise.

## Acts of Power and Love: Setting Victims Free

We are told that "God anointed Jesus of Nazareth with the Holy Spirit and with power." As a consequence, Jesus, in His earthly ministry, "went about doing good and healing all who were oppressed by the devil" (Acts 10:38, rsv).

Jesus did His liberating work by preaching, by teaching, by acts of kindness, and by acts of power, including healing the sick and casting out demons.

An immensely important fact is that evil spirits can, under certain circumstances, enter into and occupy the human body and use it as the vehicle for carrying out their own depraved intentions. They cannot, I hasten to add, do this at mere will. They must be given a basis for occupation by voluntary acts of human compliance with evil—most probably either repeated and willful acts or a venture into some extreme and forbidden thing.

I have talked with individuals who became Christians after their involvement in occultism or spiritism. Their experiences gave them an especially keen and painful awareness of the demonic supernatural and of the damage, trouble, and torment that come to a person by it.

But my first direct awareness of the reality depicted in the Bible as a contemporary fact came in a most unexpected way, during an interview with a professor at Union Theological Seminary in New York. I did not go there by choice; a magazine editor told me to go there to get what he called "another perspective" for an article. I did not expect to come away with much more than some vague or lofty theological formulations, but I came away, to my great surprise, with a heightened awareness of a biblical reality brought up to date.

The professor was a quiet man of about retirement age. After a scholarly review of healing in the first 300 years of the Christian church, he made some remarks about a young married woman in a southern state who had become deeply disturbed in her personality, for reasons that were not apparent. She had been to psychologists but had obtained no help. In a kind of stab at hope, she sought the counsel of a Presbyterian minister, who took a radically different approach to her case. Through his help she obtained relief from her distress, relief that proved to be complete.

"I have a tape recording," the professor said, "of the session in which she got relief from her trouble. It is quite remarkable. Would you like to hear it?"

In the next forty-five minutes, as the tape played, I heard two voices. The voice of the minister and the woman's voice. But it became plain that the minister was not talking to the woman. He was talking to *another intelligent personality in the woman!* He was addressing himself, intentionally and directly, to an evil spirit.

What I remember most vividly is that, about halfway through the session, the woman's voice changed. It ceased to be a natural young woman's voice and became an odd, rather high-pitched, whiny, nasal sound.

"You're hurting my head, pastor," her voice said with a kind of nasty, pleading petulance. Three or four times the phrase was repeated.

"I am not touching this young woman's head. I am not hurting her head. I am speaking to you, you foul and lying spirit," the minister said. Two or three times he reproved the evil spirit for lying through the woman's lips.

As I realized later, the demon to whom the minister was speaking was being brought out of hiding within her by stages—was, in short, beginning to be forced against its will to reveal itself as actually present in the woman.

Up to that point, the evil spirit had sought to hide its identity entirely behind that of the woman and to remain undetected. Now, however, the spirit knew that it had been discovered and identified by the minister, and it began to speak directly, with no further attempt to hide.

For a while this intruding personality was belligerent toward the minister, but as he took authority over it, an evident tremor came into the voice that spoke to the minister, and it increased until its tone was that of a nearly hysterical panic.

"You are going to go out of this young woman," the minister said in a strong, even voice.

"If I go out, I will come back in," the high-pitched voice replied.

"No. You will not come back in," the minister said. "You are going to go out today, and you will never come back in."

All challenges, all argument disappeared from the responding voice. It became considerably weaker, and it was filled with fear and pleading. The evil spirit to whom the minister spoke no longer made an issue of staying or leaving. Instead, it began to bargain for the terms of its departure! The voice begged the minister, in a pitiful manner, not to command it to go far away.

The minister took final authority. "You foul and lying spirit," he said. "I command you, in the name of Jesus Christ, to come out of this woman now and not to return."

The young woman, from that moment on, had suffered no more from her perplexing distress, the professor said. He said that what I heard had taken place some months earlier.

What had happened in the final moment was that a demonic spirit, an intelligent agent of evil, who had entered the young woman and had occupied part of her being for many months, causing her much unaccountable distress, had been *discovered, identified,* and *cast out.*

This was a modern-day instance of the casting out of demons. It was the first of which I had ever known, but in the next several years I was to learn of case after case from many different sources, all isolated but often exhibiting the most striking similarities in method, in response and result. It became impossible for me to avoid the conclusion that evil spirits do sometimes enter into human beings, entirely unsuspected and unseen, and remain until something explicit and forceful and direct is done to get them out.

I heard, from the lips of reputable and intelligent ministers and missionaries, so many accounts of their own direct experiences in dealing with evil spirits that had taken up residence within troubled individuals—and these accounts, though they were based on experiences as far removed as China from Switzerland, are so remarkably similar in their content—that I cannot doubt their validity.

While I was looking into this in the same searching way I went about my newspaper reporting, there came into my hands an invaluable book entitled *Demon Experiences in Many Lands: A Compilation,* published in paperback by Moody Press in Chicago, a thoroughly responsible Christian publishing house. It contained thirty-one separate accounts by missionaries from all over the world of personal experiences in dealing with cases of demon possession and in casting demons out. The accounts come from India, Japan, Korea, Mexico, Ecuador, Colombia, Brazil, Guatemala, Basutoland, Haiti, and many other nations. Each account is signed by the missionary relating it. It shed basic light in this much-neglected, important area. The book is not currently in print, but to those wishing to pursue the matter it probably can be found in some

Bible school and seminary libraries.

In giving His commission to the disciples, Jesus said, "And these signs shall follow them that believe: *In My name* they shall cast out devils" (Mark 16:17, KJV). The casting out of demons was to be one part of the total ministry of the Christian church to humanity. In His three years of ministry Jesus repeatedly engaged in casting demons out of people. Matthew 8:16 records that "when the evening was come, they brought to Him many who were possessed with devils, and He *cast out the spirits with His word.*" Jesus recognized them, identified them, and ordered them to depart from their victims.

It is equally true that the demons recognized Him. They often made that recognition emphatically known by speaking through the individuals in whom they dwelled.

At one point, "a great multitude from Galilee followed" Jesus, "for He had healed many, so that all who had diseases pressed upon Him to touch Him. And whenever the unclean spirits beheld Him, they fell down before Him and cried out, 'You are the Son of God.' And He strictly ordered them not to make Him known" (Mark 3:7-12, RSV).

Jesus knew who they were, and they knew who Jesus was. Jesus did not want their testimony, even though it was accurate. Atheists and agnostics exist among human beings, with minds blinded by "the god of this age," but there are no atheists among evil spirits. They have not the faintest doubt as to the deity of Jesus, and though they are liars by nature, they knew it was futile to lie to Him. Another thing of which they had no doubt is their destiny. They saw it clearly. The Scripture says that "the devils also believe and tremble" (James 2:19, RSV).

Once "in the synagogue there was a man who had the spirit of an unclean demon, who cried out with a loud voice, 'What have You to do with us, Jesus of Nazareth? Have You come to destroy us? I know who You are, the Holy One of God.' "

It was not the man speaking; it was the evil spirit speaking through the man. Knowing that Jesus had come to destroy the works of the devil, it was in anguish at His presence. "But Jesus rebuked him, saying, 'Be silent, and come out of him!' And when the demon had thrown him down in the midst, *he came out of him,* having done him no harm. And they were all amazed and said to one another, 'What a word is this! For with authority and power He commands the unclean spirits, and they come out' " (Luke 4:33-36, RSV).

This ministry of casting out demons was to continue in the church through the disciples, and indeed it did. It is part of the basic and continuing mission of the church for the alleviation of suffering, and a good many American missionaries to heathen lands have found it so.

We read in Acts that when "Philip went down to the city of Samaria, and preached Christ to them," one result was that "unclean spirits, crying with a loud voice, came out of many who were possessed with them" (Acts 8:5-7, KJV).

Evil spirits are not all alike in the particular expressions of their depravity. There are spirits who specialize in lying, in hatred, in various delusions, in depression, in fear. There are evil spirits of self-destruction, of exhibitionism, of rebellion, of fanaticism, and they produce in their victims' behavior these bizarre effects.

While on a reporting assignment for a national magazine traveling through the Midwest, I met an Episcopal rector in Illinois, an evangelical, who told me of a singular experience in his ministry.

The Rev. Richard E. Winkler said that the six-year-old son of a woman who lived near the church had become dangerously destructive, but physicians could find no cause nor offer any solution. The boy would sometimes strike matches and set fires, and he would jump out of the second-story window of his home, bruising himself in the drop.

The boy's mother brought him to the church. "The mother was beside herself," the rector said. "She had to watch the child every moment. Evidently he was possessed by a demon of destruction."

As soon as the rector took the child and put him on his lap, the boy kicked and thrashed and struggled like a wild animal. The minister had to hold him down. While several others prayed, Mr. Winkler began to deal directly with an evil spirit of destruction. He took authority over the spirit and, in the name of Jesus Christ, ordered it to leave the child.

"It was wonderful to see," the minister's wife said. "The child changed just like night and day, from a kicking, squalling kid to a peaceful, quiet little boy before our eyes." Now calm and still, the boy needed no longer to be held. The rector talked with the mother awhile. Then they left.

Mr. Winkler said that the child had never since set fires or done anything else abnormally destructive. He appeared to be a normal, happy child thereafter.

The wild struggle the boy put up just a moment or two before he was set free is typical of some cases of demonic possession. I have been told repeatedly that inordinate strength is often exercised by persons troubled by evil spirits, usually just at the point at which ministers are ready to cast the spirits out. Though the demons are not physical beings, they are sometimes able to apply great force in the physical realm when they occupy a human body, particularly at the point at which they begin to feel threatened by exposure, identification, and dispossession.

My direct experience is limited but impossible to forget. I was talking by telephone with a relative whom I greatly respected, and I was surprised at how agitated and accusatory she became. The conversation got hot and heavy and, not quite on impulse, but with only a moment's deliberation, I decided to speak directly to the spirits I believed to be at work. I said slowly, "I am not talking to this person. I am talking to the evil spirits who are troubling her. In the name of Jesus, be still."

The only response came in the next sound—the clicking of the receiver at the other end. She had hung up. Briefly the thought came to mind, "Now you've done it." I wondered what the content of our *next* conversation might be like. I did not have to wait long to know.

Within less than a minute, my phone rang. It was my relative. She made not the slightest reference to what had just happened, and never has since, but now she spoke in a calm, clear, entirely untroubled voice, and it was a pleasure to speak with her.

This was not, I think, a case of demonic possession but of evil agitation that was ended, virtually at an instant, by naming it for what it was and dealing with it that way. When Jesus sharply rebuked Peter for his misunderstanding of God's purpose by saying, "Get behind Me, Satan," He was not dealing with possession but with evil suggestion.

The act of casting out demons may sometimes be almost instantaneous. At other times, it is possible only after a considerable amount of spiritual conflict and prayer.

A man came to Jesus and said, " 'Teacher, I brought my son to You, for he has a dumb spirit, and wherever it seizes him, it dashes him down; and he foams and grinds his teeth and becomes rigid; and I asked Your disciples to cast it out, and they were not able.' " Jesus said, " 'Faithless generation, how long am I to be with you? How long am I to bear with you? Bring him to Me.'

"And they brought the boy to Him, and when the spirit saw Him, immediately it convulsed the boy, and he fell on the ground and rolled about, foaming at the mouth. And Jesus asked his father, 'How long has he had this?' And he said, 'From childhood. And it has often cast him into the fire and into the water, to destroy him. If You can do anything, have pity on us and help us.' "

Looking at the boy, Jesus said, " 'You dumb and deaf spirit, I command you, come out of him and never enter him again.' And after crying out and convulsing him terribly, it came out, and the boy was like a corpse, so that most of them said, 'He is dead.' But Jesus took him by the hand and lifted him up, and he arose. And when He had entered the house, His disciples asked Him privately, 'Why could we not cast it out?' And He said, 'This kind cannot be driven out by anything but prayer and fasting' " (Mark 9:17-29, COM).

In setting the boy free, Jesus did not stop the final convulsive act of the intruding spirit in the victim. The boy was possessed by one evil spirit that robbed him of his hearing and the power of speech. It forced him to fall into fire or water in an effort "to destroy him." At other times the demon convulsed the boy and at times it made him seem paralyzed.

Some spirits afflict or destroy those they possess. Some drive their victims to suicide. Others do not immediately cause their victims to harm themselves. Instead, they use them to torment, deceive, and even to destroy other human beings. Other demons drive their victims insane.

Two opposite dangers or failures would seem to face the church in North America. The more widespread danger takes the form of ignoring the works of evil spirits or largely relegating them to a former time, or of recognizing them *theoretically* or only in the most blatant forms, such as in persons engaged in the practices of witchcraft or voodoo. With this stance goes an ignoring or laying aside of the lawful weapons of the church in dealing with evil spirits.

The other danger or failure, instances of which I have encountered, is to become so fascinated with and centered upon the subject of demon activity as to lose balance. There is, for instance, an independent Gospel church in the Midwest whose minister moved into a ministry of helping individuals afflicted by evil spirits by casting them out and who became so caught up in the phenomenon and I think, in its more spectacular aspects, that he began to conclude most services in the church with a big session of dealing with demons in individuals who come from many distant places. Knowing of this, another minister who deals at times directly with cases of demonic possession, remarked, "Thank God our services don't come to an end with that going on!"

The total ministry of the church of Jesus Christ comes from the totality of its active and faithful members, with their varying gifts, and especially from those called to specific ministries. Among the latter, some will and do at times exercise the authority of the Lord Jesus Christ in rebuking evil spirits. They do so responsibly, for the sake of the persons affected, not for the sake of making a public show.

## Legion: A Trophy of Grace

Whether we like it or not, whether we know it or not, there is no escaping the fact that evil spirits are at work in human society. Until the coming of the Lord, the church of Jesus Christ is appointed by heaven to be the single greatest counterforce to evil powers.

Wherever the church is alive, alert, and faithful, it severely crimps demonic activity in many ways just by what it is and what it does. It also has, in its armory, specific weapons of devastating efficacy against the workings of evil powers. They are vital and not to be laid aside, but they are far from the whole. Overall, it is highly probable that more damage is done to the interests of the devil by godly lives of consistent faith, especially those called to particular vocations in faith, than by anything else.

That statement is the context in which the following close-ups of certain specifics are to be understood.

To the gainsayers of His day, Jesus said, "If I drive out demons by the finger of God, then the kingdom of God has come to you" (Luke 11:20).

The name and the authority of Jesus is the source of the only power that can fully overcome demons and, if possession has occurred, cast them out. Moreover, the name of Jesus and His authority over evil spirits can only be applied and enforced by an individual who truly believes in Him.

There is an interesting account in the Book of Acts regarding this. It says that "God did extraordinary miracles by the hands of Paul," by which some who were sick were healed and others who had evil spirits were set free. "Then some of the itinerant Jewish exorcists undertook to pronounce the name of the Lord Jesus over those who had evil spirits, saying, 'I adjure you by the Jesus whom Paul preaches.'

"Seven sons of a Jewish high priest named Sceva were doing this. But *the evil spirit answered them,* 'Jesus I know and Paul I know, but who are you?' And the man in whom the evil spirit was leaped on them, mastered all of them, and overpowered them, so that they fled out of the house naked and wounded" (Acts 19:11-16, RSV).

One man, possessed with a demon, overcame seven young men. The mistake of the young men was that they attempted to engage in a supernatural activity by imitation. They were practical men. They had observed that the demons could not hold onto their victims when Paul confronted them in the name and in the authority of Jesus. Since they were exorcists, and since they wanted results, they decided to try using the name of Jesus, but they used that name in a kind of imitative rote, in an experimental way: "I adjure you by the Jesus whom Paul preaches."

It was a secondhand sort of thing. They did not know Jesus personally, but by reputation. Their use of His name was therefore of no effect.

There is no magic in invoking the name of Jesus in such cases, but there is power to cast demons out in His name when it is spoken by one who knows Jesus and who has faith to cast them out—not in some kind of boisterous haste but with a clear, calm, Word-founded faith.

There is no primary ministry of exorcism in the New Testament. Though frequently done, it was not primary in the ministry of Jesus, nor in the work of Philip the evangelist nor Paul. It was *present* and powerful in their ministries, not primary.

Satan and demons, with no creative power, have only the power to go against what God has created, even to the point of destroying it in part. They do so largely by proxy through human beings who fall sway to their promptings, temptations, or deceptions. "You create; we destroy," is what they say, in full effect, to God. "You establish order; we overthrow it and wreak havoc."

For clear evidence of what unclean spirits do when they are able to gain extreme advantage, and a true picture of their mercilessness, the following account from the Gospel of Mark affords insight into their character and works.

Jesus and His disciples came across the Sea of Galilee. "And when Jesus had come out of the boat, there came out of the tombs a man with an unclean spirit, who lived among the tombs. No one could bind him any more, even with a chain; for he had often been bound with fetters and chains, but the chains he wrenched apart, and the fetters he broke in pieces; and no one had the strength to subdue him.

"Night and day among the tombs and on the mountains he was always crying out, and bruising himself with stones. And when he saw Jesus from afar, he ran and worshiped Him. And crying out with a loud voice, he said, 'What have You to do with me, Jesus, Son of the Most High God? I adjure You by God, do not torment me.' For Jesus had said to him, 'Come out of the man, you unclean spirit!'

"And Jesus asked him, 'What is your name?'

"He replied, 'My name is Legion, for *We are many.*' And he begged Him eagerly not to send *THEM* out of the country. . . .

"So He gave them leave. And the unclean spirits came out, and entered the swine; and the herd, numbering about 2,000, rushed down the steep bank, and were drowned in the sea" (Mark 5:1-13, com).

Notice that Jesus did not deal with the evil spirits as *conditions* but as with *intelligent beings.* There are some who are fond of saying that, in this, Jesus was merely going along with the superstitions of His time, but it is not the case.

Jesus made a distinction. He dealt with conditions as conditions, and He dealt with evil spirits as evil spirits, and He knew the difference.

Some illnesses He healed as illnesses; others He recognized as physical symptoms of demon possession, and He cast out the evil spirits.

Think for a moment of the state of the man whom Jesus met in the tombs—a man made in the image of God as to origin and, though born in sin, still bearing many aspects of that likeness, as we all do, but now reduced to a pathetic captivity, a travesty on God's design and loving intent.

Friendless and homeless, he was useless, dangerous to himself and others (Matthew adds that, fearing violence, "no one could pass that way"), utterly insane, uncontrollable, miserable. He had been consigned to permanent futility.

What a grief to the heart of God such a human spectacle must be. See him roaming the tombs and the mountaintops night and day, howling or making strange crying noises. How rarely he must have had anything like decent food. Jesus showed nothing but care for the man. He had not a word of reproof for him. He dealt solely with the evil spirits.

The man in the tombs was not his own master after unclean spirits had gained control. They drove him away from human society and made him a wild, restless, reckless, roaming recluse.

The man had more than merely human strength ("the chains he wrenched apart"). Evil spirits forced him to inflict damage on his own body, and Jesus, in a few moments' time, turned it all around. What a trophy of grace that man became!

As soon as He met him, Jesus fixed His gaze on the man and said, "Come out of the man, you unclean spirit."

It is critically important to notice that Jesus *did not address the man.* He went *beyond the man* and directly addressed the unclean spirit.

The man's voice cried out, "What have You to do with me, Jesus, Son of the Most High God? I adjure You by God, do not torment me."

It was the demons speaking, trying to hide themselves behind the identity of the man. Evil spirits seek the closest possible identification with the person they inhabit, so that their words and acts will be mistakenly ascribed to the person. The spirits were in great fear of Jesus, because He had absolute power over them, so they begged Him not to torment "me."

They used the first-person singular because they still hoped to conceal their true identity. They hoped to make it seem that the *man* was asking Jesus not to torment him.

Plainly, Jesus had not come to torment the man. The evil spirits were doing that. Jesus did not speak to the man. He addressed the demons: "What is your name?"

"My name is Legion," the man's voice answered, "for *WE* are many."

The invaders were now out in the open, forced to reveal themselves as foreign beings occupying the body of the man.

Verse 12 of this account specifically shows that it was not the possessed man who was speaking to Jesus, but the unclean spirits in the man. It says: "*They* begged Him, 'Send *us* to the swine; let us enter them.'" No man could go into swine.

Jesus made them leave the man, but He allowed them to go into the swine. Immediately two things happened.

The man out of whom the demons had gone sat there quietly, "clothed and *in his right mind.*"

The pigs on the hillside, into which the demons went, immediately "rushed down the steep bank into the sea, and were drowned in the sea." The herd ran wild. The 2,000 swine were destroyed.

When the demons, though unseen to the natural eye, entered the herd of pigs, the man was perfectly sane and rational and calm, but the pigs immediately became self-destructive, as the man had been.

Real demons had gone out of a real man and entered real pigs. When they left the man and went into the pigs, their activity was transferred from the man to the pigs. There can be no more graphic depiction than this of the reality of evil spirits and of the effects of demon possession.

The church of Jesus Christ is characterized by the fact that its many members have many differing gifts—as Paul wrote in Romans 12:6, "We have different gifts, according to the grace given us." He immediately cites such gifts as serving, teaching, giving to the needy, leadership, and acts of mercy.

In 1 Corinthians 12:29, the apostle asks, "Are all teachers? Do all work miracles?" plainly conveying that such gifts belong to some, while others have other gifts, among them administration. Every such gift is valid, grace-given, and quite actually necessary to the whole functioning of the church; and it is sheer folly to unduly exalt one over another, or to diminish one because it is unlike another.

Do not let "the foot say, 'Because I am not a hand, I do not belong to the body,'" Paul wisely counsels in 1 Corinthians 12:15. Both parts, foot and hand, and many others, all acting with due regard for the rest, make up the body of Christ, His church. Working in a complementary way, each strengthens the others and the whole.

The quiet, godly Bible teacher steeped in the wisdom of the Word and able to minister it with clarity to others, is as essential as the fiery evangelist, with a motivating passion to bring souls to Christ. We are richer for having both. Where all is evangelism, there is little growth in the knowledge of the Lord, and where all is teaching, the church grows older and wiser but lacks the fresh infusion of life that comes by the adding of new members in their newfound joy.

Since God's true economy is marked by wisdom, the gifts and ministries will exist in a reasonable and proper balance. Some will occur more frequently than others, and some will be given to relatively few. The incidence of occurrence is not what is important, but the genuineness of the gift.

A specific gift belonging to the church that relates to the demonic realm is the "discerning of spirits" named in 1 Corinthians 12:10 (KJV). Do not for a moment confuse that with keen insight, and do not confuse it with anything resembling a so-called ability to see into other people's interior lives, to sift their souls, so to speak, to see what is there. Such a rummaging "gift" would be a source of mischief more than any good.

The gift chiefly has to do, not so much with the character of any individual, but with the presence and working of evil spirits in contradistinction to the Holy Spirit. It is not given for information primarily. Where there are demonically troubled or afflicted individuals, discerning allows evil spirits to be identified so that they can be resisted in their working or, if possession has occurred, commanded to depart. This gift is more necessary where the working of the enemy is intentionally subtle so as to deceive the unwary.

In the case of a false teacher, a person working with or influenced by demonic powers, the Christian believer possessing this special ability should be able to know quickly what is at work, even in cases where the appearance of the false worker may be pleasing, lively, and seemingly genuine.

The most dangerous spiritual enemies are not those who are outright fakes, whom almost any intelligent and observant believer should be able to identify, but those who are taught or led by evil spirits, whether they are aware of it themselves or not. Their points of variance with biblical truth may be so well-disguised or subtle that many believers could not readily see their errors.

When the whole universalist lie swept in upon Protestant Christianity in North America, it did so by citing Scriptures that were accurately and even passionately quoted, yet used to form doctrine without reference to other Scriptures that had equal bearing and validity. The universalist heresy, which drew considerable numbers of people away from true faith, came in on the appearance of earnest scriptural belief. A century or more later, after it had deceived countless victims, its true nature was plain as universalism became the vehicle for all manner of antibiblical beliefs, including the outright advocacy of flagrant sins.

The enemy is a strategist. He will deceive people at the outset only as far as he senses they *can* be deceived. Once he gets a wedge of untruth in place, he will later make a hole big enough for many false and evil things to enter.

Though relatively rare in its occurrence—leaving aside those who pretend to it with flamboyance and guile—the discerning of spirits and its attendant release for the victims of evil spirits is of high value to those who have such need. I have never seen a clearer definition of the discerning of spirits than this, "The God-given ability to detect the presence, and to ascertain the identity of, evil spirits."

There is sometimes a tendency to put aside something real on the ground that it is counterfeited by certain persons. We do not do that with money. We have not done that with evangelism, though it is surely falsified by some. We should not do so with anything that belongs to the church on biblical authority.

We should, however, and we must, always insist on testing it according to the Scriptures. It is crucial to remember that Jesus, who cast out devils regularly and who gave it to His disciples, apostles, and other believers to do the same, thereby putting the seal of heaven on such acts, also warned that some who will boast that they cast out devils *in His name* are workers of iniquity who will go to the lake of fire.

Such religious practitioners insist on being known by their *acts.* There is a lamentable tendency at times in parts of the religious realm to veer that way. The Scripture says "by their *fruits* you shall know them" (Matthew 7:20, KJV), not by their acts, even when miraculous.

In no sense does that drive a barrier between the fruits of the Holy Spirit—love, joy, peace, patience, self-control, and the others seen in Galatians 5:22-23—and acts of power. That tendency has existed among some believers, to great loss. Rather it puts the two in godly unity, by which the *fruits,* not the acts themselves, give assurance that the acts are true.

I will take the fruits anytime ahead of the acts, no matter how great or impressive the acts—but let us have what God actually intends, the acts with the fruits, rather than stripping the acts away as though they were somehow contrary to the fruits. The religious Pharisees did something like that when they falsely charged that Jesus "by the prince of demons casts out the demons" (Mark 3:22). Jesus, acting with divine authority, did not fit into their theological framework, so they denied deity and despised acts of power done in love.

Over *everything* religious stands the changeless truth that, while faith, as Jesus declared, can move a mountain (Matthew 17:20), yet "if I have a faith that can move mountains, but have not love, I am nothing," as Paul wrote in 1 Corinthians 13:2.

That is heaven's own assessment of persons who do mighty faith-acts out of anything but love—absolute zero. God is of power beyond our comprehension, but "God *is* love" (1 John 4:16).

The account of the man in the tombs tells a lot about evil spirits, but primarily it shows the complete triumph of God over what had seemed to be a complete triumph of Satan. Jesus, by an act of spiritual authority, did what He came to do—to destroy the *works* of the devil (see 1 John 3:8).

## King Saul Consults a Medium

We have noted that evil spirits work to produce definite effects in human thought and behavior. Such effects are easily traced in the life of Saul, the first king of Israel.

He was, the Bible affirms, "a choice young man"—humble, gentle, exceedingly good-looking: "There was not a man among the people of Israel more handsome than he; from his shoulders upward he was taller than any of the people" (1 Samuel 9:2, RSV).

There was no royal line in Israel, but the people insisted on having a king and God allowed it. The Prophet Samuel anointed Saul for the office and gave him supernatural signs to make plain to Saul that he had been chosen by God, not man. Soon after this anointing, "the Spirit of God came mightily upon him, and he [Saul] prophesied" (1 Samuel 10:10, RSV).

The young king was greatly blessed by God. He was a modest and unassuming individual, but he was weak and only partial in his obedience to God. He began well but, through cumulative acts of disobedience, Saul lost out. The fateful transition is seen in 1 Samuel 16:14—"Now the Spirit of the Lord departed from Saul, and an evil spirit from the Lord tormented him."

The course, which had tended upward, now ran steeply downward. Saul ended as a man capable of murder. At the very end, he sank to consulting a medium.

A point came at which God withdrew His Spirit from Saul and allowed an evil spirit to go to him. This change in the spiritual realm, unobservable to the human eye, brought distinct and drastic changes in Saul's behavior. The first effect was that the evil spirit "troubled him," causing Saul to suffer internal agitation and unrest.

"And Saul's servants said to him, 'See now, an evil spirit from God troubles you. Let the king now command his servants . . . to seek out a man, who is a skillful player on an harp, and it shall come to pass, when the evil spirit from God is upon you, that he shall play with his hand, and you shall be well.' And Saul said to his servants, 'Provide me now a man who can play well, and bring him to me'" (1 Samuel 16:15-17, KJV).

The one selected for this service was a young man named David, whom God had chosen to succeed Saul as king. "And David came to Saul and stood before him, and Saul loved him greatly; and David became his armor-bearer" (1 Samuel 16:21, KJV).

Saul's immediate reaction to David was that he loved him greatly. But soon, under the incendiary influence of the demon, he would show an entirely different attitude.

As young David began to become a respected warrior for Israel, Saul felt the stirrings of jealousy within him. "And the next day an evil spirit from God rushed upon Saul, and he raved within his house, while David was playing the lyre, as he did day by day. Saul had his spear in his hand; and Saul cast the spear, for he thought, 'I will pin David to the wall.' But David evaded him twice" (1 Samuel 18:10-11, RSV).

Anger and jealousy surged up suddenly within Saul under the immediate influence of the evil spirit. The man who a short while before had held David in great affection made two impulsive attempts to murder David. Under the driving actions of the evil spirit, Saul became a man capable of blazing up to a murderous fury. He hurled his spear. If he had killed David he would perhaps have said when asked why—as others have said: "I don't know. Something came over me."

"Saul was afraid of David, because the Lord was with him but had departed from Saul" (1 Samuel 18:12). Saul made further attempts to have David killed: "Now Saul thought to make David fall by the hand of the Philistines" (1 Samuel 18:25b). Later, he made another direct attempt at murder:

"Then an evil spirit from the Lord came upon Saul, as he sat in his house with his spear in his hand; and David was playing the lyre. And Saul sought to pin David to the wall with the spear, but he eluded Saul, so that he struck the spear into the wall. And David fled, and escaped. That night Saul sent messengers to David's house to watch him, that he might kill him in the morning" (1 Samuel 19:9-11, RSV).

Anger, jealousy, rage, hatred, fear, the impulse to murder—all these were prompted in the life of Saul by the activity of an evil spirit.

These are not the only effects of evil spirits, not by far, but they are prominent among destructive things that demons stir up in men and prompt or drive them to act upon.

The last step for Saul was a deliberate and desperate encounter with occultism (1 Samuel 28). When Saul had been pursuing the will of God, he "had put the mediums and wizards out of the land," because God had commanded that these demonic substitutes have no part with the pure worship of the Jews.

"The Philistines assembled and came and encamped at Shunem. . . . When Saul saw the army of the Philistines, he was afraid, and his heart trembled greatly. And when Saul inquired of the Lord, the Lord did not answer him, either by dreams, or by Urim, or by prophets. Then Saul said to his servants, 'Seek out for me a woman who is a medium, that I may go to her and inquire of her.' And his servants said to him, 'There is a medium at Endor.'

"So Saul disguised himself and put on other garments, and went, he and two men with him, and they came to the woman by night. And he said, 'Divine for me by a spirit, and bring up for me whomever I shall name to you'" (1 Samuel 28:4-8, RSV).

Saul chose his words well, for he knew what he was talking about. A medium who is not a sheer fake, who does in fact make "contact" with an intelligent, invisible being, is one who works together with, or comes under the control of, an evil spirit.

The woman was afraid to practice her illicit craft, but she had not given it up. She said to her anonymous visitor, "Surely you know what Saul has done, how he has cut off the mediums and wizards from the land. Why then are you laying a snare for my life to bring about my death?"

"But Saul swore to her by the Lord, 'As the Lord lives, no punishment shall come upon you for this thing.'

"Then the woman said, 'Whom shall I bring up for you?' " Saul named the Prophet Samuel, who had died a short time before. The medium went to work.

"And the woman said to Saul, 'I see a god coming up out of the earth.'

"He said to her, 'What is his appearance?'

"And she said, 'An old man is coming up, and he is wrapped in a robe.' And Saul perceived that it was Samuel, and he bowed with his face to the ground and did obeisance."

Saul said, " 'I am in great distress. The Philistines are warring against me, and God has turned away from me and answers me no more, either by prophets or by dreams. Therefore I have summoned you to tell me what I shall do.'"

The spirit was soon telling Saul that the Philistines would conquer and that "tomorrow you and your sons shall be with me."

"Then Saul fell at once full length upon the ground, filled with fear" at these words (1 Samuel 28:9-15, 20, RSV).

"Now the Philistines gathered all their forces . . . and the Philistines overtook Saul and his sons, and they slew Jonathan and Abinadab and Malchishua, the sons of Saul. The battle pressed hard upon Saul, and the archers found him. . . . Thus Saul died, and his three sons, and his armor-bearer, and all his men, on the same day together.

"On the morrow, when the Philistines came to strip the slain, they found Saul and his three sons fallen on Mount Gilboa" (1 Samuel 29:1; 31:2-3, 6, 8).

It was but hours between Saul's visit to the medium and his death. He had crossed the last line of disobedience to God. The very man who had put the mediums out of business ended up asking one to "consult a spirit for me" (1 Samuel 28:8). The next day the whole house of Saul fell. Badly wounded in battle, he took his own life.

Much earlier, in a moment of true self-awareness, Saul said, "I have played the fool." Now he came flat up against a commandment of the Lord in the law: "If a person turns to mediums and wizards [sometimes called warlocks: males who practice witchcraft], playing the harlot after them, *I will set My face against that person, and will cut him off from among the people*" (Leviticus 20:6, RSV).

Young people need to become aware of the damage or danger they can incur by any traffic with these demonic inventions, even when presented in the form of a game. While writing this chapter I came upon a news report of several teenagers in different places who did away with themselves or killed friends, apparently as a result of their involvement in a popular "game" that concentrates heavily on players imagining themselves into situations of intense conflict with strange other-worldly powers. The game reportedly draws directly on witchcraft practices in some of its instructions to players.

"Do not practice divination or sorcery. . . . Do not turn to mediums or seek out spiritists, for you will be defiled by them. I am the Lord your God" (Leviticus 19:26b, 31). To do exactly the opposite of what the Scriptures command is to hand an advantage to the enemy over us. It is love that warns us away from all such things.

Avoid mediums, witches, séances, astrologers, fortune-tellers, magic, Ouija boards, and every variety of psychic practice as you would avoid fire. Whatever the come-on, the payoff is big trouble if we get involved.

The tragedy of King Saul had, in a way, a modern counterpart in the experience of a prominent American churchman, one who became nationally known while occupying the pulpit of the Cathedral of St. John the Divine in New York City, the largest Gothic cathedral in the world.

As dean of the cathedral, James A. Pike managed to attract considerable attention from the press by a combination of intellectual inquiry, quiet friendliness, and innovation—and a singular knack for coining catchy phrases on controversial matters. I encountered this Episcopal clergyman twice in my reporting, once at the New York cathedral, later in his San Francisco office, where he presided as Bishop of California.

His life was lived on a kind of spiritual roller coaster.

Pike, a devout Roman Catholic as a youth, had studied for the priesthood with Jesuits for two years, then abruptly quit and declared himself an agnostic. He earned a doctorate from the Yale Law School and launched into a successful career as a lawyer. He had a change of mind while serving in naval intelligence during wartime. Pike decided to leave the law in favor of the Episcopal ministry, in which he rapidly became a highly influential figure. Yet there is something sad and rootless, and steeply declining, about the latter years of his life.

The bishop narrowly escaped a trial for heresy not long after he had boldly used the pulpit of Manhattan's historic old Trinity Church to call the doctrine of the Trinity "excess baggage." He expressed doubts about other core doctrines. He finally quit the regular ministry to become a member of an important "think tank" or study foundation, a position of intellectual prestige, by which time he was veering sharply off into occultism.

His personal secretary who, oddly, shared his apartment, "entered Bishop Pike's bedroom late one night for a book," a published account reported, "and he sat up in bed, asleep, and delivered a discourse on the importance of selfishness, of only caring about 'Number One.'" The woman had what were interpreted as a series of spiritistic visitations, and she committed suicide.

The key turn apparently came when the bishop's son, Jim, who had experimented with psychedelic drugs in San Francisco, locked himself in a New York hotel room and shot himself dead at age twenty. Pike consulted with a minister, the Reverend Arthur Ford, a very prominent medium. It was widely reported that Ford held a séance in which the former bishop received messages from what he took to be his dead son.

Most mediums who conduct séances are, of course, outright fakes. They prey upon the gullible. We earlier remarked that a fake can be discovered in his *methods,* if they are inspected closely enough.

The late Harry Houdini, the extraordinary escape artist and stage magician, made himself a major scourge of phony mediums because he knew and could expose the contrived means by which they produced their supposedly supernatural effects.

Such phony mediums are still around, and they still deceive the ignorant; but there is another breed as well. It is unlikely that Mr. Ford was a fake. Bishop Pike surely believed in what occurred and spoke and wrote earnestly about it later. He cannot be faulted on the grounds of objective sincerity. He was simply deceived.

The term *medium* is a very apt one. One definition is: *"A person serving . . . as an instrument through which another personality or a supernatural agency is alleged to manifest itself: a spiritualistic medium."*

At this point we must ask, a medium *from* what *to* what? Mr. Ford would claim to be a medium between dead human beings and living human beings. When he conducted the séance for Bishop Pike, he apparently succeeded in accurately speaking certain facts about the dead son to Bishop Pike, facts about which Mr. Ford possibly had no prior knowledge. He seemed to bring forth words and statements of factual accuracy by supernatural means. It is yet more precise to suggest that the medium brought forth certain words by *being used* by supernatural powers. His spiritual accessibility to these powers is what made him a medium.

A medium purports to stand between the natural realm and the supernatural realm, and permits himself to become the channel through which spirits manifest themselves. The Bible clearly and repeatedly forbids this. ("Channeling," as it happens, is the name being applied to a popular upsurge of mediumistic practices, centering initially on the West Coast, but only the label has changed—a "channel" is a medium.)

Mediums commonly go into a trance before "another personality" speaks through them. It may be that a spirit took hold of Mr. Ford during this séance. But the terrible fact is the spirit that takes hold of a medium is not the spirit of a deceased human being but an evil spirit. The voice that speaks through the vocal organs of a trance medium in a séance is not the voice of a dead human being. It is the voice of an evil spirit impersonating the dead human being.

The art of a medium is the art of direct communication with demons, whether the medium is aware of that or not.

Evil spirits are at least as old as human history. Their knowledge of events and personalities of the past can be impressive. That is undoubtedly why the Bible so strictly bans dealing with what it calls "familiar spirits."

When guidance is sought, consulting a medium can be a shortcut to getting the counsel of Satan upon a matter, though that counsel is usually carefully disguised so that it will not appear to be what it is.

Bishop Pike ended his days searching into occult matters. He was last seen going on a pilgrimage, in search of something or other, with his third wife in a barren area in the Middle East, on what proved to be a futile, deadly errand. The pair became lost. The heat soared well over 100 degrees. His wife, hoping to find help, stumbled her way to safety, while Pike trudged around in scorched, desolate terrain.

As in so many previous matters, his misadventures made page one. "Searchers for Dr. Pike Will Use Guidance Provided by Mediums" a *New York Times* headline reported. Two mediums gave his wife separate but similar directions. One had used a pendulum swinging over a map and had received messages through "automatic writing," in which, the story reported, "a force or spirit moves the pen."

Both mediums directed Diane Pike to a cave where Pike was allegedly alive. The search party of over 100 desert trackers plus two aircraft accepted this mediumistic guidance, which turned out to be flat wrong.

"Dr. Pike's Body Is Found On Ledge Near Dead Sea," the next page-one *Times* headline said. It said the 56-year-old former bishop "was climbing a steep cliff, either to extricate himself from a box canyon or to get better vantage, when he slipped and fell 70 feet" to a rocky ledge.

*Time* magazine devoted two full pages to the death and life of a man who had been a Catholic, an agnostic, an Episcopal minister and bishop, a public doubter, and finally, a spiritist. "Death in the Wilderness" called his end "just one more unusual adventure in a remarkably strange career." The article told of his meteoric rise as a clergyman and of "dazzling transitions that sometimes made him seem unstable."

Pike's experiments with the supernatural were in the most explicit contradiction to the Word of God, and he ended out in an arid wasteland, tragically deceived and misled.

God told Israel there was to be no one among them "who practices *divination, a soothsayer, or an augur, or a sorcerer, or a charmer, or a medium, or a wizard, or a necromancer.*" The last had to do with attempted dealings with the dead (see Deuteronomy 18:10-12, RSV).

Does that apply to Gentiles? Consider this: God went on to tell the people of Israel that precisely "because of these abominable practices the Lord your God is driving" the Gentiles out of the land and giving it over to the Jews.

Among all those who engage in such practices, some meet and pass the test of factual accuracy at times. That does not make them any less false; it only makes them more dangerous and more deceptive to the scripturally uninformed.

In *The Great Bridge,* the book containing the epic story of the building of the Brooklyn Bridge, author David McCullough devotes a few paragraphs to the odd views held by John Roebling, designer of the bridge, on life, death, truth, the hereafter, and the nature of the universe.

Roebling scrawled out hundreds upon hundreds of pages on what he called the "Truth of Nature." The few close friends to whom he showed it found it hard to plow through or to understand—"as though some impenetrable Teutonic mysticism" from the past had taken hold of him, McCullough wrote.

Roebling had begun to open himself up to strange spiritual influences. He left the Presbyterian Church and was "swept up by the teachings of Swedenborg . . . who rejected the dogma of original sin and eternal damnation . . . [and] had embraced spiritualism."

The human mind, undefensed by scriptural truth, can be led very far astray. The engineer became engrossed in concepts of an afterworld, which he called "the Spirit Land and Spheres." It existed "above, and concentric with, the earth's surface" and was heavily populated with the spirits of deceased human beings. (Roebling thus named an area where the biblically described "prince of the power of the air" is at work with evil spirits.)

All of this led to many séances with a medium and what Roebling accepted as direct communications with dead relatives, chiefly his late wife. The communications took the form of knockings and rappings by an unseen presence, which could be asked questions. The response was obtained by presenting the alphabet and waiting for either silence or an answering rap. The medium was a cousin, Edward Riedel, whom Roebling trusted.

The answers reportedly given by the spirit are more than a little revealing. The spirit was asked if it attended "public lectures." Yes, it replied. "Who is your favorite lecturer? Spell out his name," Roebling asked.

"C-H-A-N-N-I-N-G," came the answer, one that was especially acceptable to Roebling. It referred to the late William Ellery Channing, a noted ministerial freethinker, a denier of the Trinity and of other basic scriptural truths, for which Channing had substituted his own concepts. He gained great influence with scholars and certain writers, and Roebling had eagerly read his writings.

Asked if "the Christian Bible, the Jewish Scriptures" were merely human compositions subject to error, the spirit genially answered, "Yes," Roebling wrote.

"Every man has a spark of divine principle within himself, which alone can save him and elevate him—is this so?" he inquired, to which the recorded answer was, "Yes."

There you have a whole false doctrine of salvation in a nutshell—the *only thing* that can save a man is "a spark of divine principle within him."

In short order Roebling got what he took to be supernatural confirmations of the erroneous and merely human nature of the holy Scriptures, the correctness of Channings' heresies, and the assurance that Jesus Christ has nothing to do with salvation, which comes only by an inner "spark of divine principle." It is wonderfully interesting that the Bible should happen to be fallible and erroneous, while Channing's concoctions out of his own head drew approval.

We cannot know with any certainty how all this happened. What is certain is that Roebling was further deceived on the most important spiritual matters as a result of these séances. He felt himself confirmed in his delusive outlook by unseen authorities on what he called "the other side."

"How shall we escape if we neglect such a great salvation" bought for us by Jesus, by turning aside to fables and lies? That is what the Scripture asks—and warns in Hebrews 2:3.

The strong-minded Roebling, whose passion was to build the Brooklyn Bridge, died when it was scarcely started. His family, friends, and associates saw him "destroyed before their eyes," McCullough wrote. The engineer had an infection (as the result of a small misstep near the water's edge), yet one that was within the capacity of physicians to treat.

Perhaps with the same bent of willfulness and pride that had led him to abandon true religion and to pursue spiritism, he now rejected the advice of doctors and insisted on treating his injury his own way, until the "muscles around his face, neck, and jaws grew rigid as iron . . . and his mouth was pulled back in a terrible grimace, the teeth all showing and locked tight." Soon "seizures began . . . his whole body would lift off the bed and double backward with a fierce, awful jerk," and he died in a convulsion.

Of such practices as divination, soothsaying, sorcery, consulting with mediums, the Scriptures say that "*whoever* does these things is an abomination to the Lord."

To the people of Israel, the Lord said, "Do not defile yourself by any of these things. . . . The persons that do them shall be cut off from among their people. . . . A man or a woman who is a medium or a wizard shall be put to death." (See Deuteronomy 18:9-14; Leviticus 18:24-30 and 20:27.)

On relatively few matters do the Scriptures speak in terms this severe. Stepping into such things, when they are not sheer fakery, is to deal with evil spirits, giving them special access to human affairs. To do so is a great spiritual transgression.

Speaking of the apparent "harshness of God's punishments," the fine Christian writer Philip Yancey wrote: "I find myself gazing into the grieving eyes of a parent whose children are destroying themselves."

If some insist upon so doing, their example is held up to persuade the others not to stray into the path of ruin. Any crossing over into or dealing with the realm of demons has its consequences. Remember Bishop Pike. Remember Saul.

## Mysticism, Mediums, Witchcraft, and Magic

"White Collar Witches." The words came at me from the top of page one of the weekly newspaper in my neighborhood. A box referring to an article inside said: "By day, they are rock publicists and radio reporters. By night they practice ancient rituals in witches' covens."

"Your friendly neighborhood witch," I thought sarcastically, opening the issue. The block headline that met my eye inside was set in bigger type than any I had seen in this paper before.

"TODAY'S WITCHES," it blared. Then below: "Witches tend to be male and female, educated, white, and middle-class."

A photograph showed several books on witchcraft, including *Natural Magic, The Quest,* and *Witchcraft for Tomorrow,* each undoubtedly designed to draw readers toward or into such practices.

Another photograph showed a "practitioner of witchcraft in her office at National Public Radio," where she works as a reporter. She looked intelligent, serious, and natural—that is, without cosmetics or artificial adornment. She was listed as the author of a book with the strange title *Drawing Down the Moon.*

Nothing about her in the photo or the article suggested any kind of put-on. Here was a career woman in the late 1980s who was in earnest about witchcraft.

The woman, who looked to be in her early 40s, was reported to have "found her way to what witches call 'the craft' through the values of the 1960s."

During that period of seething unrest and college campus turmoil, she had been involved in both the so-called Free Speech movement and the very radical Students for a Democratic Society or SDS—both major elements in a movement that, for a while in the 1960s, threatened to shake the country and that did, in fact, lead some young people very far astray.

"Witchcraft is a full-fledged religion," the article said, "predating Judaism and Christianity. Derived from the pagan religions of Northern Europe, it's very similar to other polytheistic folk religions. . . . In the 1960s, Englishman Gerald Gardner brought a witchcraft tradition to the U.S. and witchcraft covens have multiplied here ever since.

"Feminists have also played an important role in reviving witchcraft in this country," the article said, quoting the radio reporter this way: "The feminist spirituality movement, of which the craft is a big part, grew out of the consciousness-raising groups in the late '60s.

"Witchcraft is essentially a matriarchal religion, where the woman is the primary power seed," the article continued. Quoting these statements is in no sense intended to brush all of feminism with such associations, but rather to make clear that some of it, particularly at points where its aims and convictions go expressly counter to what the Bible teaches, connects to witchcraft.

Rebellion against human injustice and human imbalance can, if it does not go wild and turn evil, bring about critically needed awareness and cure injustice. But rebellion against the decrees of God and His wise plans for mankind leads only to bondage and to misery masquerading as liberty.

Every believer needs to be aware of the words the Prophet Samuel spoke to the self-willed King Saul: "For rebellion is as the sin of divination, and stubbornness is as iniquity and idolatry." Note those words carefully in 1 Samuel 15:23 (RSV) for they are a key warning to the human soul as it reaches out for what it wants.

Radical feminism rolls right over such biblical statements as: "Now I want you to realize that the head of every man is Christ, and the head of the woman is man, and the head of Christ is God. . . . A man . . . is the image and glory of God, but the woman is the glory of man. For man did not come from woman, but woman from man; neither was man created for woman, but woman for man. . . . In the Lord, however, woman is not independent of man, nor is man independent of woman. For as woman came from man, so also man is born of woman. But everything comes from God" (see 1 Corinthians 11:1-16).

A shallow male interpretation of such truths, by which the woman becomes unduly subordinate and is made more a possession or a serf than the companion and helper and partner that she is ordained to be, is a cruel distortion—the reflection of sheer selfishness, not spirituality—and it is thoroughly invalid.

This biblical injunction—"Wives, submit to your husbands as to the Lord. For the husband is the head of the wife as Christ is the head of the church, His body, of which He is the Saviour. Now as the church submits to Christ, so also wives should submit to their husbands in everything" (Ephesians 5:22-24)—is in no sense a call to the husband to hammer his wife into submissiveness. It is a summons to the wife to submit herself voluntarily to her husband, and this can only be rightly understood in the context of the following verse, "Husbands, love your wives, just as Christ loved the church and gave Himself up for her."

No submission to cruelty, or to truly untoward or evil demands, is in any way called for. Moreover the biblical instructions that clearly distinguish male and female roles, to important and godly effect, must be understood in true balance with the declaration in Galatians 3:27-28, "... for all of you who were baptized into Christ have been clothed with Christ. There is neither Jew nor Greek, slave nor free, male nor female, for you are all one in Christ Jesus."

Similarly, any effort to make that spiritual truth a warrant to abrogate or overthrow the male/female distinguishing verses is an arrogant distortion. On the woman's side, the kicking over of these fundamental and changeless truths of nature and the creation is a grievous error.

So when "feminist spirituality" turns to the practice of witchcraft, it is no total surprise, since the wilder persuasions of that sort of feminism fit very well with the doctrines of demons behind witchcraft. The modern witch featured in the previously mentioned news article traced "her transition from radicalism to paganism" from her earlier involvement in two of the most radical student rebellion movements.

The article also described a witchcraft ritual held in front of an occult bookstore in New York, a store said to have "the perfect atmosphere for an occult shop: dim, dusty and cavernous, every available corner is crammed with arcane items like magical herbs, magic wands, skulls, bones, statues of Pan, jewelry with magical symbols, oils, bats, gargoyles, censers, tarot cards, and hordes of other unidentifiable objects."

Carefully assembled "spell kits" are sold at the store. There are "kits for love (either gay or straight), success, money, protection and separation, plus a black arts kit to put the whammy on someone. If you buy a kit with the potentiality to do harm, the owner will ask you to sign a 'karmic disclaimer,' so he won't be held responsible for the results."

Karma is an old Hindu and Buddhist notion having to do with the so-called transmigration of souls and a person's state or destiny after death.

What does this sort of thing amount to? Both less and more, I suspect, than some may think. Less for some who dabble in it, only to find a kind of endless teasing suggestiveness that always seems to promise what it never delivers. A newspaper circulation executive I knew—and to whom I spoke plain warnings about it—had been doing experiments in spiritualism and psychic phenomena for close to fifteen years. The *total* conclusion he drew from it all came to, "There's something out there"—something that was always elusive, never conclusive, never satisfying. He was always hoping that the next experiment might help pin it down. He had wasted countless hundreds of hours in the chase.

But for those who, by such means, connect to evil spirits or to what they wrongly call natural "powers" and "forces," and who either "use" them or "control" them, it leads to quite a lot, all of it as bad as it can be. And they use exactly the kind of formulas, rituals, objects, and spells in which the occult shop so busily deals.

To some it may seem a kind of sport. To others it is the avenue to the magnification of self-will—what the self wants to get or do—so that self-will is enforced or exacted upon other people by such unseen "forces."

What is magic? One definition says magic is "the art of producing a desired effect or result through the use of various techniques, as incantation, that presumably assure human control of supernatural agencies or the forces of nature." With it go magic spells, magic rites, magic words, enchantments, witchcraft, hexes, charms, so-called communications with the "dead," and a wide variety of other practices and means. There is plenty of quackery and fakery in it, but there is also a potent realm of magic that sometimes produces real effects.

Colin Wilson, author of thirty books including *Religion and the Rebel* and *The Age of Defeat*, boldly wrote that man "must somehow return to the recognition that he is potentially a 'mage,' one of those magical figures who can hurl thunderbolts or command spirits." He added that "civilizations cannot evolve further until 'the occult' is taken for granted on the same level as atomic energy." Ah, what a likening!

The stream of junk mail that empties into my mailbox included one day, unsolicited by me, the catalog of a dealer in the occult. As I leafed through it, I read of promises of mysterious powers and of various practices alleged to deliver quick gratifications and obtain irresistible results. When any power capable of producing an impact on individuals and events comes from such practices, that power derives from their nexus with evil spirits.

Many of these rituals and practices and spells and incantations have a religious character, entirely on the enemy's side. As prayer is an appeal to heaven, based on faith in God through Christ; as intercession is prevailing with God on behalf of mankind, these practices appeal, whether done knowingly or ignorantly, to wicked spirits. They stir up such spirits, give them room to maneuver in, and hand them advantages they seek over those who engage in them, and sometimes, over other individuals or events.

Though there are heaps of it in print, I read very little, and extremely selectively in any of the literature of occultism, magic, and witchcraft while investigating some of the matters in this book, because such material is a sinkhole.

I paid heed to the testimonies of Christian ministers and missionaries about their encounters with ensnared or demonized persons and the means used to help them; the accounts of Christians who had been delivered from occult bondage; and historical accounts.

Those who had come to Christ from especially bad spiritual backgrounds told of the extreme holds that evil powers had obtained in their lives—and of the desperate resistance of those powers to the lessening and final vacating of their claims brought about through the power of the Lord Jesus. They experienced demonic oppositions of an intensity that others know nothing of.

While details differed, there were important similarities in such accounts concerning certain results of spells, curses, and other evil practices.

A missionary who had long worked near a center of European witchcraft and who had succeeded, at high personal cost, in helping free several of its practitioners and victims, told of one such effect of an exceedingly strange and evil character. Several months later I read the account, written in another country at another time, of a minister who had done similar work, and there I found the exact same thing carefully described.

Such things fall, I think, into the category of "the deep things of Satan," to which Revelation 2:24 refers in warning believers against certain practices—practices which are not truly deep, though seductively presented as such, but just cheap and wicked enticements. There is no need to go into them here. They do, however, have to do with the strength of some of the warnings in these pages, and they justify it thoroughly.

Recent years have brought a rising vogue in occultism, astrology, magic, witchcraft, and the like in our culture.

In his sweeping survey of modern occultism, Colin Wilson called it "safe to say that there are now more witches in England and America than at any time since the Reformation." He wrote of Alex Sanders, who was initiated into a witchcraft coven by his grandmother at age seven: Sanders had "deliberately used black magic to achieve money and sexual success. 'It worked all right,' he explained. But he then made the discovery that it all had to be paid for: several members of his family died of cancer, and his girlfriend committed suicide."

For many decades spiritualism and witchcraft were off in remote and obscure corners of our national life. For quite a while it was entirely the fashion in this society to hold that there were no such things as witches—individuals who practice various kinds of magic or black magic—and I dare say that anyone who had ventured to assert that there *were* such individuals would have been regarded as hopelessly medieval. Now we are faced with the fact that there are witches who publicly say they are witches.

Though it is still decidedly a minority phenomenon, witchcraft is now practiced quite openly and it has been getting a fair amount of publicity. The *Daily News,* the New York tabloid newspaper with the largest circulation in the nation, carried a full-page story by Lisa Hoffman, from which I quote in part:

"It may come as a disturbing surprise to learn that there really are such things as witches' covens, one of which now operates in an otherwise typical suburban town on the South Shore of Long Island. Long Island holds no monopoly. In fact, [covens exist] elsewhere in New York, in New Jersey, Kentucky, California, Ohio, Washington, D.C. . . . Being what it is, the Craft, as it is known to its practitioners, keeps its membership rolls understandably secret and also the sites of most covens, [each] compromised of twelve couples presided over by a high priestess.

"Don't make the mistake of thinking all this is a piece of arcane flummery. Twentieth-century witches are deadly serious. The chants, the swords, the music, the symbols, the herbs, and the incense are all pretty much what they were in the pre-Christian era of nature cults when the bizarre practice was born.

"The Long Island cult [is] headed by Lady Rowen, 32, and her husband Robat, 34, to give them their cultist names. . . . [They] are white, or good witches [who own] a large collection of books on the occult. . . . The couple, it seems, dropped out of the Church of England thirteen years ago to become disciples of Dr. Gerald Gardner, who, until he keeled over on his breakfast tray while reading a book on magic four years ago, was considered the grand old man of British witchcraft.

"... They were 'remarried' with a ponderous sermon called 'Handfasting.' This boils down to a simple promise to be true to each other for 'as long as love shall last.' If love doesn't last, either party is free to go his own way.

"That expedient philosophy is laid down in *The Book of Shadows,* which ... contains all the rites, spells, charms, cures, and chants. 'Once a month,' the book says, 'gather in some secret place and adore me who am the Queen of all witcheries ...'

"The Long Island coven holds its rituals in Robat's basement. ... On Halloween, the major festival among the eight holidays on every witch's calendar, ... the witches, all nude, will begin singing and dancing." The writer comments that the witches "seem to share a common faith in reincarnation."

The United Press International newswire carried a story from San Francisco on a wedding rite of a witchcraft cult: "Asking the blessings of Lucifer, Beelzebub, a priest of Satan, performed a marriage ceremony last night using a naked woman as an altar. ... The bridegroom, thirty-five, had been married twice before. The rite consisted of bells, gongs, chanting in a magic language from an old book, *The Equinox,* and some play with a sword and chalice. ... Stuffed ravens, wolves, owls, and rats looked down from shelves everywhere."

There are similarities in the practices of the so-called white and the Satanist witches. Both have a book of mysteries whose formulas they follow. Both make a point of nudity and both twist matrimony into little more than an interim alliance for lust.

A Satanist cult worships the devil. The Long Island coven meets in secret to adore "the Queen of all witcheries"—addressing worship not to God, but to a demon spirit.

*Mademoiselle* magazine made witchcraft the theme of a "Special Magical Mystery Issue" whose cover promised: "Sorcery and Sex: A terrific tour of spells, charms, witchcraft, and the mysterious East ... Yoga ... India's exciting Tantric art. Chilling occult novel complete in this issue."

Tantric art derives from a secret cult within Hinduism centering on "erotic, magical, and mystical rites" in which female deities are worshiped, according to the *Columbia Encyclopedia.* In a single issue the magazine scooped up a heap of such things, concentrated them into its pages, and spread them to several million readers. This illustrates the power of a spiritually undiscerning press, in its eagerness for novelty, to reach into darkness and deposit it at will over the national landscape.

The issue included an interview with Dr. Harry E. Wedeck, a college professor with an extensive knowledge of the history of witchcraft. Unless witches practiced "white magic," according to Dr. Wedeck, "their intentions and operations were evil. Commonly they attempted ruin and destruction, even if they didn't always succeed."

"Are there many witches around now?" he was asked.

"In the Far East and India, naturally, but there are some in England, rural France, all over Europe, and everyone knows about Haiti." Dr. Wedeck said that "India is full of fakirs and mystic writings and magic."

"It's old. It's all so old," Dr. Wedeck said, observing that he had recently read a book translated from a sixteenth-century manuscript, *Chin P'ing Mei,* which mentioned "witchcraft practices, astrological lore, and spells that were precisely those found in Theocritus and Vergil" (writers of Greece and Rome who lived before Christ).

"Vergil to a sixteenth-century Chinese text—that's quite a jump, isn't it?" the interviewer said, to which the scholar gave this significant reply: "These beliefs are so pervasive that I feel they are not necessarily transmitted one to the other, but develop independently."

It is important to catch the essence of that. It appears that these practices are *not transmitted* from culture to culture, but that they sprang up spontaneously. The same practices of magic, divination, and the worship of many gods or spirits are discovered in culture after culture.

Dr. Wedeck rather weakly assigned this repetitive coincidence in practices, reaching across broad barriers of time and space and language, to a similarity in human thoughts. That misses the core of it. Some of these practices have their origin outside of the mind of man in a single supernatural source.

Demons have access to every culture, and it is in their power to communicate mysteries of Satan to individuals in each. Certain practices appear to have been separately revealed to various cultures by evil spirits from the earliest history of civilization.

That these practices are often identical is an evidence of their supernatural origin and design.

Certain it is that nearly identical religious ceremonies and trappings have been found in the last century among tribes in South America, in Africa, and in the far Pacific. These tribes have never had contact with the outside world, but they have had contact with evil spirits.

Witches and witch doctors are priests of Satan, and they obtain certain powers from him. It is not surprising, as Dr. Wedeck said, that they sometimes attempt "ruin and destruction," since those are exactly the purposes of Satan.

The interviewer told Dr. Wedeck, "Whenever I've read about witches, there always seem to be strong links between sorcery and sex—and very sick sex at that," to which Dr. Wedeck replied: "You couldn't be a witch unless you gave yourself completely to it. Which meant involving yourself with your coven—twelve disciples . . . sometimes including 'a ceremonial orgy.' "

Certain things crop up repeatedly in various forms of witchcraft, occultism as well as in Eastern religions, including Hinduism, Shintoism, some forms of Buddhism, and Lamaism. One of these is sex in rites. One ugly variant of this is authoritatively described as being "one of the oldest and most universal cults in the world." It has broken out in place after place.

The enemy loves to corrupt humans sexually, and sexual sins of the grossest kinds are spawned and promoted in direct association with certain occult practices.

Other strands running through the fabric of his religious inventions include: the worship of sundry deities and gods; the obtaining of good luck by charms and the promotion of bad luck for enemies by spells; idols and images; the sale of religious articles and objects intended to procure help, safety, or good fortune for the user; the burning of candles before statues and shrines; obtaining blessings by purchase; dancing into a frenzy; the participation in mysteries through prescribed rituals; some forms of chanting and incantations; extremes of asceticism and of indulgence (in the Islamic observances of Ramadan, a strict fast is required from sunup to sunset for a month, including sexual abstinence, but at night one may take his fill of the things avoided by day; the Bible calls this "will worship" and declares it devoid of value).

These things belong to the house of idolatry that Satan has set up for all mankind. The whole vast supermarket of magic, idolatry, superstition, and false religion is his substitute for the placing of human trust in the living God. God hates these substitutes with fury since they are devised to misdirect men spiritually and to separate human souls from Him forever.

"God made mankind upright, but men have gone in search of many schemes," Ecclesiastes 7:29 laments.

To some the surge of interest in witchcraft and the like may seem to be a bit of a lark, a mild dabbling in the fantastic, a form of escapism, perhaps, in a crowded and perplexing age. Yet any of these ancient occult practices can open up a dangerous avenue into the supernatural for a person who becomes involved in them.

The same issue of the popular magazine listed a score of books on witchcraft for young women to read, and recommended a Chinese system of divination over 3,000 years old, calling it "absolutely dependable divination: a method you can live by."

A person throws three coins six times and then, using the result in connection with a particular section of a book, receives guidance. Divination of any kind is part of a demonically revealed system by which men can put themselves in the hands of something beyond themselves for direction or help. The intelligence activating spiritistic devices of divination is demonic.

Hear the Word of the Lord: "For the terephim [small images or household gods used by disobedient Jews] utter nonsense, and the diviners see lies; the dreamers tell false dreams, and give empty consolation. Therefore the people wander like sheep; they are afflicted for want of a shepherd" (Zechariah 10:2, RSV). Occultism is costly not only to those who engage in it, but also to the nation that becomes rife with it.

*Time* magazine did a cover story on the many eruptions of occultism in the American culture. Witchcraft and magic are suddenly and prominently with us. These things have not thronged upon the scene by any mere coincidence, and curiosity about them runs highest among the young.

Satan, who could not widely foist such practices upon the American public when biblical faith had great influence among the people, has now found the time ripe to bring these dark mysteries swarming in from the East to a decadent American culture.

It is all timed and carefully planned for the weakening of the society and the damaging of thousands in it. It will be reversed only if there is an awareness of its source and an awakening to faith in the living God.

Johann C. Blumhardt, a minister of the Lutheran State Church in Germany a century and a half ago, was a man who learned, by force of direct experience with an insane demonized parishioner, a great deal about certain occult operations. Magic has its root, he wrote, in "the sin of idolatry which by steps leads up to magic and complete black magic."

"Idolatry may be considered *every reliance* on a supernatural, invisible power, based upon which a man is attempting to obtain either health, honor, gain, or pleasure, as long as this power is not purely divine," he wrote, adding:

"Slowly I learned to get a glimpse into the horrible consequences of all of this idolatry . . . a man becomes more or less bound to a sinister Satanic power. This happens through a demon which wins influence over him because it is enticed through the acts of idolatry.

"Most of the witches and warlocks . . . are what they are in this capacity, without their knowledge. The most would be that once in a while they have a feeling of what they do in the spirit without being able to explain this feeling. In any case, they are highly unfortunate people. . . ."

Magic has, Pastor Blumhardt perceived, "a series of steps: On the lowest level are those who become ensnared without being conscious of it. The highest level is black magic proper in which the person serves Satan with full consciousness and who grants him these powers.

"In the middle . . . are those who make a trade out of the use of magic means. . . . Usually they use printed booklets . . . which are revelations of Satan proper."

Some, he wrote, "receive, if I may say so, demons from the devil which become their counselors . . . and through which the magicians inquire. These demons appear to them, either visibly or invisibly, through certain means which they use, including mirrors.

"The demons answer the questions asked of them, not without an interest in the reign of darkness. Thus it comes that Christians ask advice at the mouth of Beelzebub (2 Kings 1:2-4).

"Black magicians proper are those who, so to speak, have made a formal pact with the devil. This can happen individually or through joining certain societies whose foundation is such a secret pact. In both cases the signing of the name in blood takes place."

The possessed parishioner whose state drew Pastor Blumhardt into spiritual warfare for her deliverance had evidently been marked early in life. The child was "sent to a cousin who was generally feared as an evil person and she once said to the seven-year-old child, 'When you are ten years old, I will teach you something worthwhile.' This age is usually mentioned as the time of possible initiation into magic."

The cousin objected to the fact that the child's name translated into "lover of God or beloved of God" and said that if conditions were more advantageous than they were, "I would give you great power in the world."

That and similar sayings caused the child concern. "In her quiet thoughts she always remembered the words, 'Our Lord is great and of great power, and it is beyond understanding how He rules.'" Magic means were used on the child when she was ill. "That is why, like others, she was pulled into the net," Blumhardt believed.

"But her spirit . . . withstood the insinuations of darkness. . . . There resulted, it appears, a sort of tension between her and the sinister realm. She felt herself bound to one side, the Satanic, with a certain power and her heart sought for the other side, the divine."

The point eventually came, the minister wrote, when the object apparently was "to ensnare her really into magic . . . or to do away with her."

Seasons of insanity and extremity rendered her life as a young woman miserable, and her minister determined in his heart not to let her "become the victim of darkness at any price." Initially, the only means used was "prayer which held fast to the invisible divine power." Much later, demons were cast out. While this went on, "Satan," he wrote, "was constantly trying to do away" with the victim. Her attempts to kill herself were carried out without her conscious awareness, it seemed.

Then one afternoon she "heatedly demanded a knife. Her frightened brother and sister would not allow a knife to get into her hands. She ran to the attic, jumped on the window sill, and already was hanging outside in the free air, only holding on to the inside, when the first flash of lightning of the approaching thunderstorm met her eye, frightened, and awakened her. She came to and cried, 'I don't want to do that!' "

In a delirium the young woman later "took hold of a rope . . . and tied it skillfully around the beams of the attic. She made a noose which easily pulled tight. She had nearly forced her whole head through the noose" when she came to consciousness. "A stream of tears flowed from her eyes the following day when she looked at the noose hanging from the beam. She could never have tied it as skillfully in the best of consciousness."

At one decisive point, Pastor Blumhardt, who always worked with other believers present as witnesses, took her stiff hands, pulled them together as for prayer and was emboldened to state aloud, "We have seen long enough what the devil is doing. Now we want to see what Jesus can do!"

There followed "days the likes of which I hope I never have to live through again," the minister wrote. "I clearly felt a divine protection so that I did not feel the slightest tiredness or weariness, not even after forty hours of waking, fasting, and wrestling" in prayer. Freedom then came in a moment's time, and the victim slowly came to complete health thereafter.

She became a teacher of children marked by "insight, love, patience, and kindness." She embarked on a sane, free, normal existence. Six years later the minister wrote of her continued stability, health, and usefulness, and over the whole experience he wrote these sure words, "Jesus is victor!"

# THE CHALLENGE TO
# SELF-POSSESSION

## Spirit, Soul, Body—
## Knowing Yourself

As living human beings, you and I are set in certain relationships to the seen and unseen worlds. Our understanding of these relationships may be clear, or murky and obscure, or even baffling, depending on the accuracy of our knowledge, and upon how we stand, act, and live in terms of *total reality*—meaning *all* that *is* real and that bears on life and being and eternity.

The Christian is in a far better position to understand this, if he will exercise himself to do so, than even a brilliant, unbelieving psychologist or rational thinker. No one who believes there is no God, or who thinks there is no devil or evil spirits, no heaven or hell, lives in reality, even if realism lies at the heart of his intention. He lives in severely truncated reality, limited to what he sees and understands, and he is not finally able to handle his true existential situation.

A blind man lives *in* total visible reality but cannot see any of it and so must grope. A spiritually blind individual lives *in* total reality without being aware of vast and powerful elements in it. That robs and disarms him with respect to truth and evil, but changes nothing except his own ability to deal adequately with reality.

Unregenerate man is ever thus disarmed. The Greeks, in their love of wisdom—philosophy—had one great motto for their intellectual pursuits: Know yourself. Yet neither the Greeks with their many philosophies, nor any of the succeeding nations that engaged in this pursuit of wisdom, have been able to find this understanding of self.

Otherwise there would be no need for the constant rise of new philosophies, and the discarding of others, nor would man be at an ever more apparent loss in understanding himself, despite the many modern schools of psychology and psychiatry.

The knowledge of self eludes us, remaining always beyond our grasp. The attempts of man to arrive at it purely by reason fail, as they do, because there is more to man than reason can account for. Put biblical truth at the center of the human equation, however, and many things about man and his situation that were elusive come into focus.

Since man lost his communion with God through sin and thereby lost a true understanding of himself and his reason for being, and since all attempts by unregenerate man to regain this understanding (who am I, and where did I come from, why am I here, and where am I going?) have so obviously failed, is it truly possible for man to understand himself?

There is a way. What man cannot find out, God has chosen to reveal to him.

The Bible says, *"For what man knows the things of man, save the spirit of man which is in him?"* (1 Corinthians 2:11, KJV)

In these words we are given the clear beginning of an understanding of man. In form, the verse is a question, but actually it is a statement of an essential fact. It says that what cannot be imparted to us by our minds can be given to us by another faculty. A man cannot truly know the things of a man by the mind alone, but he can know by "the spirit of man which is in him."

Few people would be able to explain this because the very term "spirit of man" is not understood by most. Vague religious notions attached to such terms only impede our understanding. With respect to the essential nature of human beings, some people confound spirit and soul and think they are the same.

It is of great importance to understand the makeup of man, the structure of his being.

God created man in His own image; therefore man is tripartite or, more accurately, triune: spirit, soul, and body. In closing his first letter to the Thessalonians, Paul wrote: "I pray God your whole *spirit* and *soul* and *body* be kept blameless" (1 Thessalonians 5:23, COM).

That is the sum of what man is. Fail to understand this, and it can be guaranteed that we will fail to understand the nature of man.

Someone may ask what makes it so vital for a person to possess this understanding. There are several reasons. Satan is always working to keep man deceived about himself, because by such common deceptions he is able to keep millions in bondage and under the power of sin or demons.

Some people are drawn, in the vanity of their minds, to estimate man above his true station, even to magnify man against God. Others are led to take such a diminished view of man that they refuse to believe that God would take an interest in such a lowly creature. Either extreme denies man a true understanding of himself. Either extreme denies him an understanding of himself in relationship to God.

To understand how evil spirits work to undermine human well-being, it is necessary to have some grasp of the nature of man: the nature of man as God intended him to be, and the nature of man as he is.

If you were to get a wrong set of instructions for a mechanism with which you were unfamiliar, your understanding of it would not correspond to the actual nature of the thing itself. A wrong understanding of the nature of man—even when that understanding is satisfyingly complex and apparently profound—can, when it is applied in an effort to help a man, do him little good, and it may do him considerable harm.

In this, the good *intentions* of the one attempting to help are of little account; what really counts is the *accuracy of his understanding* as far as it goes.

Shakespeare was moved to write the exclamatory phrase, "What a piece of work is a man!" Man is, indeed, an incomparable piece of work, created in the image of God, and the Bible teaches very clearly that he is: spirit/soul/body.

These terms are not self-explanatory, except in the case of the body, about which most of us have some basic understanding.

It is no accident that Paul mentioned these terms in the order in which he did, for that order places them in their right relationships to man's whole being. In regard to their mutual functions it also sets them in their right relationship to each other. Finally, it places them in their right relationship to the living God. The progression as he gives it— spirit, soul, body—proceeds from the innermost to the outermost parts of a human being.

For a crude illustration of man's nature, we might think of a peach. The core of the peach is the nut, which is surrounded by the pit, which in turn is surrounded by the fruit flesh—corresponding in this order to spirit, soul, and body.

That gives you some picture of the elements of a man in their actual arrangement. The soul is set within the body, and the spirit is deeply set within the soul.

The spirit is the very core of man. It is in the spirit that man has his God-given primary capacity to commune with God, who is Spirit and who must be worshiped in spirit and in truth. It is the shrine in which spiritual life is centered.

The spirit expresses itself through the soul. The soul, in turn, expresses itself through the physical body.

The body is the outer man, the soul is the inner man, the spirit is the innermost man. When all three of these are fully alive and free of sin, and functioning in their right relationships to each other, you have a human being as God made him to be.

But that is not what you find. Instead, you find human beings with all kinds of impairments and distortions and imbalances, and you find men in whom the wrong part of their being exercises undue control over their whole being.

To fully understand the rather simple basics that are set forth above and that immediately follow, it may be necessary for you to read these lines slowly and with deliberate, thoughtful concentration; perhaps to read them carefully a second time. For unless these basics are understood, the applications that follow will not be understood.

Dr. Andrew Murray, a superlative Bible expositor, wrote that *it is through the spirit that man stands "related to the spiritual world."*

Dr. Murray also penned these telling lines:

"The spirit is the seat of our God-consciousness; the soul of our self-consciousness; the body of our world-consciousness. In the spirit, God dwells; in the soul, self; in the body, sense."

Understand these words, and you will be well on your way to an understanding of the nature of man.

In this, Dr. Murray was speaking of man as he was meant to be. Self dwells in the soul and sense in the body in every case, but God does not dwell in the spirit of an unsaved man. The fact is that evil spirits may dwell in the part of a man meant for the indwelling of God, or it may be an empty, darkened faculty.

We tend to think—I know I did for a long time—of the soul as some extremely vague inner principle—a kind of pale ghost that you can't quite put your finger on. That renders the expression "saving the soul" virtually unintelligible because we don't know what it is that is being saved.

The soul is the human being within the body. It is the you resident in your body. It is the real you. The self.

Your mind, your will, your emotions, and the ability to express personality are all powers and aspects of your soul. (So also are your gifts and talents, except the chiefly physical.)

The soul includes the mind and the will of a man—all the powers of intellect and volition. In its whole makeup, the soul is the essential and distinctive you, the true inner person. At the resurrection, your saved soul will be united with a new immortal body: "For the trumpet will sound, and the dead will be raised imperishable, and we shall be changed. For this perishable . . . mortal nature must put on immortality" (1 Corinthians 15:52-53, RSV).

A man's personality and his emotions reside in the soul. It can be accurately said that a man's personality is the expression *of* his soul, but a man's personality is expressed *by* his body.

The soul expresses itself through the physical body. The emotions are expressed by facial expressions and physical gestures and words, and the thoughts are expressed in words and actions. If the emotions of a man's soul are agitated by anger or fear, his face and body will reflect that, or if his emotions are joyful, his countenance will reflect that.

The human soul is the seat of the emotions. The emotions are felt and experienced in the soul, but they are expressed, insofar as they are outwardly expressed, by the body.

So the term "saving the soul" refers to the saving of the essential you—mind, will, personality, character—as distinguished from your physical body.


Genesis 2:7 shows that man had a body, which God formed out of the dust, *before* man had life. It was when God "breathed into his nostrils the breath of life" that "man became *a living soul.*"

"A living soul" is the essential man. It has been helpfully said that "man *is* a soul, and he *has* a body."

The mouth, the larynx, the tongue, the lips speak—but do the lips really speak? No. It is the man in the body who is speaking, and his soul is employing his bodily equipment through which to speak. You can use your lips by an act of will to form any words you wish. When your lips speak, it is not your body primarily that is talking; it is you, the real you, the inner man, the soul.

The outward members of your body are instruments you use to carry out the intentions of your soul. If, in an accident, I were to lose the use of an arm, I would after recovery not be essentially any less myself. My soul would remain intact. It would simply have fewer bodily mechanisms to use, by which to express itself.

Ultimately the soul will be transferred, once, from house to house! The present body will perish (or, if Christ returns while we are yet alive, it will be changed in a moment) and the redeemed soul will dwell forever in a new spiritual body subject to no pain or deterioration—a body similar in form to the mortal body, yet different, new and perfect.

"Our commonwealth is in heaven, and from it we await a Saviour, the Lord Jesus Christ, *who will change our lowly body to be like His glorious body,* by the power which enables Him to subject all things to Himself" (Philippians 3:20-21, RSV).

Though man is tripartite in his makeup, and though each of these three parts is distinct, man's trinity is fused into a true union.

The brain, for example, is the seat of the mind. The brain is part of the body. The mind is a part of the soul.

The mind is certainly greater than the brain. The thoughts that come to us come to our minds. They are received, stored, or dispatched by the brain as instructions to our members. *The brain is the command center of the mind for the body.* The brain relates the mind to the body.

Even a dictionary definition helps show this:

*The Random House Dictionary* defines the word *mind* as "the element, part, substance, or process that reasons, thinks, feels, wills, perceives, judges, etc."

Of the word *brain* it says: "The part of the central nervous system enclosed in the cranium of man and other vertebrates, consisting of a soft, convoluted mass of gray and white matter and serving to control and coordinate the mental and physical actions."

Alternatively, it speaks of the "brain as the *center* of thought, understanding, etc.; mind, intellect" (italics added).

The will of the human soul controls the thought processes of the brain. It is able to direct the brain, to redirect it, to check it.

A thought flies into your mind, seemingly out of nowhere. It may be an idle thought, a creative thought, an unpleasant thought, or an evil thought. It may be about virtually anything from the label on a soup can to the nature of the universe. When the thought comes to mind, the will can direct the brain to receive it, reject it, ponder it, expand on it, or it can redirect the brain to some other, more useful avenue of thought.

It is through the body that man—man's soul—stands related to the external world. His physical senses apprehend—see, hear, taste, touch, or smell—the realm of nature and his surroundings. His physical powers enable a man to act upon his environment.

Then there is the spirit. It is this, above all, that makes man unique. By this part of his being, a man may be in touch with the spiritual realm.

The human spirit gives man his spiritual capacity. It is by this that people may worship God as He desires to be worshiped "in spirit and in truth." Yet this part of man was ruined, in terms of its primary purpose, by the Fall.

In God's perfect design for man, the human spirit—indwelt and filled by the Holy Spirit and enjoying a full and free communion with the living God—was to govern all the activities and powers of the soul—intellect, will, and emotions. In this plan, man would always act in agreement with the will of his Creator, and he would enjoy the fruits of the creation in abundant activity and leisure, and in peace.

When man sinned, the spiritual lifeline between heaven and earth snapped. Man was cut off from the life of God. The communion between the Creator and His creature was gone. The human spirit became dead toward God—not totally inactive, but utterly unable to perform its proper function.

Man, meant to be the express reflection of the beauty and wisdom of God, was orphaned. Emptied of the life of God, yet still possessing the capacities and energies of his body and soul, man became even a menace to himself and to the earth. This is the tragedy of the Fall.

Man's spirit, meant to be the dwelling place of God, became at best dead to God, and at worst it became an abode of evil spirits. The intention of God was that man, walking in perfect communion and unforced agreement with Him—the human spirit and the Holy Spirit wholly at one—would *jointly rule with God outward from the spirit, through the soul and body, to the whole natural environment.* Everywhere man went, then, the will of God would be done.

Instead we see another condition entirely. Man, dead in his spirit and lacking communion with God, carries on in the powers of his soul, which inevitably come under some degree of influence by demons (even in the best of men) or, at the worst, he comes under the actual control of evil spirits and spreads chaos and misery in his environment.

It is the spirit of man, not the soul, that God intended to govern his life! The soul is not capable of governing the life aright. With the soul in charge, the center of man's government is misplaced—from God to self.

Man, created for communion with God, was never meant to walk alone, apart from God, independent of his Creator. Yet that is his condition. Just as confusion besets the body politic when the lines of command are disoriented, confusion has plagued human affairs because of this dislocation.

Yet in his lost condition man, with very few exceptions, does not seek God. It is God who seeks man, for He has made a way of restoration for us. He has made a way back to Himself.

The extent of the Fall cannot be measured solely by the lack of communion with God, though this is central, because it manifests itself in countless aspects of human life. Let us look for a moment at man as he is.

An individual may become primarily or highly developed in any of the three parts of his being: body, soul, or spirit. Or he may remain underdeveloped in one or more. He may be badly lopsided, as some are.

God evidently intended for all three sectors to develop and function in a kind of balance, with no area to be developed at the excessive expense of another.

Possibly the majority of mankind are those centered in the body, the senses. Pleasure and appetites and cravings often dominate and rob men of the dignity God desires for them.

We have all met sensual men and women whose talk is centered on bodily appetites and needs. They talk a great deal of eating, drinking, of sex, of relaxing, and sleeping. They may be people whose minds are thick, but there are intelligent individuals whose interests are centered in the gratification of their senses, even if in a refined style.

I remember a man of the sensual kind saying to me one evening toward the end of a day's work: "You know what I'm going to do? I'm going to go down and get me some tall drinks, and then I'm going to get me 'bout the biggest steak in town, and then I'm going to roll into that hay and get me 'bout twelve hours of solid shut-eye!" Except for the necessary interruption of work, his chief pursuit in life was in procuring for his senses the next thing they wanted.

Such men are ruled by their bodily appetites inward, in an exact reversal of God's intention that the spirit rule both soul and body.

The mind can be sensual too in a fleshly, or in a worldly, way. Bodily sensuality is likely to be stirred up initially in and through the mind. Knowing the truth that "when lust has conceived, it brings forth sin; and sin, when it is finished, brings forth death" (James 1:15, KJV), evil powers must rejoice to see the human mind plied by the depictions of pornography in its many facets and sordid extremes. By it the mind receives highly sensual impressions and passes them through to the body to be acted on in some sinful way.

"Beloved, I beseech you . . . to abstain from the passions of the flesh that *wage war against your soul,*" we read in 1 Peter 2:11 (RSV).

But sensuality need not be gross to be spiritually undermining. Even a Christian may be unduly ruled by his appetites. John warns believers that "if any one loves the world, love for the Father is not in him. For all that is in the world, the lust of the flesh and the lust of the eyes and the pride of life, is not of the Father but is of the world. And the world passes away, and the lust of it; but he who does the will of God abides forever" (1 John 2:15-16, RSV).

Believers, alert to the pitfalls of fleshliness, are more readily beguiled, and weakened, by the somewhat more subtle lures of worldliness.

Unlike the physically centered or the sensual man, another man might be highly developed in his soul—in the department of the intellect, or in the appreciative emotions. He gives a heavy proportion of his time to cultivating his mind, or to cultivating such of the finer soulish emotions as attend great music. Various aspects of his soul—emotions, thoughts, cognitive capacity, creative genius, artistic talent, and so on—may be brought to a point of marvelous sensibility and refinement.

There are men whose interests are centered in the life of the intellect. For the sake of pursuing knowledge, they may greatly rein in their sensual drives. They live primarily in the mind, not in the body. The extreme of this is the frail, pale, stooped scholar who neglects his body, feeding it haphazardly and giving it no exercise but that which daily routine necessarily imposes.

There are men who strike a balance between intellect and the aesthetic emotions and cultivate them both in very useful ways.

There are some more truly rounded men who bring their bodies, their minds, and their sentient emotions all to fairly high states of development. The able athlete with a Phi Beta Kappa key who devotes some of his spare time to chess, scientific reading, and Spanish poetry might fall into this class.

In North America there are large numbers of fleshly men, devoted to their bodily desires, and possibly larger numbers of soulish men, occupied with the worldly uses of their minds or the enjoyment of their emotions, but there are far fewer spiritual men who are developed or keenly exercised in this part.

That is not surprising, since man died in his spirit when his first father sinned. If any man who is, as the Bible puts it, spiritually "dead in trespasses and sins" undertakes to develop his darkened spirit, he does so only by the agency and activity of demonic spirits. Imams, shamans, dervishes, priests of the heathen religions, and individuals who seek to cultivate themselves spiritually apart from the Holy Spirit and the Word of God, are usually in this category. So are occult practitioners.

Some, who go to extremes in their religious or spiritual practices, receive certain powers, "revelations," and special connections to the demonic realm from the enemy. By various rigors, by asceticism and fasts, by neglecting the body, by chanting and slavishly repeating certain formulas, these individuals obtain special status and so become wonder men and women or acknowledged "saints" in some regions of the world. They, in effect, stir up the underworld by their illegitimate exertions, though they may be unaware of the real source of their fetchings.

North Americans, by and large, have developed the mind and the body but have neglected the spirit. This is not true of many men of India, who have assiduously cultivated and developed the spiritual faculty, yet almost exclusively through demonic influence. A relatively small number in our society are psychically "sensitive," as they say. They are often full of spiritual perceptions and intuitions of various kinds as a result of their commerce with evil spirits.

In recent times we have seen some young people becoming active in this way. They *know* that there is a spiritual and supernatural realm. They have had experiences with it.

Speaking of believers who had stayed too long on a diet of spiritual milk—basic or foundational biblical truths—and had failed to go on to spiritual meat, the writer of the Book of Hebrews supplied a key to real spiritual maturity with these words: "But strong meat belongs to those who are of full age, even those who *by reason of use* have their senses exercised to discern both good and evil" (Hebrews 5:14, KJV).

The lawful use and exercise of any faculty makes it keen and leads to its full development. Neglect, disuse, or inadequate use cheat the possessor of what is potentially his.

In a misguided quest to be spiritual, certain believers in the early history of the church put themselves under excessive rigors or disciplines and others deliberately neglected the body. By such religious practices they hoped to make themselves better.

Regarding these practices, Paul wrote these telling words: "Such regulations indeed have an appearance of wisdom, with their self-imposed worship, their false humility, and their harsh treatment of the body, but they lack any value in restraining sensual indulgence" (Colossians 2:23). Another translation says that these "are of no value in checking the indulgence of the flesh."

Why? Because they *are* fleshly and soulish and willful, not spiritual, in origin and nature. They have "an appearance of wisdom," but it is empty. Not all indulgence of a fleshly nature is for pleasure. Some of it feeds pride, or aims at special or superior self-attainment, or at getting ahead. But since it is all of the flesh and of the natural soul, the Bible says it has no spiritual value.

Does that mean that fasting is therefore excessive or uncalled for? No, not at all, so long as it is truly spiritual in motivation, in application and purpose—lifted up above the level of spiritual self-interest. True fasts are not mere exercises in heroic self-discipline, designed to cultivate the spiritual self. The latter comes from the flesh, and it goes to the flesh.

We too easily tend to think of the term *flesh* as referring chiefly to sensuality in pleasurable or sinful forms. That is an extremely limited definition. The "flesh" actually is *everything that man is, and can be, apart from the life of God.* It is man carrying on with fleshly and soulish life (sometimes with demonic collaboration or inspiration) yet without true spiritual life.

The "works of the flesh" identified in Galatians 5:16-21 more accurately tell what the "flesh" is in God's sight. The passage says, "Now the works of the flesh are plain: immorality, impurity, licentiousness, idolatry, sorcery, enmity, strife, jealousy, anger, selfishness, dissension, party spirit, envy, drunkenness, carousing, and the like. I warn you, as I warned you before, that those who do such things shall not inherit the kingdom of God" (RSV).

As you inspect each of those, you will quickly see that, though they include sensual indulgence, they go well beyond it to things that are much more of the soul and the spirit than of the body. Taken together they give a pretty good profile of what man is without God.

Charles G. Finney, the young lawyer who became a great American evangelist, demonstrated brilliantly in his preaching that self—self-interest, self-gratification, self-promotion, and self-preferment—lie at the heart of most human actions, though they take exceedingly differing forms of expression.

Finney showed that an individual will absolutely sacrifice or submerge one desirable thing for another that is still more desirable. The deeply greedy man may sacrifice pleasure so as to dedicate himself more fully to the hot pursuit of gain. Another man may abstain from certain enticing but publicly disfavored sins, not out of any regard for God, but solely so that his position in society, on which his esteem and livelihood depend, can be maintained. He is wiser than the immoral man, and temporarily safer, but no less alien to God.

The very nature of God—and hence the nature seen in the lives of those who really belong to God—is love, defined as "disinterested benevolence" in action, Finney declared. That is the opposite of selfishness as an animating principle.

As a born-again individual abides in the light of God, and pays heed to the Word, he will gradually begin to understand himself and his reason for being.

The Word of God, when it is applied to our lives in its function as a sharp "double-edged sword," has this effect: "It penetrates even to dividing soul from spirit, joints and marrow; it judges the thoughts and attitudes of the heart" (Hebrews 4:12).

Only the living Word can slice, so to speak, with such unerring accuracy among and between things in the complex nature of man. When it divides soul from spirit, it diminishes not the functions, but the authority, of the former in favor of the latter. It makes us spiritual.

Since self is centered in the soul, that dividing action is highly necessary. Some persons, tightly grasping certain areas of sheer self-interest, will not let that operation take place. Their tenacious grasp on the desired state of their soulish life obstructs their spiritual development. It leads also to self-deception.

"Do not merely listen to the Word, and so deceive yourselves," James 1:22-24 warns. "Anyone who listens to the Word but does not do what it says is like a man who looks at his face in a mirror and, after looking at himself, goes away and immediately forgets what he looks like." The Word is a true spiritual mirror.

Such believers do not fully face the fact that Jesus said that among the things that must go if anyone is to follow Him is a man's "own life," i.e., the self-life. They forget that "everything is uncovered and laid bare before the eyes of Him to whom we must give account" (Hebrews 4:13). We can fool ourselves, if we insist on it, but we cannot fool Him.

Our society is not marked by a lack of Christians—there are millions of them—but it is short of spiritually mature, spiritually discerning, and spiritually motivated believers who live the exchanged life (the Christ life for the self-life) daily.

Happy are the individuals who are alive and active in their spirits, who truly worship God and know Him because they have been reawakened, made alive in the spirit. New life began for them and, with it, a new peace, a new power to live above sin and temptation.

Those who follow through, becoming lovers of God and counting His will more precious than their own desires, become men as men truly ought to be—governed by God through the awakened human spirit and exercising their capacities of soul and body in a way that pleases Him.

When Paul wrote, "I pray God that your whole spirit and soul and body be kept blameless," he was expressing God's desire that a man's whole being be free of sin, so that he may enjoy unhindered fellowship with God and be filled with light in the spiritual part.

## Reality, "*Reality*," and REALITY

Believers are told the glorious fact that "he who is united to the Lord *becomes one spirit with Him*." There is no higher earthly privilege than that. The declaration comes in the middle of a warning against the immoral use of the body and says:

"Do you not know that your body is a temple of the Holy Spirit within you, which you have from God? You are not your own; you were bought with a price. So glorify God in your body" (1 Corinthians 6:17-20, RSV).

Your body is a temple, a dwelling place, of the Holy Spirit. Though it serves you marvelously well when in health, it is meant to be a house for the Lord, a place from which worship ascends to Him. In its use, the body is to be "a living sacrifice"—daily yielded deliberately to God for the carrying out of His good will, according to Romans 12:1-2.

When that is the case, the will of God is advanced through the human vessel whether the fact is immediately visible or not. Advanced not so much through the pursuit of some *program* of service to God or to men as by a mysteriously powerful co-working of earth with heaven, of heaven interacting with those who are "one spirit" with the Lord.

It is that which really grinds the enemy, which tells against his work in the long run and hews it down. And it is that which draws opposition and interference from him.

Martin Luther in his grand hymn "A Mighty Fortress" spoke from experience when he wrote: "And though this world, with devils filled, should threaten to undo us"—he is speaking of believers here—"we will not fear, for God has willed His truth to triumph through us." The hymn also states, "For still our ancient foe doth seek to work us woe. . . ."

In his program against the unbelievers, the enemy aims for their maximum strategic victimization (chiefly through spiritual deception and moral ruination, but in some cases reaching all the way to demonic occupation).

His approach to believers is necessarily adapted to the very different spiritual circumstances. It might be said that his aim is maximum strategic interference—with their godly purposes, their patterns of thought, and their *peace.*

He sometimes seeks to turn what might be called "environmental evidence" against our trust in God.

We who believe are living on two levels at once. One of those levels surrounds us at nearly all times. It is out of accord with the higher, and it bears its testimony in upon us continually. God has "raised us up with Christ and seated us with Him in the heavenly realms" (Ephesians 2:6) but our feet are planted on *plain old sod.*

Like all other human beings, believers live on the natural plane; we see, feel, hear, taste, smell, and have knowledge there. But we go far beyond that. We who believe are living, by faith, on unseen reality—the reality of the existence and redeeming love and providence of God.

The devil is acutely aware of that fact and he hates it. He is also aware that life on the natural plane and the act of living by faith are not always in smooth agreement. They clash at times in a way that pulls us between living by what we see, and living by faith in the God we do not see.

One of Satan's classic tactics against believers is to try to seduce us with what I call the argument from reality—an argument *against faith* based on objective, or seen, reality. It is one of his strongest arguments and the reason it is so strong is that, quite often, the thing he directs our attention to is manifestly, and inarguably, *real*. When that happens to be the case, it is what he *says* about it that is false.

He tries at times to pile up objective reality so high against us that it seems to mock and overwhelm our faith. The enemy, pointing at visible circumstances, reasons or urges upon our minds the total irrelevance and powerlessness of God in our particular situation.

His presentation of such circumstances to the mind may happen to be highly accurate or factual—in which case he interprets the facts to us in a false or threatening way—or it may appear to be so when it is only *partly* so.

Since Satan is a liar, he is not entirely scrupulous about whether he comes at us with actual, or *perceived,* or even merely *predicted* reality. His purpose is to dishearten us, to avert our gaze from God on high.

Never forget the fact that powers of darkness lie to us *through,* and about, reality. They use lies as powerfully as they can to reduce our outlook at earth level to that of a practical atheist. They seek to put us in fear through lies, and then to bring us into bondage to circumstances.

"How are you doing?" a believer of abounding faith, whose life was full of delight in God and frequently marked by the acts of God in response to faith, said one day to a fellow believer.

"Okay, under the circumstances," the second replied.

"Well," said the first with a huge smile, "what are you doing under *those old things!"* It was not a manner of speaking; the man was talking from long experience in walking above circumstances with God.

We must live *in* the world and in reality, of course, while living above it, as Jesus did. The enemy wants the world to pull us down to its level, and fix its claims upon us, but he surely knows that believers have the power to lift sectors of the world toward heaven and the atmosphere of heaven. He knows that it is true of believers that, "Blessed are those whose strength is in You. . . . As they pass through the Valley of Baca, they make it a place of springs. . . . They go from strength to strength" (Psalm 84:5-7).

So Satan tries to pound us down by what we see about us. He says that the visible reality is *the* governing and controlling factor in our situation. He assures us that faith is totally powerless with regard to it. He pressures us to surrender to the momentous or mountainous circumstance.

Denying the reality, when it really is real, would be fanaticism. What we must do is to set truth over against it by faith. We must remeasure it. The thing is so close to us it seems bigger than God, but faith gives it its right proportions under God.

There is at times a battle within the human soul to assert faith. Quite often, in fact, the main battle of the Christian's life is not so much to accomplish a certain thing as it is to maintain unbroken faith in the face of all appearances and feelings, contradictions, adversities, and delays.

The psalms, especially those of David, are often a record of a successful, recurrent struggle to assert truth and the sovereignty of God (and also the inevitability of victory for believers and defeat for evil workers) against strong evidences to the contrary.

A few of these psalms are poetic expressions of pastoral serenity, but many of them are declarations of victory wrested out of danger, inner turmoil, and spiritual conflict. They make up a soaring chronicle of faith triumphant.

When David, as a young warrior, went out alone against Israel's brashly defiant enemy Goliath, the giant's huge bulk and loud declarations of his prowess had stopped the army of Israel cold. They did not dare move against him.

David took Goliath's measure by faith and asked, "Who is this uncircumcised Philistine that he should defy the armies of the living God?" Acting alone, in the power of God, David quickly brought Goliath down and silenced him forever.

Out of faith exercised in demanding situations, David wrote, "I have set the Lord always before me. Because He is at my right hand, I will not be shaken." It wasn't that there was nothing to shake him, there was plenty; it was that he would not be shaken. "Find rest, O my soul, in God alone; my hope comes from Him. He alone is my rock and my salvation; He is my fortress, I will not be shaken" (Psalms 16:8 and 62:5-6). "In God I have put my trust; I will not fear what man can do to me" (Psalm 56:11, com).

## Rejecting Invitations to Despair
If the enemy cannot separate us from our basic faith, he will do what he can to separate us from our peace—a peace to which we have a divinely bestowed right. Yet the possession of that peace must be enforced *by*

*faith* in the face of whatever may confront us.

Something had occurred—it took the form of a doctrinal lie—that had disturbed and distressed the believers at Thessalonica. Paul counseled them with these words: "We beg you, brethren, not to be quickly *shaken in mind* or excited, either *by spirit* or *by word,* or by letter purporting to be from us . . ." (2 Thessalonians 2:1-3, RSV).

A deception had sown a certain amount of confusion, uncertainty, and anxiety among the believers, separating them for a time from inner peace. They had suffered intrusive interference. They were delivered by Paul's exposing of its nature.

The Bible is distinctly not a record of the nonexistence of things contrary to God as, for example, Christian Science tries to make it, but it is a record of how even those things must yield to God and be subject to Him.

The trouble with the devil's reality argument is that it is based only on partial reality, never on total reality. It leaves God out, and is based on godless materialism.

Faith in God alters the effect and the power of antagonizing circumstances. How fast that happens is usually not the key fact but that it happens. The Red Sea was a thoroughly forbidding barrier when the people of Israel were fleeing the pursuing Egyptians, but the supernatural opening of a dry path through the waters became the prevailing reality in that situation.

The result of faith in God is not always as outwardly spectacular as that; what counts is that it is wonderfully effective. Sometimes faith is all we have in a situation. It is all we need. Faith brings the applied resources of God to bear upon it.

If we accept a demonic interpretation of circumstances, we deny faith and go under. By doing so we, to some real extent, prevent God from lifting us above our circumstances. Among the saddest words of Scripture are: "The men of Ephraim, though armed with bows, turned back on the day of battle." God was ready that day to go with them, to see them through to victory, but He could not because they would not. "They forgot what He had done, the wonders He had shown them. . . . They did not remember His power" (Psalm 78:9, 11, 42).

They had God, and they had earthly means as well, but without faith, neither did them a speck of good. They cheated themselves, and they cheated God. They tasted none of the exhilaration of co-conquest with Him.

The enemy is always ready to issue his invitations to doubt, discouragement, or despair. Since faith is our actual spiritual lifeline to and from the throne of God, the adversary goes all out at times to persuade us to cut it. The only thing he can hope for is *a voluntary abandonment* of faith by the believer.

If we hold fast to faith and assert truth, he loses the argument and slinks away. He has no option. He is entirely overcome.

If the adversary sought to tempt the Lord Jesus Christ, it is certain that he will seek to tempt us.

Jesus overcame the three great temptations—specifically devised and aimed by Satan to undermine Jesus at the heart of His being, as God in human form—by applying whole truths from the Scriptures, honestly quoted, against half-truths, malignantly misapplied (see Matthew 4:1-11).

The trouble at Thessalonica mentioned earlier was no less artfully adapted to the believers' spiritual situation. It was a deception having to do with a precious doctrine, the coming again of Jesus. It did not deny that hope; it twisted and misapplied it. That doctrinal lie, made to resemble truth, shook the believers in their minds for a time.

The enemy was aware that he could not blatantly deny the doctrine to these believers, so he came around another way to distort it and confuse them. He is a master of the calculated tactic.

Satan had persuasive access to the person of Jesus, just as his agents do at times to us. Having that, they can get no further than that—unless we yield to them.

The victory of Jesus in the matter of the threefold temptation—in which each element was a direct attack on His divinity-in-humanity—brought freedom and relief.

The result of Jesus' resistance was that the devil "left Him." Take note that this relief from opposition-via-temptation was total in the matters immediately at issue, but not final in its effect on the tempter, for we are told another important fact—that the devil left Jesus "for a season," or, as the NIV puts it, "he left Him until an opportune time" (Luke 4:13).

We are not going to get in our earthly lifetimes total relief or exemption from such opposition, but we will enjoy seasons and periods of freedom from it, especially after meeting a temptation or deception or attempt at interference and overcoming it.

Some have said that this Christ-defeated enemy is now a kind of straw man. That is far from true, but in his work he must, and does, resort to bluff and bluster—and he seeks to be a master psychologist.

Soon after his sudden, terrible losses and bodily affliction, the good man named Job was brought under accusation; and the whole ensuing psychological and spiritual thrust against him was argued *from reality*.

He was told that since he was in great suffering and appalling loss, God was severely chastising him for some hidden, unconfessed fault.

Reams and reams of that very reasoning were thrown at him by his God-fearing "friends."

It was plenty hard for Job to stand against these persuasive arguments, yet he mounted up above them magnificently when he declared to those who were accusing him in this high-toned way:

"How long will you torment me and crush me with words? . . . If it is true that I have gone astray, my error remains my concern alone. . . . Have pity on me, my friends, have pity. . . . I know that my Redeemer lives, and that in the end He will stand upon the earth. And after my skin has been destroyed, yet in my flesh I will see God. I myself will see Him with my own eyes—I, and not another" (Job 19).

Job was being terrifically tested in his faith, but he was *not* being punished for his faults. It was a masterstroke of Satan's attack on him for godly men to sit next to Job and put him through the grinder of eloquent and lengthy theological reasonings which said the opposite of what was true.

Job prophesied mighty truths about the coming Redeemer. He saw through death to bodily resurrection and life after the grave and eternal fellowship with God. His words have been set to glorious music. We can speak truth after Job in the face of anything that comes against us, of whatever shape or size or kind.

Unquenchable faith honors God greatly and rebuffs powers of darkness. It brings God into action on our behalf in the way that He knows is best. "You have heard of Job's perseverance and have seen what the Lord finally brought about" (James 5:11; see Job 42:7-9, 12-17).

The more a believer serves the Lord, the more he knows of three things—of opposition by unseen powers at times, of overcoming the enemy, and of the reality of divine protection and assistance. All of it has the effect of maturing a believer spiritually.

"Faith must be tested, because it can be turned into a personal possession only through conflict," Oswald Chambers, the luminous British Christian teacher, wisely said.


The best definition of faith I have ever seen, outside of the Bible, is that of the lawyer-evangelist Charles G. Finney, who wrote, "Faith is a voluntary *act* of trust in God." You would do well to memorize that, for it is truth distilled in very few words.

Faith is volitional in nature, not a mysterious disposition that is sometimes ours, sometimes not. It can be deliberately asserted and held to. Because a believer must at times choose between what he *sees* and what he believes, the enemy seeks to pressure us on that very issue.

Faith in God is nothing more than faith in what *is*. It is merely normative. If the enemy can separate us from our faith, he can separate us from our heavenly resources in part and delude us out of victory.

Newspaper editors, often acting under severe time constraints as well as tough news competition, want what they want when they want it. The degree of its possibility is of little interest to them, especially since they do not have to go and get it themselves but assign reporters to do it.

In newspaper reporting for *The New York Times*, I was quite often assigned to do the very difficult and to do it fast, but on several occasions I was assigned to do what had every appearance of being impossible. Those assignments were slammed at me, with considerable impact on my soul and nerves.

Each time, by a deliberate act, I put aside my emotions and refused feelings of panic and hopelessness. Once, turning to the water fountain for a quick drink, I lifted the whole assignment to the Lord and told Him that I trusted Him for it.

What ensued was awesome. I tell the cold truth when I say that I did not go out to get that story. That story came in and got me! I never left the office. I did hardly a lick of work until I started writing. I think I may have made one phone call, but I am not even sure of that. Within three hours, on a subject of remarkable complexity and remoteness, I found myself loaded with information from two expert sources, and I wrote two and a half full columns that had the ring of authority and were filled with facts.

The editors found it remarkable, as, indeed, I did myself. They gave *me* the credit for it, since they did not know anywhere else to put it. But I knew *who* had done it. All I had done was reject panic and assert faith. Then I watched God go to work on the assignment. God is finally the biggest fact in any situation, and faith brings Him into it.

Again, hear Oswald Chambers: "We act like pagans in a crisis. . . . All our fret and worry is caused by calculating without God."

" 'Commit your way to the Lord; trust in Him, and *He will act*. . . . For the wicked shall be cut off; but those who wait for the Lord shall possess the land' (Psalm 37:5, 9). Don't calculate without God. . . . When we choose deliberately to obey God, then He will tax the remotest star and the last grain of sand to assist us with all His almighty power."

What has all of this to do with the supernatural? Absolutely everything, because faith is *the* means by which we overcome the enemy and carry out God's will. God acts for us when we cast our faith, our case, our hope on Him.

Abraham, called the father of faith, obtained that station by the simple yet profound act of simply believing God in a matter where the facts and circumstances said the opposite of what God said.

He was old and his wife was way past childbearing years. When he told the Lord, " 'I remain childless.' ... the Lord ... took him outside and said, 'Look at the heavens and count the stars. ... So shall your offspring be.'

"Abram believed the Lord, and He credited it to him as righteousness" (Genesis 15:1-6).

He had absolutely nothing to go on, no evidence apart from the promise of God.

As time went on, and no son came, his faith was tried. He stood between the promise of the invisible God and the flat fact that nothing was happening.

His wife came up with a workable "solution." She advised him to strike a sensible compromise between faith and fact by letting a maidservant bear him a child, and he did so, becoming the father of Ishmael—a pink and wailing living substitute for God's not-yet-fulfilled promise.

God had not forgotten. Thirteen long years later, when Abraham was ninety-nine years old, the Lord spoke to him again and assured him that, even at ninety, his wife would bear him a son—Isaac, the son of promise. A year later the child was born. Abraham was 100 years old (Genesis 15–17; 18:9-15; and 21:1-12).

Along the way Abraham had wobbled somewhat under the testimony of his senses. And he had learned something about what Chambers called "the enormous leisure of God."

Temptation to abandon faith, and to live by sight, comes to us at the crucial point when reality speaks so loudly that faith is made to seem unreasonable, weak, stupid, or beside the point. Then the voice of the evil one may come to us by a thought that flashes into our mind, or by a human voice that gives faithless counsel.

### The Master Tactic

A godly king of Judah, Hezekiah, came up against a terrific crisis during his reign (2 Kings 18:17–19:35). The king of Assyria sent a large army to Jerusalem with three commanders. Judah and Jerusalem were about to be invaded by a force many times stronger than any King Hezekiah had.

That was the *fact*. It wasn't any dream; it was absolutely and cruelly real. That big foreign army was poised to strike.

The king and the people were confronted by two things. One was a picture of reality—that powerful force drawn up against Jerusalem. The other was words—the *interpretation* put upon the fact. That is quite precisely the twofold combination that the enemy will use against us.

The Assyrian field commander was a hulk of a man with a booming voice, and he bellowed out a message for King Hezekiah:

" 'This is what the great king ... of Assyria says: "On what are you basing this confidence of yours? You say you have strategy and military strength—but you speak only empty words." ' "

That barrel-chested warrior mocked any hope of Judah getting help from Egypt, and he was bold enough to say, "The Lord Himself told me to march against this country and destroy it."

The field commander turned next to the men of Judah and did everything he could to put fear into them, even saying that if they resisted him they would be forced to "eat their own filth and drink their own urine."

His voice seemed to grow louder as he "stood and called out in Hebrew: 'Hear the word of the great king, the king of Assyria! This is what the king says: Do not let Hezekiah deceive you. He cannot deliver you from my hand. Do not let Hezekiah persuade you to trust in the Lord when he says, "The Lord will surely deliver us." ... Make peace with me. ... Choose life and not death!

" 'Do not listen to Hezekiah, for he is misleading you when he says, "The Lord will deliver us." ' "

At just this point, the field commander spouted out the capstone of his argument from reality: "Has the god of any nation ever delivered his land from the hand of the king of Assyria?" He reeled off the names of six nations that had been overrun by the Assyrian army.

"Who of all the gods of these countries has been able to save his land from me? How then can the Lord deliver Jerusalem from my hand?" the field commander demanded. It was strong stuff, and *facts* backed it up.

The men of Judah were up against tremendous psychological pressure on the key point of faith. The whole argument was *don't trust God for this.*

The tactic was to pile up facts that were well known, sprinkle them with lies, throw in some taunts and threats, interpret them with a very powerful line of false reasoning—all aimed at precisely one thing, at getting Hezekiah and the people of Judah to act apart from faith.

Their *only* strength against these belligerent invaders was their faith in the living God. If they gave it up, they would be defenseless. The enemy would march in by sheer default.

This was potent antifaith propaganda based on *facts* and on threats. The enemy's message to believers is, "Give up, give up, give in. Don't lean on something as feeble as faith in the face of all this." Yes—he warns us not to be deceived by faith, while he is in the very act of doing all he can to deceive us by facts!

Faith, based on the sacrifice of the cross and the resurrection, is what defeats him. In fact, Satan is predefeated by what Jesus did, and by what He does today in response to faith. So the enemy's *only* hope is to turn certain defeat into stolen victory by false persuasion. He cannot *get* victory unless *we give it* to him, so that becomes his entire tactic.

The people of Judah immediately employed the right counter-strategy. The account says, "But the people remained silent and said nothing in reply, because the king had commanded, 'Do not answer him.'"

Whether with our lips, or just in our minds, the enemy wants us to get down on his level and talk it over with him. That is always a losing game. The only answer given the enemy commander was total silence.

Then Hezekiah went into the house of the Lord to pray. He saw that everything the Assyrian warrior had said, even when it was indisputably factual, amounted to "ridiculing the living God."

The king sent men to the great Prophet Isaiah, who sent word back: "This is what the Lord says: Do not be afraid of what you have heard— these words with which the underlings of the king of Assyria have blasphemed Me . . . he will return to his own country, and there I will have him cut down with the sword."

*Reality* as it *is* was now overshadowing reality as it seemed to be.

The whole enemy production—big army backing up big boasts based on a long string of conquests—was a precanceled zero. He who had said that Hezekiah's hope was only "empty words" had himself spoken only haughty, empty words. With all their fact-based appeal, there was *nothing to them!*

In God, Judah and Hezekiah were impregnable and unconquerable. Our spiritual enemy knows that in God, we cannot be overcome. That is why he works so hard to break the line of faith from our hearts to God's throne. If we throw faith over in the crunch, we allow the enemy to strip us.

Some men in this world walk in the greatness of their own strength— the Assyrian commander surely did—while some walk in the strength of the Lord. The former often *feel* very secure. The latter sometimes feel extremely weak.

These are those of whom the Scripture says "out of weakness were made strong" (Hebrews 11:34, KJV).

It is one thing to be strong; it is another to be "made strong." The worldly, godless man often does not know or sense his own weakness. It comes upon him suddenly; he is taken unawares.

"When I am weak," wrote the Apostle Paul, "then I am strong" (2 Corinthians 12:10). Does that make sense? To the spiritual man, yes.

None of us are sufficient in ourselves for the spiritual conflict in our day. We either avoid it, or we enter in and learn that "our sufficiency is from God" (2 Corinthians 3:5, RSV).

It was when Paul trembled in himself that he preached wonderfully well to others: "I was with you in weakness and in much fear and trembling . . . that your faith might not rest in the wisdom of men but in the power of God" (1 Corinthians 2:3-5, RSV).

"I will boast all the more gladly about my weaknesses," he wrote, "so that Christ's power may rest on me. That is why, for Christ's sake, I delight in weaknesses, in insults, in hardships, in persecutions, in difficulties. For when I am weak, then I am strong."

He precedes these words with the Lord's great promise: "My grace is sufficient for you, for My power is made perfect in weakness" (2 Corinthians 12:9-10).

No believer who walks as a natural man in the natural world, by sight more than by faith, by self-determination more than by God's appointment, counts very much for Christ in his hour. But when the believer, led by the Holy Spirit, follows the Lord in the path of service chosen *for* him, not *by* him, and steps beyond natural things into spiritual territory, he discovers his own weakness and something more: the strength and the power of God meet him there.

In personal weakness, the trusting Christian becomes the channel of God's power into the situation in which he walks. By such faith, God's power is applied to earthly realities, to reshape or remake them as God wants them.

Let faith always be foremost. Give God the opportunity to show Himself strong. Against everything the enemy says, or does, or throws, faith is our shield—and it always shuts the enemy out—troops, commanders, noise, and all!

# Natural to Supernatural— Glimpses of the Wider Picture

You are endowed with certain faculties—mental, physical, emotional, and spiritual. Each is a trust from God. He wants you to enjoy full control and command of those faculties for all their right uses, up to the limits imposed by the fact of mortality.

The enemy does not. If he cannot steal your victory or your peace in the manner described in the previous chapter, he may at some point seek to cut in against your full, free governance of some area of your being.

It is easy enough, even for believers, to take these faculties nearly for granted, since they are ours so naturally, yet the fact is that they are far beyond price. They deserve to be guarded. Those who do so often find themselves in the keenest and freest enjoyment of them through many decades and even late in life.

That is in line with the design of the Creator, who gave them. Evil spirits take a contrary aim. They seek at times to impede or encroach upon a person's own power over his actions and thoughts and even physical functioning, to hinder or impair these to whatever degree they can.

Because mankind is under ongoing attack by the powers of darkness, and is often susceptible to demonic initiatives, there is a constant tension between what God intended and what *is*.

Though its scale is relatively vast, man stands close to the center and apex of this conflict. He is its object on both sides.

Before getting to certain helpful specifics on the actual effects of this tension, let us take a moment to see the wider picture.

In making man in His own image, the Creator meant for humans to have progressive dominion over the whole earth—its lesser creatures, territories, resources. Man was told to "fill the earth and subdue it," to "rule . . . over all the earth" and "over every living creature"—an adventure to be freely enjoyed in daily fellowship with God (see Genesis 1:26-30).

To rule well over the realm to which he was appointed, man had first, under God, to be able to *rule himself.* Man was made to be a balanced, rational, creative, healthy, able, productive, loving, and—without the least strain—*holy* being.

When God's enemy found the way to infect man with the poison of sin, he brought a threefold divine curse—upon himself, on man, and the earth. Out of it came sorrows, pains, hardships, limitations, disease, rebellion, destructiveness, and death.

Much that blights both the social and natural landscapes simply reflects man's badly damaged—and spiritually opposed—capacity for true authority, which is embedded in self-rule.

In this crisis, God did not vacate man's primary position of authority over the earth. In fact, He specifically renewed it with Noah and his family after the Flood (see Genesis 9:1-3). Though we sometimes use it perversely, even destructively, we exercise it all the time to great personal and collective advantage.

When sin took its death-grip, it did not catch heaven off guard. God intervened—for man, the earth, and His own design.

By acting savingly toward His creation as soon as the curse took effect, God set in motion mighty countervailing facts to check and throwback and to *undo* the effects of the curse, of sin, and of Satan—a plan reaching from Eden to the end of the world.

It centers on His Son, and the unvarying principle behind it is that it goes *for* man and the earth, and it goes *against* the enemy. The only inevitable objects of God's wrath are Satan and evil spirits, whose fixed destiny is total banishment to the lake of fire.

God's plan will conquer exactly as He has promised, but *it is not all future.* It is on the move all the time. Powerful, liberating aspects of it belong to Christ's church *now.*

Never picture God as just waiting for the grand climax. Through the risen Christ, the living Word, and the Holy Spirit, He is undoing the undoer now. He is setting people free every day! Jesus came to loose the bands of wickedness and to let the oppressed *go free.*

God's strategy against all evil—in which He invites us to have a dynamic part—is so grand in scope, and total in intent, that it will finally lift all human beings who are willing to have it so *out of* the region of death and sin and suffering forever and establish them as co-heirs with Christ, not over earth only, but over the entire creation (see Romans 8:17; Galatians 4:7; Revelation 5:9-10; 22:3-5).

In that process—wonder of wonders—even bodily death itself, the direct result of Adam and Eve's fall, as dire as it is, becomes for the saved the final stage of deliverance from sin! (The war between flesh and spirit—see Galatians 5:17—ceases forever precisely there.)

God is the great Conservator, and He will save everything that can be saved. His primary purpose toward everything that sin has touched is not judgment—it is liberation, redemption, restoration.

Indeed, the Bible tells us that "the whole creation has been groaning" and awaits the day when "the creation itself will be *liberated* from its bondage to decay and brought into the freedom of the children of God" (Romans 8:18-23).

Meanwhile, the great issue in the earth is between things as God designed them and things as Satan distorts and corrupts them. The entire natural order is affected by this fact.

The earth itself strikingly illustrates one facet of truth about this ongoing conflict.

When man joined Satan in sin, God acted on man's environment. In all its beauty and fruitfulness, it became partly alien and hostile to him, somewhat resistant to his will. It brought forth abundant good—but now it had a hidden sting. Acute dangers lurked in it, including debilitating and deadly diseases.

These were often mysterious, stubborn, and severe. Yet they were ultimately subject to discovery, identification, and cure. The very environment out of which they came in many cases also supplied a canceling or ameliorating antidote—a specific remedy to check the specific affliction.

God let nature itself become a living statement of the struggle that exists between sin and holiness, disease and health, blessing and cursing.

Even before the curse came it appears that God, in His love for us, had folded into nature many substances with the power to alleviate and thwart infection and disease. Nature is thus a mirror, a distant reflection of God's redeeming love, which stood ready "before the foundation of the world" to give His only Son to bleed and die.

When a large pot of stew, full of herbs and gourds and vegetables from the fields, was served to the young prophets studying under Elisha, something went wrong. As they began to eat, the younger men cried out, "O man of God, there is *death* in the pot!" What was meant to sustain them had poison in it strong enough to kill them.

Death itself was brewing in that stew, yet something else from nature was put into the pot that, spiritually as well as naturally, rendered the poison powerless and canceled its deadly effect (2 Kings 4:38-41).

This is a figure of Christ—the total antidote, of which all other antidotes testify. The poison of sin, absolutely fatal, had got into everyone. Yet because of Jesus millions of its victims will ultimately be delivered from every effect of sin and the curse, including the "last enemy," death.

For believers there are many deliverances along life's way. We are kept out of traps and preserved in ways that go beyond our knowledge.

When Adam and Eve ignored the warning God had given them, "You shall surely die," and ate what was forbidden, spiritual death fell upon the human race and, with it, the fact of mortality. Even the best of saints are at some point vulnerable to bodily attacks, but there is a real shield in godliness.

After parading between the divided waters of the Red Sea, the people of Israel trudged three days through the desert. They got powerfully thirsty and were glad to reach Marah—but its water was too bitter to drink, so they got powerfully discouraged.

The place was called Marah because of its bad water, Exodus 15:23-25 tells us. Moses cried to the Lord, who "showed him a piece of wood. He threw it into the water and the water became sweet." God's thirsty people eagerly drank it.

Now they were ready to listen to the Lord. It was at Marah that God told the Israelites that if they would heed His voice and "do what is right" in His eyes and "keep all His decrees, *I will not bring on you any of the diseases* I brought on the Egyptians, for I am the Lord who heals you" (Exodus 15:26-27).

There was for this people, under God, a *conditional exemption* from many diseases, and the condition was simply obedience. Obedience brings many real exemptions to God's people, and their families, today. But disobedience can strip such protections away.

Consider the lovely litany of promises God gave to the people of Israel on another occasion. They began with the key word *IF:*

"If you pay attention to these laws and are careful to follow them, then the Lord your God will keep His covenant of love with you." (Though codified in laws, it *was* a covenant of love.)

"He will bless the fruit of your womb, the crops of your land—your grain, new wine and oil—the calves of your herds and the lambs . . . none of your men or women will be childless . . . the Lord will keep you free from every disease" (Deuteronomy 7:12-15).

Sometimes we walk closer to the lines of disease or death than we know, but biological defenses work with precision in our bodies to counteract the afflicting agent. Or we have the appropriate pharmacological remedy prescribed for us. For believers, there is more. Christians are told in Romans 8:11 that, "if the Spirit of Him who raised up Jesus from the dead dwell in you, He that raised up Christ from the dead shall also quicken your mortal bodies by His Spirit that dwells in you" (KJV).

### Refreshment, Renewal, Release

I knew a missionary of long overseas service who, when she was aged, would at times come into a prayer meeting looking drawn, hollow-eyed and sunken-cheeked, suggesting desperate weariness, even the closeness of death. Yet forty minutes later her face would look almost full and fresh, with the soft sure glow of health upon it. The change went way beyond the merely natural; she received a quickening *in her body.*

She lived to great age, sometimes in weakness or pain, and all but her very last few weeks were filled with vital service to the Lord. She made three significant missionary journeys while in her 80s, one of them to Egypt, when she was feeble and could only go on strength that was supplied.

"Though outwardly we are wasting away, yet inwardly we are being renewed day by day," Paul wrote in 2 Corinthians 4:16.

As a young man, when he should have been at the peak of strength,

A.B. Simpson, the founder of the Christian and Missionary Alliance, was pathetically frail. The story is told in his biography *A.B. Simpson: His Life and Work* by A.E. Thompson (Christian Publications). Extremes of weakness put him so near death that, while he stood at grave sites as the presiding minister, he thought at times that he himself would "drop into that open grave."

Over twenty years' time he had a collapse that put him out of action for months, he suffered "many physical infirmities and disabilities," took "constant remedies," and went through three physical breakdowns because of heart trouble. Just going up a flight of stairs often brought on a feeling of "suffocating agony." Only "a frail thread held the vital chain" of his life from snapping, he later wrote.

A "prominent physician in New York told me I had not constitutional strength enough to last more than a few months." At that stage, "all things in life looked dark and withered" to Simpson's eyes. Yet God had important plans for this servant of His.

This same sickly minister and candidate for the grave was to devote the last thirty-five years of his life to vigorous, demanding, sustained labor as preacher, evangelist, editor, author, and chiefly as a great leader of the worldwide missionary cause.

After prolonged seeking the Lord and searching the Scriptures, Simpson believed that he could "take the Lord Jesus as my physical life, for all the needs of my body until all my lifework is done," and he did so. As his biography recounts, he found that "one of the provisions of redemption is 'that the life also of Jesus might be made manifest in our body'" (see 2 Corinthians 4:10-11, KJV).

One day Simpson climbed a 3,000-foot mountain. He knew it was far beyond his strength to attempt it, yet he sensed that he must do so. "I found," he wrote, "I had in myself no more strength than ever," yet taking "divine strength" by faith he reached the mountaintop and "seemed to be at the gate of heaven, and the world of weakness and fear was lying at my feet."

In his weakness, a point had come, he declared, when Christ became "my life and strength from this moment on." Dr. Simpson did not experience a onetime healing by which he was left strong and able thereafter to do the work of several men. He did not walk in reconstituted natural strength, but in the power of a continual provision.

"Physically I do not think I am any more robust than ever," he wrote. It was by faith every day, all the way, yet he experienced an "unwearied buoyancy and energy, and in that light and life of God I am working without exhaustion."

The Holy Spirit had led him to see in the Word that he "had a right to the life of Christ for body, mind, and spirit." Simpson's testimony was that "I am drawing my vitality from a directly supernatural source, and it keeps pace with all the ... necessities of my work."

That vitality was no mere luxury. The burden of a Christless world was on him, expressed in hymns Simpson wrote with words like these: "A hundred thousand souls a day/Are passing one by one away ... With future dark as endless night."

Because of those thirty-five years of strength received, scores and scores of believers were inspired to carry the light of Christ's salvation to distant fields overseas, while many thousands in the homeland were motivated to stand behind them. A.B. Simpson died in a good old age, active to the full up to his final months—a man redeemed in soul, reclaimed in body, restored in vitality.

As long as there is life, there is hope for almost everything. Even stubborn, long-standing difficulties can yield to the motions of grace, suddenly at times, progressively and more slowly but just as surely in other cases.

The Bible warns believers not to neglect meeting together for worship (see Hebrews 10:25), as some did then and some unwisely do now. In any church that is alive with faith, there is no knowing in advance when some importantly applicable scriptural understanding will be received, when some key insight will be imparted, a "word of wisdom" spoken, an act of power done, a call given, a soul saved, a wavering faith strengthened, a mind and heart freshly edified.

There is a divine element to biblically true worship meetings, a moving of the Holy Spirit in and through what is done. This brings a wisdom to bear on life that is surely greater than the sum of its human instruments. It is folly for a believer to remove himself or herself from that scene.

The workings of the natural and the supernatural in the lives of believers are varied and often closely interwoven, so that the latter affects the former more than can be calculated.

In understanding the essential *separateness* of the natural and the supernatural realms, it is equally important to understand their *inter-relatedness*. It is so close that in many cases there is virtually no telling them apart.

Surely evil spirits carry out nearly all of their direct and practical operations among mankind unobserved and, in most cases, unsuspected. The special "gift of the discerning of spirits" available to believers throws a kind of laser beam upon them that sharply distinguishes them from the natural.

Most of the work of angels in or toward the natural realm is unseen and unknown, while the Holy Spirit often works in a way that cannot be directly observed. (Whenever the human body becomes the dwelling place of the Holy Spirit, the natural and the supernatural come together in a closely working union.)

There is a great tendency to think of the supernatural in terms of what is spectacular, and sometimes it is, but for the most part supernatural workings are not at all so. They are so closely aligned with the natural as usually to seem part of a single whole.

How little unbelievers know the extent to which evil spirits have had impact on their lives! The demonic supernatural is quietly folded into many lives, mostly without it being the least suspected.

The mind is especially accessible to supernatural workings. Thoughts are subject to demonic suggestions, among believers and unbelievers. Accepting them, regardless of how plausible they may seem, can be terrifically costly.

It is entirely possible for an individual to think his or her way into defeat, discouragement, unbelief, various evils and sins, hostility, inferiority, and other bad mental states, often with the hidden aid of evil spirits that skillfully act to reinforce such lines of thought, just as long as the thoughts are accepted.

Death worked its way into Eve and the whole race *by the thought processes.* Unless we stay alert, we are also vulnerable. Discouraging thoughts can eat away at the vitals of life, and steal emotional and mental health.

That is why the response of which Paul speaks in 2 Corinthians 10:5 is essential: "Casting down imaginations, and every high thing that exalts itself against the knowledge of God, and bringing into captivity every thought to the obedience of Christ" (KJV).

There is a whole lot of health and safety in obeying that imperative counsel. Catching bad thoughts early and quickly casting them away will keep them from becoming deeply embedded, at which point they become more resistant to dislodging. This cannot be done casually; it requires sharp alertness and decisive mental action.

The mind has to have a healthy, nontoxic diet just as the stomach does. A good diet is prescribed in Philippians 4:6-8.

The biblical truth that, "The mind of sinful man is death, but the mind controlled by the Spirit is life and peace" is not just roughly or generally so, it is profoundly, directly and consequentially so (Romans 8:6).

It is also a fact that if your eye is single to the Lord, "your whole body will be full of light" (see Luke 11:33-36, KJV).

A mind that is frequently centered on pure scriptural truth will tend

**176**

to peace and health and good balance. As *The Living Bible* expresses Isaiah 26:3, God "will keep in perfect peace all those who trust in Him, whose thoughts turn often to the Lord!"

## Guarding the Endowment

Parables sometimes pass before our eyes.

Consider two brothers, a little over a year apart in age, reared in the home of a Gospel minister. Both had able minds and unusually strong bodies. Both were ace students who went through high school as if it were an ice-cream eating contest, running up virtually unbroken strings of A's. Both got admitted to Yale.

To that point there could not have been a greater equality between them of upbringing, of opportunity and achievement. Both had received Jesus and had given good evidence of changed lives in their teens. Yet one, after a brief brush with shaky faith, recovered and decided to go the way of the Lord Jesus.

The other slipped almost imperceptibly away from faith and drifted into rebellion just as he entered college. It took barely a year for him to be sadly adrift and unable to deal in practical terms with life.

Fifteen years after they entered college, the slightly older son had a prime education, a bright and pleasant outlook on life, and he was fruitfully engaged in teaching. He had also developed a good ministry to university students.

The slightly younger son was a wasted being. His education was cut short, his mind was clouded and unable to deal effectively with reality. He rarely was able to work, and then only at low-demand, part-time jobs, and he was a grief and burden to his loving and patient parents.

He was generally disinclined to talk, all drawn up within himself and darkened, yet he ought to have been a first-rate guy. He had lost primary control over parts of his being. That fact was outwardly visible at all times.

This is not to say that all unfaithfulness to the Lord has equal and observable immediate consequences; it does not. But in this case darkness closed in fast and stole away parts of what had, prior to then, been in his free control.

Jesus once exclaimed, "If then the light within you is darkness, how great is that darkness!" (Matthew 6:23)

Just as there is a steep downgrade for the rejecter of given light, so there is a swift upgrade for the sinner who repents.

I know a young man who, if you saw him today, you might think to be as fine looking as it is possible to be. He has a face that looks like a piece of chiseled sculpture, he glows with happiness, and he is engagingly vital. Yet only two years earlier, this young man was so under the power of sin that he had no dwelling. He lived in misery out on the sidewalks and, as he graphically puts it, "I smelled."

What hope was there for this near-wreck, in bondage to something he had to have that was destroying his body and being?

Five times he went into a hospital for detoxification, and he got the full treatment each time. But when he came out he was soon sucked back into what had taken him over.

One day someone handed him a piece of Scripture on the street—just words on paper, some might say. But when he read it, light came flooding in!

Those words gave him a glimpse of Someone he had never known, the liberating Jesus. As he reached out to the Saviour, his inward being was filled with new understanding—and new power.

Satan had the guy down and halfway to the grave, a captive to a destroying substance, a slave in an evil kingdom. You should see him now! What men who tried their best were helpless to do for him, Jesus did in hardly any time at all. He looks like he might have graduated from West Point—so crisp and clean, alert and sharp.

He enrolled in practical studies at which he excels. I saw him happily court and win a lovely young Christian woman. Like those who are forgiven much, he has a bright-faced love for Jesus that comes out all the time.

The curse and power of addiction was broken—broken supernaturally, not by the hand of man. In this case, the release seems remarkably complete. Not even lingering effects are apparent, as in some cases they are because, even when forgiveness is entire and deliverance real, visible marks of previous damage remain.

Remember that you cannot always get back something that is thrown away, even when you want it with all your heart. Here is a crude illustration, yet one that approximates a loss suffered by a young believer in Texas who went out and committed one act of deliberate disobedience. If, by a rash act, an individual lost two fingers, he could be sewn up and restored to health, but he would never grow his two fingers back.

The one thing that defies hope and pushes it away is rebellion against God and its close cousin, willful sin.

Yet invitations to sin abound. There is a massive assault upon the minds of young people in our culture. Some of it connects to the supernatural realm. There are individuals who receive various evils by demonic suggestion, then use mass organs of communication to spread them. Evil ideas sometimes have a dynamic, propelling energy that impresses them forcefully upon the soul.

The Bible repeatedly warns believers concerning worldliness and the sins that go with it, and lust and the sins that it leads to. Sectors of the entertainment media bring young people smack up against the attractions and deceptions of worldliness and fleshly sin—urgently drumming out their vivid invitations to fornication, to drug taking, even to raw satanism.

Certain of these media convey demonic messages to millions—saying exactly the opposite of what God's Word says concerning behavior, and drawing some into an entangling net of evil by it.

By allowing themselves to be unduly exposed to such readily available influences, young Christians weaken themselves. It is critical to remember a key spiritual fact—whoever "breaks an hedge, a serpent shall bite him" (Ecclesiastes 10:8, KJV).

God's hedges are not meant to confine but to protect, though the enemy always mocks them and says they are unnecessary boundaries.

Never, never listen to the demonic argument that God doesn't want you to have any fun or, indeed, to be "free." There is not a single real pleasure or enjoyment of which God is not at base the author! The enemy's sole purpose is diversion, distortion, excess, and perversion! He takes what is given as a blessing and does his best to make it over into a curse. What he calls "freedom" is only license for the fallen nature to indulge itself in sin, to defy God's natural and moral laws. That is not freedom, it is the route to sure enslavement. God offers and leads in a freedom that is real and that lasts—and has no hidden sting.

None of us can escape the law of sowing and reaping. "Do not be deceived," the Scripture warns, "God cannot be mocked. A man reaps what he sows. The one who sows to please his sinful nature, from that nature will reap destruction; the one who sows to please the Spirit, from the Spirit will reap eternal life" (Galatians 6:4-5).

Certain bodily afflictions have a particularly close identification with sin, such as venereal diseases that basically only afflict humans when they step over the line of God's good decrees for sexual behavior. They are a curse attending sin.

A young woman in her twenties, a believer, had backslidden, and she consented one night to do what she knew to be wrong. Even as she began, she said later, "God warned me," but she went ahead. She came down later with AIDS, the terrible cost of one big act of disobedience.

Simply obeying the Lord would have kept her entirely free of that. See the huge difference in *all the rest of her life* that sprang from one faithless decision.

By his tactics, Satan trivializes, reduces, betrays, wastes human beings and, where possible, ultimately destroys them. His offers have no other purpose.

God's protective hedges do not put believers beyond, or outside of, reality or the spiritual conflict. They enable believers to be equipped and positioned to take their rightful part. They are called into conflict on the Lord's side, but if they grow passive, indifferent, spiritually lazy, absorbed with self or worldly things, or permit themselves to be drawn into sin, they will fail.

Samson is a vivid picture of this. What a calling he had! He was expressly set apart, by divine appointment, from his birth to be a deliverer for Israel, and he was specially empowered to fulfill his mission—to make major strikes against the enemies of God's people.

He began to do so brilliantly. His life ought to have been a string of notable victories and conquests for the Lord. But Samson was a young believer who dabbled and dabbled in fleshly sin *without intending to lose out.*

He seemed to be able for a time to have it both ways, to be strong for the Lord and to indulge, but a day came when he suddenly found himself out of strength. He was stripped. The vanquisher was taken captive by the enemy and blinded.

The man whose lifework was to deliver Israel *from* the enemy, spent long, hard years as a slave, grinding out grain to *feed* that enemy. He is a clear warning of the ultimate binding and enslaving effect upon a believer of "just a little" continuing sin.

The enemy took it all away from Samson—he wasn't even a tenth of what he was meant to be—because Samson let him. He had a right to be free but he sold it—sold it cheap, and the cost was high.

In his role as a thief, one who works by stealth, the enemy will steal away anything that he can from us, if we let him. The powers of evil understand the nature of man quite well. They know the interrelatedness of all the parts of a man's being, so if they can't get him in one way, they will seek to get him in another. They know that by goading an individual to do what is morally wrong they will damage him spiritually and may also adversely affect his emotional or physical well-being.

Fix it in mind that evil spirits work to damage human beings spiritually, morally, mentally, physically, and emotionally. They are skilled at turning an advantage gained in one area into expanded gains.

## Two Objectives of the Thief

Just as at the beginning of his work against man in Eden, Satan wants human beings to do two big things—to *think his thoughts* and to *do his deeds*. The mission of evil spirits is to accomplish that.

What his agents aim at specifically is obtaining *influence* or even *control* over the thoughts, the beliefs, and the actions of human beings.

To the extent that a man becomes involved with demons, to that extent he ceases to be his own master.

When it is impossible for these agents of evil to have control over human beliefs and actions, they will aim for influence *in any available measure*. People have differing levels of susceptibility and receptivity to various temptations, deceptions, enticements, and lies. At times every individual is, inescapably, an object of their attention.

The varieties of working and the stages and degrees of demonic influence and control cannot entirely be categorized. Among the many stages are those that have been described as oppression, obsession, and possession. Suppression and delusion should be added to that list.

When precise knowledge is needed in a certain area, it is useful to have an *index*. The Bible provides us with a kind of index of demonic workings and effects. It does so in two ways, by definition and by illustration.

These enable believers to see them clearly and to define them quite accurately.

The Bible speaks of many kinds of evil spirits, identifying them by the effects they produce in those they afflict. There are spirits of fear . . . foul spirits . . . spirits of error . . . perverse spirits . . . unclean spirits . . . spirits of jealousy . . . spirits of whoredom . . . lying spirits . . . spirits of infirmity.

There are also deceiving spirits, sadistic spirits, spirits of murder, suicide, destruction, rage, accusation, malice, hatred. There are spirits of divination. The Bible speaks many times, and sharply warns against, "familiar spirits."

All of the above effects are by no means attributable solely to the activity of evil spirits, for such spirits make their appeal to, and link closely with, the natural man in his fallen state. We are dealing with two distinct, yet related, things here: the works of the flesh and particular workings of evil spirits.

The Bible lists witchcraft or sorcery as among the works of the flesh or the sinful nature, as well as "fits of rage" (Galatians 5:19-21). That is entirely accurate. The flesh is the seat of such things and only the sinful nature indulges in them, yet this does not suggest a divorce between such works and demonic activity.

When the sorcerers and magicians of Egypt stood against Moses on the side of Pharaoh and supernaturally produced wonders, they did so by demonic inspiration and coworking—fallen flesh in league with evil spirits, and they directly sought to thwart and overthrow God's purposes by their acts.

The key question is how do demons succeed in putting into practical effect their programs for man? There has to be a basis for them to do so. There are five major avenues through which evil spirits gain a certain access to, and a degree of advantage over, human beings:

Through sin.

Through unbelief or belief in lies.

Through false religion, false worship, and occult practices.

Through alcohol, narcotics, hallucinogenic drugs.

Through giving vent to extreme emotions.

When a man's will gives way repeatedly to temptations to sin, a basis for demonic activity in his life exists in that area. Temptation is the most common work of evil spirits and, as it proves effective, it may be succeeded by more severe stages of demonic activity—oppression or obsession.

Suddenly, out of nowhere, a surprising evil thought or impulse flies into the mind. We become aware of it with a mild shock of recognition. It is not native to us; it is foreign. It did not originate with us; it was introduced. Satan wishes to get the human mind down under the power of such conceptions.

Certain kinds of popular music, satanically inspired in their flagrant and filthy insistence on contact with things the Bible calls perversion and lust, can be an avenue to such mind control, as can all pornography.

A believer who fails to guard his heart and mind and allows himself to receive an evil influence from any source needs to recover spiritually by turning straight away from it in an act of obedience to God, thereby taking himself out of the devil's trouble zone. If that is not done quickly, and influence takes a hold on the individual, then confession and repentance will be needed.

Especially beware of the enemy's invitation to "just a little" dipping into areas of sin. It is a classic tactic, an opening wedge. He has no intention of keeping it there. Unless it is seen and pulled away from quickly as the deception it is, he will work to draw the cords of sin more tightly.

There are many, many degrees of demonic interference with human faculties—from occasional and partial all the way to total.

Some individuals who are afflicted in this way must engage in a painful and difficult struggle for the free and efficient use of their faculties. At times certain people must somehow limp along with half, or less than half, of the full use of some parts of their beings.

Sudden experiences of acute nervousness, unexplained by any immediate or outward circumstances, may be caused by demonic attacks. If this proceeds far enough, it can sometimes lead to nervous collapse. Some people are kept in an almost constant state of agitation or nervousness. They rarely enjoy intervals of full relief. Demonic suggestions to the mind may have a part in this.

In gaining advantage over human faculties, demons sometimes affect them in extreme and speeded-up, or violent ways, and sometimes they do almost the opposite. They slow them down or stop their functioning. Both of these effects can be seen at times in a single individual.

On one occasion, Jesus said, " 'You dumb and deaf spirit, I command you, come out of him, and never enter him again.' And after crying out and convulsing him terribly, it came out" (Mark 9:25-26, RSV). The same evil spirit produced two extreme, but opposite, effects. While it went undetected it blocked hearing and speech in the victim. Then it cried out through the victim and convulsed him. When the spirit came out, the boy could hear and speak. Soon he was in full motor control of his body.

Not all deafness or muteness, of course, is demonic in its cause.

The demonic action opposite to convulsions is that in which evil spirits freeze human faculties, so to speak, rendering them partly or wholly immobile. This is best described as binding. In some forms, binding even takes the mode of a deformity of posture.

There are varying stages of demonic occupation. Just as physical paralysis can be anywhere from partial to total—from a hand up to most of the body, involving one part, several parts or more—so it is with evil spirits.

The number of demonic spirits involved with a victim may be one or many. Mary Magdalene, to whom Jesus appeared first after His resurrection, is described as a woman "out of whom He had driven seven demons" (see Mark 16:9; Luke 8:2). When Jesus asked the man in the tombs his name, he said, "My name is Legion, for we are many" (Mark 5:9-13).

Jesus once spoke of a man who becomes free of an evil spirit, which then goes and finds "seven other spirits more wicked than itself " and takes them with it into the man so that "the final condition of that man is worse than the first" (see Luke 11:24-26).

As the specific effects of such spirits vary greatly, Jesus here indicates that some are more wicked than others in their evil working, not entirely surprising since, among humans who are evil, the degrees and kinds of depravity vary markedly.

Jesus was "teaching in one of the synagogues on the Sabbath. And there was a woman who had had *a spirit of infirmity* for eighteen years; she was bent over and could not fully straighten herself. And when Jesus saw her, He called to her, 'Woman, you are freed from your infirmity.' And He laid hands upon her, and immediately she was made straight, and she praised God."

When the ruler of the synagogue protested what he regarded as work on the Sabbath Day, Jesus said, "You hypocrites! Does not each of you on the Sabbath untie his ox or his ass from the manger, and lead it away to water it? And ought not this woman, a daughter of Abraham *whom Satan bound for eighteen years,* be loosed from this bond on the Sabbath Day?" (Luke 13:10-16, RSV)

The way Jesus spoke of, and handled, this binding effect reveals a physical infirmity that, in this case, had a satanic source.

It is clear that when the Lord Jesus cast spirits out of sorely afflicted individuals, they immediately came into the easy, natural, and unhindered control of all their faculties. They became what God intended them to be, not what the enemy had betrayed them into being.

What the demons did to such individuals tells us very accurately what they desire to do today. The pathetic states such people were in under demonic attack illustrates two things—certain works of evil spirits *and* the intentions of Satan toward humans.

Such persons displayed the enemy's works of binding, tormenting, afflicting, and driving human beings. They suffered everything from paralysis to convulsions, each an attack on their faculties—until they met Jesus.

When Jesus sent the spirits out, these terrible effects ceased. Jesus' restoration of the free, unimpeded use of their faculties perfectly illustrates God's intentions for man.

So the will of God in the person of Jesus, and the will of Satan in the activities of evil spirits, met head-on in the lives of these individuals.

Using rough yet plain terms here, Satan's agents engineer slowdowns and shutdowns and bindings in human beings; speedups and drivings and breakdowns; freezings and fiery uncontrolled outbursts of temper—a variegated array of deliberate interferences with normal, sane, free human functioning.

The results are not always extreme or total, because evil spirits take advantage and move in as people give way to their devices. Many people experience certain limited effects of demonic workings, usually without knowing the source.

Evil spirits do not go for all *or* nothing. They do, of course, go for all, but in many cases they must settle for less. It is extremely unlikely that unbelievers who end up possessed by evil spirits become so at a single rush. It happens by a series of stages proceeding from initial and partial to complete.

Yet as bad as it may be, such persons are rarely beyond hope or reclamation if they will turn to Jesus for deliverance, as the fearfully possessed man in the tombs did.

In a world in which demons are on the loose, there is deliverance and freedom for the captive unbeliever. For the obedient believer there is continual and abundant protection by the blood of Jesus Christ.

Though the powers of darkness have a host of ways, some of them very potent, of getting human beings to cooperate in damaging, or even destroying themselves, God has given mankind the strongest line of defense possible. Through Jesus and the Holy Spirit, and the counsel of His Word, the Creator does all that can be done to safeguard and preserve and to deliver.

Jesus is man's sin-bearer, liberator, deliverer—He is God's total answer to every satanic initiative according to 1 John 3:8. The great fact remains for every member of the human race that, in spite of everything the enemy can do, "if the Son sets you free, you will be free indeed" (John 8:36).

## Getting to the Nitty-Gritty

A young woman, a believer, had a vexing problem. She was in a university fellowship group that held open meetings for students at which believers told of salvation in personal terms or spoke of scriptural truths.

Though she loved the Lord and wished to speak for Him, this young woman found that, when she went into the meeting, a fear of speaking came upon her and kept her mouth shut, often leaving her feeling unhappy afterward that she had not spoken of her Lord.

How did she try to solve this problem? By prayer. Then more prayer. Then more *earnest* prayer, beseeching prayer, even prayers in which she *felt* that she had the victory and would surely speak in the upcoming meeting—but every time she got to the meeting the fear-clamp remained on her lips.

Why, she asked, had the Lord not delivered her when she had so carefully sought Him for it? Why was there no answer to her prayers?

I explained to her that when the enemy does a particular work against a believer, it does not especially trouble him to see the believer do *anything* that surrounds the problem but does not get at its root and core.

There was nothing wrong with prayer certainly, but prayer must soon be followed by faith-action or it can become itself a holy means of evading the issue and the actual problem. It was certain that God was not going to speak *for* her in the university meeting, nor would He force her to speak.

He had given her a love for Himself and He had given her the *capacity* to speak—a voice, lips, a tongue, a knowledge of language. The enemy had worked a work that kept her from speaking, placing a kind of barrier right at her mouth that gave her the false impression that she really could not speak in the meetings.

As long as she kept silent, that fear-barrier would be kept right in place, and it would lead only to bondage. Since the specific enemy action against her was to keep her from speaking, the specific overcoming of that opposition required the act of speaking. I counseled her to break through the fear-barrier and speak, no matter how difficult.

She saw it and she did it. She took hold of that situation and spoke in the next meeting, though it was not easy. It took courage to follow through and speak in a subsequent meeting, but she did.

After a short time, speaking in those meetings seemed almost as natural and easy to her as speaking in her home. The problem was gone because it had been taken on exactly where it was, and the power of the enemy to reinforce and continue the problem was entirely broken.

When the whole army of Israel was paralyzed with fear at the threats and boasts and taunts of Goliath, the "ruddy and handsome" teenage shepherd, David, could have come on the scene and prayed up a storm for the Lord to overcome that surly giant and deliver Israel. David could have prayed day after day after day about it.

Instead, he quickly sized the situation up with precise spiritual accuracy—"Who is this uncircumcised Philistine that he should defy the armies of *the living God?*"—that is faith speaking—and David went at the giant *directly* "in the name of the Lord almighty," slung a stone at him and put a sudden, final end to all his false, intimidating power (1 Samuel 17:4-12, 26, 40-52).

God acted with and for David as that young man acted in faith against the precise center of the crisis. The fear-paralysis that had stopped the Israeli army cold was broken, and that army came surging out of its trenches to chase the fleeing enemy troops.

God is ever pleased to act for those who act in faith for Him. If David, no matter how well-motivated and sincere, had done anything *other* than what he did, no change in that situation would have resulted. The problem was Goliath and his defiance of Israel and of God; so Goliath had to be dealt with frontally, directly, quickly.

Saints can wear themselves out and considerably deepen their adverse conditions if they do everything but *the one thing* that has to be done, the one thing that specifically and totally targets the problem itself and goes against it to conquer it. Lesser actions, if you strip them down to their essence, might be called a *holy avoidance* of the actual issue.

David did not, thank heaven, chase off to three seminars in three cities on how to overcome the enemy, learning every theoretical thing there is to know about it and a lot more. He did not buy the best six books on overcoming and study them down to the finest points until he knew them nearly by heart. He did not obtain the three most outstanding series of tapes on overcoming by three of the best Bible teachers of his day, and, though he surely prayed, he did not pray until he had worked himself up into a lather.

Praying, even lengthy praying, is in many cases good, but the instant it becomes a substitute for doing the thing that has to be done, it becomes a holy exercise, largely void of real faith, and it is likely to lead to some extreme of largely empty self-exertion.

"Physician, heal yourself," Jesus once said, and in many cases believers can obtain great relief from various troubles associated with demonic activity by understanding them and then by acting in faith to put an end to them—a faith placed in the Lord Jesus Christ as a result of His victory at Calvary.

Victory in personal matters consists in overcoming what has to be overcome, when it has to be overcome, where it has to be overcome, not in doing an elaborate rain dance around it. Believers can often break the power of enemy resistance and interference by going *directly* against it.

Anything else, anything less, will not conquer the enemy and his workings.

Observation leads me to conclude that, in fact, the enemy will *cooperate* with a victim in his or her pursuit of near-miss solutions—will, in effect, suggest and encourage lines of further such pursuit, because the net result is to allow him to prolong the problem.

The enemy appears to be especially adept in holding out false solutions to real problems, solutions that have two chief characteristics: (1) They will not solve the problem, and (2) they will have a particular appeal to the needy individual. Thus they deflect him from the actual issue, while occupying him in basically irrelevant actions.

A third characteristic that is often present is that the "solution" itself, though carefully disguised, will actually contribute to the adversity and trouble it is supposed to relieve. That is so because, while it appeals to the individual to whom it is proffered, it has *something of the nature of the root problem in it.*

It is not from the Lord. It is from the enemy. It is not a cure. It is a well-calculated device. But it appears to be good.

A genuine believer, yet one who happens to be of a slightly fanatical bent, finds himself under inescapable nervousness and strain in his workplace and nothing seems to remove that unhappy fact. It is almost always there. Prayer has not changed the situation. The believer finds himself thinking that he needs to set his alarm clock for 5 A.M. so he can get up and really seek the Lord for ninety solid minutes every day before work.

What a holy solution! How really exemplary! But for the slightly fanatical individual affected by *strain* and nervousness at work, it is likely to put a further burden of fanaticism upon him and, if anything, set him under more strain during the day. He could as well be heading for a crackup as for the desired release.

If the Lord clearly showed a believer that he was to rise early and seek Him, then God would specially bless that time. But if this is self-suggestion in the hot pursuit of an answer to a need, it is likely going to be wearing, not relieving.

If the same man were to decide to spend about fifteen minutes every morning before work prayerfully reading the Bible and taking its words with him as he went, he would at least be making sense. He would not be adding strain to strain, a game the enemy is more than willing to have him play.

I have noted how often the troubled person who is given to self-sacrificing actions will be led into further such actions, how often the troubled person given to highly energetic activity will be led out toward hyperactivity, how often the earnest seeker will be drawn toward excesses of seeking—each a "solution" that appeals and seems good, yet each leading away from balance and poise toward bondage and perplexity.

Such answers bear the mark of a crafty, conniving enemy, not of our wise and loving Lord. He knows that where there is a fire, water is the answer, not another torch, even when it carries seemingly holy fire.

Our enemy does not relent or give up until he is obliged to. He will hold an adverse work fast upon a believer as long as he can get away with it. He will seek to deepen its hold over time and make the bondage it causes stronger.

What a believer who is in this situation does not need is another turn of the screw. Knowing how difficult it can be to persuade a real believer to commit some evil act that will increase bondage or difficulty, the enemy will point the believer into something evidently *good* that is either beside the point or that is a means of perpetuating the problem. That good thing becomes not a source of relief, but a reinforcing agent for the trouble.

In matters such as this, do not underestimate three things: the enemy's desire and determination to keep a harassing difficulty going and to add to it indefinitely; his utter practicality in doing so; and the slyness of deception he will use to keep the focus on *everything but* the heart of the trouble and its actual solution.

If we become aware that something is physically wrong, we usually take notice of it and act as intelligently and effectively and directly as we can to have it diagnosed, treated, and reversed. We know very well that, no matter how artfully it is applied, a tourniquet around the ankle will not help us if we need a flesh wound cleansed and sewn up just below the ear.

We would never say, "Well, I had a tourniquet put on my ankle, beautifully done, but it didn't help my wound at all." Yet believers often become frustrated at the equal ineffectiveness of a similar process in spiritual things.

The need for precision, for accurate, godly diagnosis in spiritual matters, is just as great. Resources are available to believers in such matters, if they are rightly understood, drawn upon, and applied.

When we do not know where to begin, it is good to begin in prayer, asking for the specific help we need, not help in general. If the matter is presented to the Lord and kept before Him, in calm faith, and not in the expression of frustration, He will usually lead us to the bull's-eye solution. That may happen quickly, or it may take considerable time.

"If you trust and never doubt/He will surely bring you out," Charles Tindley's Gospel song affirms.

Over quite some time your writer sought understanding and relief regarding a problem. One day the Lord drew special attention to a verse of Scripture. But the verse seemed to have no special connection to the matter. The verse mainly mentioned the names of two men.

Why was the Lord pointing, in effect, to *that* verse? It seemed to contain a fact or two but no essential message. As I was pondering this, it occurred to me to look up the meaning of those two names in a concordance.

What a difference doing that made! Those two names had two specific meanings, and both identified the problem with pinpoint exactness. There was no mystery why the Lord had called attention to that verse, just a little difficulty in finding the way to understand what it meant. From that moment, I knew what to go against, and I did so. While the problem was not routed in a moment, it gave way to informed and alert resistance.

I knew a woman of real spiritual quality who was quite knotted up psychologically and tense. Her life seemed to be a virtually endless series of sufferings, many of which were unattached to objective reality. She had a strong propelling urge toward high-powered spiritual solutions. Invariably those "solutions" took the form of some intense quest or lengthy searching through spiritual literature or overly strenuous praying. Her greatest need was to do the opposite—to relax, to ease up and off, to repose a quiet trust in God, to allow herself some pleasant recreation, but her basic nature and bent ever led her to *reintensify*.

Our enemy is an expert at false solutions to problems as a way of pointing *away from* the true crux. When the false answer has a "spiritual" character, it then pitches a particular appeal to the person who is spiritual in outlook.

How often the enemy just leads a person across the same street and points him or her in the same direction, under a differing appearance.

Intensity, hyperactivity, a degree of fanaticism, a going to extremes is one line of difficulty that the enemy is pleased to push. Another is passivity, apathy, slackness.

Though the latter may begin as a mere disposition, it can also be demonically reinforced until the condition has a quite strong grip that robs the individual of the due use of his or her faculties, notably including the spiritual faculties.

Unless it has become deeply entrenched, *the* solution for passivity is *activity* in right measures, but unless it is actually engaged in, passivity will lie like a damp blanket upon individuals for years on end. They do not feel inclined to summon the strength to go against it with the activity that breaks it. Later these people are put so far out of action that it feels to them that only a mighty effort would bring any change, an effort that they do not feel able to make.

Another big robbing agent is fear. Fear is very often directly produced by the activity of demons, and it is to be rejected. There can be vague, almost nameless fears, and there can be knife-sharp, highly distressing fears. Fears have a tremendous inhibiting power. They can stop a person from doing what he or she needs to do and would do if fear were not there.

A believer may find himself beset by what can most accurately be termed a spirit of fear. Spirits are messengers, and fear is one of their favorite messages to believers. Such a fear sets into the soul and wants to lodge there, affecting the believer, including his outlook and his capacity to act. If caught before it really has a hold, a fear of this kind can be ousted by an act of the will.

The believing mind can say to the soul, "*I will not fear*," and that fear must depart as quickly as it came in. If it tries to reenter, the same act can send it away, leaving the soul in the settled peace of trust in God. I have done this a number of times in my life, with immediate and total effect.

Such fear borne in upon the soul—when it is not a reaction to a circumstance or fact in which fear is at least initially warranted, or in which it serves usefully to modify conduct to avert real danger—is an enemy. It steals away what is ours in Christ and puts us under false constraints.

It can be and must be rejected by faith and overcome. The issue centering on fear is critical because it is connected to unbelief, and the Scriptures warn that "the fearful [*cowardly* in some versions] and unbelieving" among men will lose out (see Revelation 21:7-8, KJV).

The big difference between the brave man and the coward is that one acts against, or in spite of fears, and gets past them into freedom, while the other allows himself to be ruled by fear.

Knowing *what* a thing is, and what it does, often tells us where it comes from. Paul reminded the gifted but possibly somewhat too cautious Timothy that "God did not give us a spirit of timidity, but a spirit of power, of love, and of self-discipline" (see 2 Timothy 1:6-8). So liberty is the result of taking what belongs to us in the Lord and consistently refusing to stay under the power of anything else.

## Openings to Liberty and Joy

How important it is for believers to watch the interior dialogue—what they "listen to" or think about. A play on words may help make the point: sometimes that dialogue may be diabolical.

Every individual will at some point experience the transference of thought from the spiritual realm to the human mind. Evil spirits—liars, deceivers, accusers, tempters—convey various ideas to individuals. That is how "doctrines of demons" spoken of in 1 Timothy 4:1 get into circulation among men.

No individual is obliged to accept such thoughts—they can be swept aside and given no leave to occupy the mind—but many do receive them.

In their work as accusers, Satan and his emissaries accuse believers before God (see Revelation 12:10); they accuse believers to unbelievers, they accuse one believer to another believer, and they accuse individuals directly.

These evil messengers are experts at persuading individuals to believe some false conception about themselves. By repeating it continually to the consciousness of a victim, they turn it into a fixation. Though the conception is not fact, it becomes as good as fact. It is partly disabling by its nature.

These agents may suggest to a person directly, "You are worthless," or "You are ugly and unloved." They repeat it and repeat it until it is adopted as truth and acted on as objective fact.

They do, it seems, one thing more. They sometimes orchestrate what might be called real-world confirmations of the prevailing lie. They will at times succeed in pointing to something specific in the immediate environment that strongly confirms the counterfeit outlook, so that it seems to be mirrored in objective reality.

We saw in a previous chapter how astutely the enemy fortified his big lie that Israel could not prevail against an invading army by pointing to the objective *fact* that many other nations had already been overpowered by that army. And we know the biblical truth that "the whole world is under the control of the wicked one" (1 John 5:19). Satan can at times make reality itself *seem* to give evidence of the validity of his lies.

At times harassed individuals get apparent outside confirmations of their disabling misconceptions. For example, people seem to snub them. A whole pattern seems to develop. Walking down the street, a woman hears someone remark, "Well, look at *her*," and she fits it right into the pattern, as proof of the delusion.

Sometimes the facial expression or the overheard remark that feeds right into the false conception is, in fact, entirely irrelevant because it is in no way connected to the person who observes or hears it. It has to do with something else, or someone else, entirely. Yet it is picked up and read as more negative proof.

When a person believes a lie of any kind and acts upon it as though it were true, he walks in deception or delusion. This becomes especially painful when he thoroughly believes some lie about himself.

There are some people who are physical cripples and everyone can see that, but there are other people who are emotional or psychological cripples. They cannot use their nonphysical faculties any more freely than a man with a sprained ankle can use his foot and leg. The interior pain of that condition is, in its way, as severe as the physical pain of the man with the sprain.

Some people bear crushing loads of inferiority, and this false conception imposes much suffering upon them. It obstructs, limits, and hampers their lives. It either makes them far less than they could be if they were not so weighted, or it drives them constantly and fiercely to overachieve so that they can begin to feel equal to others.

In nearly all cases such a self-concept is an outright lie. It is a devaluation of the person that keeps him from clearly understanding the fact of the divine origin of the human being, his innate capacities, special aptitudes or gifts. Whatever its initial source, such a continued state of mind and feelings may be the direct, intentional work of afflicting spirits acting upon the thoughts and the emotions.

It is unlikely that a victim can break such a pattern by a single act of will, or by a general praying to the Lord. The pattern needs to be clearly recognized, identified, then resisted, and rejected in the name, and by the power of, the Lord Jesus. Opposing spirits are thus put on notice that the scheme has been discovered and is going to be spiritually overcome.

A young man named Roy was a brilliant electronics specialist who somehow did not have the confidence to take the work he was fully able to do. Instead he took odd jobs in electrical and television repair shops. He was living under a delusion that checked him from ever rising to his normal level of achievement. He was not bound in his body, but he was bound in his conceptions. That bind put an entirely unnecessary limitation upon his life.

A bind becomes stronger and harder to break out of the longer the misconception that prompts it is accepted and obeyed, until at last it becomes a fixation and has the force of law upon its victim.

A young believer on his way to the mission field was a guest for six weeks in the building where I lived. His dedication to the Lord and godly purpose, his faith in the Word, all seemed evident, but his posture and bearing were strangely rigid, and his face was, in terms of expression, nearly a frozen mask. There was nothing directly unpleasant about him, but he made a stiff and unpleasing appearance.

He was clearly somewhat bound. Though it was reflected outwardly, he was no doubt bound inwardly in the soul.

A variety of causes may lie behind such a bound condition. Sometimes a contradiction between what one believes and some unconquered inward problem creates a constant tension. The effort to hide it from view or to deny its existence obliges one to behave very cautiously or to put up a wall.

Perfectionism is an extreme to which one is driven, and it always results in some degree of binding.

I know a young woman, a believer, whose father had taken great pains to rear her as a little living picture of absolute perfection. He had especially trained her in posture, movements, gestures, and manners. By the time she was eighteen, almost everything about her had a practiced, measured, cadenced look. She had been taught to be graceful, but her gracefulness had just that hint of staged exaggeration that made it seem slightly comic. She was not natural, easy, or free in her behavior.

Prior to her conversion to Christ, she had been active in a couple of common occult practices. She came to understand that the outward mechanical perfection that had been so insistently imposed upon her had been reinforced by the demonic elements in her occult practices, so that she was quite severely bound.

Understanding itself was not enough for her to be able to throw this unnatural covering off. It took repeated prayer, plus the specific stated disavowing in the name of Jesus of what had been done to her by her occultic and behavioral practices, and a refusal to be held by either. She discovered, for instance, that her walking was precisely paced, almost arithmetical—a part of the whole false business of put-on perfection. She deliberately broke that pattern.

Slowly, and visibly, her boundness diminished, the artificial covering was taken away, and she got largely, if not yet entirely, free. When her arm and hand reached out for something, it was no longer like a lever coming out of its place and making three moves to take it. It had been unthinkable under her training for the gesture of receiving to be done spontaneously and easily, without conscious thought as to its appearance.

You may know young people who are oppressed by demons, without clearly seeing what is troubling them. You may know older people obsessed by demons. One excellent definition of the word *obsess* is: "to dominate or preoccupy the thoughts, feelings, or desires of a person; beset, trouble, or haunt persistently or abnormally."

No sharp or final line can be drawn between oppression and obsession. Obsession is oppression amplified and intensified.

Oppression may take many forms; it is usually experienced in the moods, in the feelings, in the emotional state, as well as in the mind. It may be cyclic, coming and going. Obsession bears down hard and knows little, if any, relief.

The latter may take the interior form of demonic persecution of the soul, or the exterior form of driving or compelling a person to engage in bad or undesirable behavior.

Some men are driven by extreme ambition, or driven to dominate others and, if possible, to hold them in fear. Some are preoccupied with and driven by lust. Driven individuals are often, though not always, miserable, and they have an unusual capacity for inflicting misery on others.

Addiction to liquor or narcotics in the physical realm is a kind of parallel to obsession in the realm of the soul. Both can have the strength of compulsion. People can be obsessed with things far less material and visible than narcotics but not a whole lot less potent in their effects.

Demonic obsession may express itself in phobias, extreme complexes, fetishes, fixations, besetting moods, and acute plaguing fears. Some of the things shown in films and videotapes center strongly on the abnormalities and perversions that can lead to obsession.

Since opening oneself to such influences of evil is initially a matter of choice, the only thing to do is to avoid and keep free of them. If the eye and ear take them in, they make their impact on the soul. A while later, they may assert and affix their claim because of the disobedience that allowed them in.

A young fellow, reared in a strong Christian home, found and became secretly fascinated with an evil movie theater in the downtown section of his city when he was fifteen. Some of the things he saw there became incorporated into his behavior later. By age twenty-four he was both physically damaged and psychologically miserable, both of which he fully acknowledged with sorrow. Yet, though he felt a certain degree of attraction to the Lord, he now lacked either the strength or the capacity to turn completely away from these wicked influences.

God's purpose for man was that the body should be nothing less than the dwelling of the Holy Spirit, so Satan's counterplan was to wrest that body and those faculties for his own desires, even to violate and defile the human body.

The devil cannot do that, or any part of it, at will, so he must seek to do it by strategy; and his strategy is nearly always some combination of deception with temptation. When temptation is presented to your mind and will, it is an evil power seeking an entrance into your being for sin.

Take the bait, whatever it is, and sooner or later you are likely to discover you are on a hook. Later, that same behavior may no longer be truly voluntary, but forced or compulsive.

Temptation is the wedge and, as it works, it will in some cases be succeeded by more severe stages of demonic activity—in the forms of oppression, suppression, and obsession.

Oppression may take the form of various moods that come upon a person, a spell of gloom or deep melancholy perhaps. It may come suddenly, sometimes without any apparent reason. It occupies the seat of the emotions and to some extent governs a person's actions, perceptions, and responses. For a time an individual walks under a cloud of melancholy, or experiences a kind of flooding of the emotions.

Human beings were never intended to be ruled or run by transient emotions and moods, but that has become part of their victimization. We are not implying that such disturbances are necessarily demonic: some may be natural and fleshly, some may be demonic in instigation or aggravation, and others are likely to be a compound of the two, in the working alliance that exists between the flesh and evil spirits.

The Psalms, because they are often a record of human triumph (over persecution or trouble or bafflement or sorrows and psychological downcasting), are, when read reverently and carefully, wonderfully clarifying and lifting to the soul. They help dispel gloom or distorted perspectives, and they can give us handles by which to take hold of such things and rid ourselves of them. The right kind of music can also help, sometimes just by its own beauty but especially when it is empowered by the Holy Spirit as a means of ministry to the soul.

Though we go to worship to honor God, one reason why believers need to be regularly in the atmosphere of true and biblical worship is that it helps balance us internally, brings us under the power of truth in the presence of the Lord, restores our worn or weary souls, enlivens our spirits, enlightens our minds, lifts us, helps us to become free. That atmosphere also oppresses the oppressor; it is much harder for opposing spirits to maintain their work upon an individual who is often found in worship with other born-again believers.

The emotions are a region of the soul that evil spirits seek to exploit for their own ends. Emotions are powerful, but if they are let go too far, they become damaging inwardly and outwardly. Evil spirits ride right in upon emotional extremes, taking advantage of them. They work to instigate such excesses, to inflame them, even propel them toward violence.

When individuals give way repeatedly, they find that emotions become a matter of such bondage that they can no longer restrain them and so become ruled by emotional tempests. Sometimes they go through enervating cycles of fury followed by remorse, as did the master composer Beethoven who at times got so angry he hurled dishes at his servants.

At the opposite end of the spectrum, the enemy will work to suppress or shut down the emotions, robbing people of emotional wealth and well-being.

Man was not created to be a sinner; before he became one, he had an emotional nature in which all his emotions were beneficent and godly. After he yielded to the deceiver, some of the evils in his fallen nature were hooked into his emotional being.

Some emotions, both at their core and in their expressions, are only evil. They reflect their source of origin. Demons of envy and anger and other passions drive some human beings. When they do, they can cause their own perversion of spirit to agitate and rule the human soul and spirit on a virtually uninterrupted basis.

It is the privilege of a man to rule over, to govern, his own spirit, forbidding evil passions—envy, anger, hatred, bitterness, jealousy, carnal lusts or a lust for power—to reign within him and to use his faculties as outlets. If a person gives way to such things and permits them, he may eventually give occasion to demons to govern part of his being.

Proverbs 25:28 says that "a man who lacks self-control" is "like a city whose walls are broken down." In biblical times a city's walls were its first line of defense; if they were broken down, an enemy could come in.

That explains why the following truth is so important in God's sight. "He who rules his spirit," the Scripture asserts, is better "than he who takes a city" (Proverbs 16:32, KJV). Ruling means keeping within bounds; it *does not mean* tightfisted, heavy-handed, grim-lipped suppression. That is not ruling; it is forced denial.

The enemy makes capital out of the distortion of human emotions. Some people become frozen in their emotions so that they neither experience nor sense them, and are consequently unable to express them. They may become this way by a tight-lipped resistance to and denial of emotions, by a sudden severe shock to the emotions, or by a subtler series of enemy actions that imprison the emotions. By whatever means, this constitutes theft of normal emotional functioning.

So it is that the enemy aims to push emotions to either of two extremes—to freeze them and shut them down (fathers who never directly express love for their children reflect this) or to stir them up to excess, so that they take us over, or to great excess, so that they spill over in outbursts of infuriation, or uncontrolled grief, or violent acts.

Emotions that are out of control are the storms of the soul. Virtually everyone at some point experiences anger. That is hardly abnormal. It is what we do with it that makes the difference, how far we let it go.

"In your anger do not sin," the Scripture says; "do not let the sun go down while you are still angry, and do not give the devil a foothold" (Ephesians 4:26-27).

Because of some provoking circumstance or factor, anger may rise. We cannot afford to let it run away with us. It must be limited in duration and in expression. Before it has gone too far or run too long, we must check it and put it aside or surrender it to the Lord. If we allow it to continue, our enemy will stoke it until he has turned it against us and those around us.

The Word prescribes the surest cure—self-control. Self-control is a fruit of the Holy Spirit, as is temperance.

Emotions are not some accident of the human soul. They are bestowed by God. In their capacity for joys and sorrows, they reflect His own being, and they are important to us. They enrich life, they motivate, reward, provoke sympathy for and outreach to others, enable love to be most tenderly expressed to wives and husbands and children, and they deepen us. Together with our gifts and intellect, they are also a fruitful source of much of the best artistic expression.

God commanded His people Israel to observe seasons of mourning. He also appointed feasts of joyous, singing celebration. Speaking by revelation, the Prophet Zephaniah told Zion that "the Lord . . . will take great delight in you . . . He will rejoice over you with singing" (Zephaniah 3:17).

There is "a time to weep and a time to laugh, a time to mourn, and a time to dance," Ecclesiastes 3:4 assures us.

When Haman's plot to destroy the Jews was broken, the account of it says, "For the Jews it was a time of happiness and joy, gladness and honor. In every province and . . . city . . . there was joy and gladness among the Jews, with feasting and celebrating" (Esther 8:16-17).

The Psalms are fragrant with hymns of rejoicing and gladness in God and His salvation. Psalm 95:1 says, "Come, let us sing for joy to the Lord; let us shout aloud to the Rock of our salvation. Let us come before Him with thanksgiving and extol Him with music and song."

"Let the saints rejoice . . . and sing for joy upon their beds," Psalm 149:5 proposes.

"My servants will sing out of the joy of their hearts," Isaiah 65:14 affirms.

There are scores of similar declarations—and not only for Israel. "May the nations be glad and sing for joy," Psalm 67:4 anticipates. The Bible refers several times to "the oil of joy" or "the oil of gladness." Oil typifies the Holy Spirit.

The idea some have that emotion does not belong in Christian worship—that it is somehow unseemly and beneath it—but that it should be very staid and proper and intellectual, does not come from the Bible. It is a concept falsely imposed on worship to stifle it, make it cold and formal and, finally, unsatisfying because it does not reach our deepest inner places and needs.

As enlightening as it is to the mind, Christianity is a religion of the heart, a religion in which "first love," refreshed and sustained, is never intended to be lost. If Old Testament worship was to be full of singers and singing, harps and lyres, dancing and rejoicing under the strictures of the Law, it is grotesque to suppose that worship in the age of grace, when all who belong to Christ have a one-to-One relationship with the living God, should be high and dry.

In speaking of "the fruit of the Spirit," Galatians 5:22 begins with "love" and "joy," both necessarily engaging, or flowing out of, the emotions. These are in a dynamic balance with "patience" and "gentleness and self-control," each speaking of a right ruling of our inner selves.

Christianity is chiefly a religion of regeneration that establishes an exchange of love between a human heart and God, with joy. It is not a religion of raw or unrestrained, or *selfish*, emotions. In their keenest state, linked to sheer willfulness, selfish emotions reflect anything but patience, gentleness, and self-control. Godly love is distinguished from everything else called love in these words: "Love is patient, love is kind. It does not envy ... it is not rude, it is not self-seeking" from 1 Corinthians 13:4-7.

The Song of Solomon celebrates the ardent exchange of love. It speaks with glowing tenderness of male-female human love, and it speaks of the love between man and God, showing believers as the bride of the heavenly Bridegroom.

Happy is the believer whose mind is attuned to truth, who keeps his thoughts from the subversions of deception, delusion, and accusation.

Happy is the believer who keeps the romance of the soul fresh with God!

# Drugs and the Supernatural

There is a direct and mysterious relationship between certain chemical agents and the supernatural. Certain drugs can carry the user into the realm of demonic experience. I call them chemical-supernatural agents because these drugs can, and often do, introduce people to the reality of the supernatural realm.

That is not a mere assertion. It is a fact based on the written testimony of many individuals who have directly experienced it.

A person who takes such chemicals into his body opens up avenues into his inner being for the working of evil spirits. He also opens his body, particularly his nerves and muscular system, to functional interference and to physical damage.

Alcohol, narcotics, and hallucinogens are potent elements for cutting in on a person's own control of his body and mind. Powers of darkness therefore widely promote their use among populations of the world. Some narcotics are central to tribal religious practices: they provide a shortcut to the supernatural.

That is no secret; it is an advertised and well-known facet of the narcotics experience. William James, author of *The Varieties of Religious Experience*, who is said to have used nitrous oxide as an hallucinogenic agent, wrote:

"Our normal waking consciousness . . . is but one special type of consciousness: whilst all about it, parted from it by the filmiest of screens, there lie potential forms of consciousness entirely different. . . . No account of the universe in its totality can be final" which ignores them.

James stressed that the existence of these forms "forbid a premature closing of our accounts with reality." Timothy Leary, who for a time acted as the "high priest of LSD," the mass evangelist of dope among young people in our society, spoke beguilingly of "consciousness expansion."

When he formulated his passion for drug-induced experiences into a cult, he significantly called it the League for Spiritual Discovery—for LSD, a high-powered, extremely dangerous hallucinogenic drug. He promoted it, along with peyote and marijuana, for what he called "sacramental use" in reaching altered states of consciousness.

The claim is often made that reaching such levels of consciousness is good, broadening, beneficial, liberating. A closer look shows that it is quite exactly the opposite.

There are pleasures of a sort available and there are terrors also. Evil spirits are able to produce stunning supernatural effects, unsuspected dimensions of the weird, full of color and radiance and silvered lightning—and they are equally able to produce extremes of terror and chaotic, crashing misperceptions. Therein lies the difference between a so-called "good trip" and a "bad trip."

Havelock Ellis wrote enticingly of "the artificial paradise of mescal" (peyote), but that is not quite what it is. It is a counterfeit paradise, and that paradise can turn in an instant into a living hell.

The use of certain narcotics as spiritual agents (expressly in order to be put into contact with the supernatural) is a deeply entrenched practice in certain parts of the world, usually among people of low achievement, slack culture, and little or no education. Some of these agents have been central to the worship of demon cults going back several thousand years.

Peyote is among the best known of the natural hallucinogens. Some people use it as a means of getting into a visionary state.

"Visions and other mystical experiences are part of the regular spiritual diet of the 50,000-odd members of the Native American Church, thanks to what they consider a special gift from God: peyote, a small cactus," one report said. "The Indians of the Native American Church cut off and dry the cactus tops, then eat the 'buttons' in nightlong ceremonies to the accompaniment of sacred fire and chanting.

"The faith's adherents believe that the partaking of peyote brings one into direct contact with God. They also address prayers to it, and consider it to be a protector." They carry it for good luck.

Yet there is no plant or drug that can put a person into "direct contact with God." The living God does not reveal Himself to a person on the basis of his taking a chemical into his system. Peyote can, however, open up an avenue of contact with unseen spirits.

Peyote has a place in Satan's great arsenal of idolatry. It is not a sacred substance; it is a cursed substance. It can damage people mentally, physically, and spiritually. There have been repeated reports of sex crimes, some against children, committed under the influence of peyote.

In Eden, God told man, "You may freely eat of every tree of the garden" with the one exception of the "tree of the knowledge of good and evil." When Adam followed Satan in sin, one of the things God said was, "Cursed is the ground because of you." Things entered into the natural realm that would never have been there apart from sin, including poisons.

Since a curse lies upon the earth, there are things that grow in the soil upon which Satan has a claim. Certain narcotic plants are inimical to the welfare and health of human beings in many ways. They are like fountains of evils. Their power for evil is strangely versatile. When you take one you can never know how it will affect you. The same plant may affect one person one way, another in a radically different way, and others in still other ways. These effects go far beyond that produced by their natural chemistry.

The link between the hallucinogenic drugs and the supernatural activity of demons is seen in the spiritual and supernatural effects experienced through their use. Whether those experiences seem lovely, or terrifying beyond description, they are demonic. It is a sad but inescapable fact that evil spirits gain advantage over human beings through alcohol, narcotics, and hallucinogens.

In addition to triggering hallucinations, these fearful chemicals sometimes induce psychoses. Of 114 LSD users hospitalized in one eighteen-month period at New York's Bellevue Hospital, 13 percent suffered *overwhelming panic*, 12 percent exhibited *uncontrolled violence*, nearly 9 percent had attempted *homicides or suicides*. Some suffered acute schizophrenia. Several "withdrew from society into a totally solipsistic existence," according to a news account.

"Half had no history of underlying psychiatric disorder," a physician reported. Another report told of a boy who, after taking LSD, threw himself off a cliff because he believed he could fly.

LSD users have suffered uncontrollable spasms and convulsions, including *grand mal* convulsions. There are delayed reactions, some coming long after LSD has been ingested.

A news report told of "a young man driving on a highway, a year after his only LSD experience." Suddenly an hallucination seized him. He saw "a hundred headlights coming at him, and he crashed." The hallucination was of a specially dangerous kind and it came, without warning, when it could do him great harm.

In a report on "The Medical View: Not What the Doctor Ordered," concerning marijuana, *Newsweek* magazine said "marijuana can be a mild hallucinogen. . . . When inhaled, the drug quickly passes into the blood stream and *takes effect on brain centers* in a matter of minutes. . . . A high dose may produce vivid hallucinations similar to an LSD trip."

As to physical effects, medical observation has shown that "marijuana can hinder the individual's ability to function. Even small doses produce unsteadiness. Since *spatial perception, as well as coordination, is affected*, a marijuana user may be as dangerous as a drunk behind the wheel."

"A marijuana smoker behind the wheel of an automobile," said Dr. Donald B. Louria of the Cornell University Medical College, "is in a sense more dangerous—because [he is] less liable to detection—than a drunken driver."

Tests have shown that an individual under the influence of marijuana tends to *lose his coordination*, yet he often has *a feeling of omnipotence*. This is a strategic attack on two centers—the brain and the muscular-nervous systems—having opposite effects of a kind that increases personal hazard.

There is some loss of actual efficiency in the bodily mechanisms; at the same time one feels more in command, more relaxed, tremendously able to handle whatever situation is at hand. The misimpression encourages risk-taking at the very time when the mechanisms of the body are less sure. Up goes the inclination for risk and down goes the capacity to handle it, so the margin of danger is increased while the margin of safety shrinks.

One of Satan's most efficient instruments is the narcotics parlay: an "innocent" flirtation with marijuana now, a deadly alliance with heroin (or some other hard narcotic) later.

It is energetically argued that using marijuana has no connection with, in the sense that it may lead to, the use of stronger stuff. That is a lie—as those who work closely with narcotics victims know.

A study made in New York City found that, out of 168 young people who had used marijuana, "at least 40 percent later began using heroin." People who wouldn't think of taking heroin will try marijuana, and some later graduate to more potent stuff.

Satan is not interested at all in immediately selling you narcotics addiction, any more than he was interested in selling the woman in the garden death. His aim is to get a person to take the first bite, or the first puffs, or the first jab, or the first lungful. If you are not a user of any drug, he wants to get you from where you are now—out of the drug scene—over into it, if only "slightly" at the start.

If you do step into it, there are numerous ways it can turn to your disadvantage and loss, some of them drastic.

You may know several people, possibly more, who have used "grass" or something else who still seem able to function perfectly well. That is right. Yet it may not be the case with you! Even if you knew 100, you cannot project that into a guarantee of a similar immunity for yourself.

The fact is that some people can't take the stuff without suffering damage; some can't take it without going out of their minds. If you're one of those, it doesn't make any difference how many people you know who can.

With all of these potent chemicals, the only sure thing is that if you don't bother with them, they won't bother you. *That is the only guarantee you have.* Everything else is playing a kind of Russian roulette with chemicals that may act like small charges of dynamite in your body or in your mind.

Some drugs have a slow, cumulative way of taking toll. You fly now, but you pay later. You may have to pay much more than you can afford. You may have to pay with your life.

Sitting one day in the first-floor office of a man on the West Side of Manhattan, I looked out the window as he said, "Do you see that man walking by?" I saw a tall man about thirty-two years old in a tan jacket.

"Two years ago," he said, "that man had a full-time job. One day he showed signs of having dope in him. Pretty soon he had a part-time job. Some days he'd be all right, and some days he'd be doped up. Now he doesn't have any job. He's doped up nearly all the time."

That illustrates, in a graphic way, the steps that lead some individuals from freedom and self-possession to bondage. The man had formerly enjoyed the use of his faculties and could apply them rationally to meet his needs, but now his faculties were devoted to the procurement and injection of a narcotic. He had become a slave.

There are more than eight million severe alcoholics in the United States. What a state for a person to be in! It is often said that alcoholism is a disease. If that is so, there is only *one* way to catch it—by drinking liquor. No one who doesn't drink has ever caught it.

An alcoholic is a liquor addict. The stuff messes him up but he's *got* to have it. With alcohol the damage can be, and often is, a slow process of deterioration. Or it can be as sudden and disastrous as a head-on collision. Alcoholism can lead eventually to the terrifying hallucinations of delirium tremers. In the worst state of alcoholism, a person is out of his mind, lying in some doorway, blabbering out gibberish, urinating like a baby. He is a living wreck, as bleak and rotting as a long-abandoned house.

At first the tremors and slurry speech are occasional; later, they become frequent; at the end they are always there.

In an abstract on alcohol, the *World Almanac* gives clues to why this is so. Alcohol is "a central nervous system depressant . . . that first acts on those parts of the brain which affect self-control." After prolonged overuse, which is often involuntary and habitual, "alcohol can damage the liver and heart and can cause permanent brain damage."

For biblical wisdom on the effects of intoxicating liquor, read Proverbs 23:19-21, 29-35 carefully. Remember that "drunkards" are among those the Scriptures say will not enter the kingdom of God. For examples, consider 1 Corinthians 6:9-11. For some the first glass of booze they ever drink leads on to the state that bars them from heaven for eternity.

### Drugs in Mystery Religions

R. Gordon Wasson, a New York mycologist (a botanist specializing in the study of fungi, including mushrooms), took the lead in the rediscovery of the religious role of the hallucinogenic mushrooms of Mexico.

"When we first went down to Mexico, we felt certain, my wife and I, that we were on the trail of an ancient and holy mystery and we went as pilgrims seeking the Grail," he said in a subsequent lecture. An ancient mystery, yes—but not a holy one.

The Wassons became probably "the first outsiders . . . to be invited to partake in the *agape* of the sacred mushroom." They had learned from sixteenth-century writers that "certain mushrooms played a divinatory role" in tribal religion. They found that this "cult of a divine mushroom, this cult of 'God's flesh' . . . can be traced back to about 1500 B.C. . . . Thus we find a mushroom in the center of the cult with perhaps the oldest continuous history in the world."

Mr. Wasson presented this rite of demons to the United States when *Life* opened its pages to a major article by him called "Seeking the Magic Mushroom."

Mr. Wasson lamented that language was insufficient to describe "the nature of the psychic disturbance the eating of the mushroom causes. . . . What we need is a vocabulary to describe all the modalities of a Divine Inebriant," he wrote. It is an inebriant, to be sure, but it is the very opposite of divine.

Mr. Wasson, banker and mushroom pilgrim, notes that the mushroom enables a man "to travel backwards and forwards in time, to enter other planes of existence, even [as the Indians say] to know God."

Or, as the Greek scholar Mary Barnard wrote in *The American Scholar*, concerning a dozen plants used in religious practices, "Some of them are open doors to the otherworld. . . . They are sacred plants, magic herbs or shrubs . . . magic carpets on which the spirit of the shaman can travel through time and space. . . . The magic plants are vehicles for a special kind of [religious] experience."

"If there were such a field as theo-botany," Miss Barnard suggests, "the study of these plants and their cults would be the work of a theo-botanist." Of peyote she wrote, "The god, being rendered fit for eating, presides over the meeting where peyote is taken and 'sends' the songs sung and the visions seen. . . ."

The scholar cites some of the other supernatural aspects of the cult: ". . . the shaman's journey . . . the food of occult knowledge . . . the disembodied soul, the communication with the dead" by means of "plant-deities."

Spirits, posing as gods, gain access to human beings through the religious use of such substances. Miss Barnard writes concerning a sick child, "When the shaman has swallowed the sacred mushroom, the mushroom-deity takes possession of the shaman's body and speaks with the shaman's lips. The shaman does not say whether the sick child will live or die; *the mushroom says.*"

The same writer lists as among the effects of these drugs: "a displaced center of consciousness seemingly outside the body . . . hallucinations of some sort—visual or auditory or both . . . divination . . . ceremonial communion with the gods ... [trances in which] the shaman's body is said to be emptied of his soul."

Drugs are a means by which satanic powers can thrust to the center of a person's being and begin to bring him under the effects of his spiritual agents, demons. Drug experiences can be the means of taking a user into regions of fantasy, euphoria, terror, passivity, anxiety, apathy, lethargy, mental and spiritual confusion, false worship, and insanity.

Among the false religions those centered on drugs feature quite sensational effects, including all kinds of interior fireworks shows and a dervish-like frenzy at times—creations of the special effects department of hell, intended to deceive. One thing these tribal religions do not do is relieve hardship and suffering and poverty and ignorance. They perpetuate them, offering occasional soul flights as escapism. If tribal murder is rampant, these religions provide a base of ceremony and excitation from which it flows.

Another common note is that of possession: the experience of being taken over by the will of the leader or by an outside force or spirit.

In a review called "The Magic of Peyote," Dudley Young discussed *The Teachings of Don Juan* by Carlos Castañeda, giving glimpses into the nightmare experiences an individual can suffer through involvement with drug plants, especially through a religious involvement. He wrote:

"This book is the record of a young anthropologist's experience as the apprentice of a Mexican Indian sorcerer. Over a period of four years, Mr. Castañeda paid intermittent visits to Don Juan, first in Arizona, then in Sonora, Mexico. The aim of his initiation was to gain power over the demonic world through the ritualized ingestion of peyote and other hallucinogenic plants."

Peyote made Mr. Castañeda "violently ill and disclosed to him both terror and ecstasy. Toward the end of his fourth year he began to have what the layman might describe as a nervous breakdown, and after a particularly shattering evening with the Don, he abruptly broke off relations.

"Don Juan emerges as an enigmatic, ultimately sinister guru figure; ascetic and authoritarian. . . .

"The spirits of his underworld, contacted through drugs, can protect . . . those they fancy, but destroy" others. "The Don was convinced that his disciple was well-favored by the gods, but if this is so, one shudders to think what happens to the ill-favored ones."

Mr. Young says that it was not clear whether Don Juan was "seeking a corrupting kind of power over his disciple," but "certainly the author's final hallucination, during which he threw a rock at his master who seemed bent on destroying him, would support such a suggestion."

Mr. Castañeda apparently broke with his misadventure at just the point at which the takeover was about to be completed, and it is a significant sign of the sharpness of his resistance that he threw a rock at the sorcerer leading him on.

This experience of a loss of control over one's own person is a rather common one. It may be seen in the experience of Frederick Swain, who was one of the first to follow through on Mr. Wasson's research, and who decided to investigate for himself. He learned that there was a shaman in the village of Huautla de Jiménez in Mexico named Santa Maria Sabina and, with much difficulty, he found his way to where she lived.

"The hut was only one room, with a dirt floor, thatched roof and mud walls"—with seven adults and "numerous children, all living in the same drafty room. They all slept, ate, and lived on the floor.

"In one corner of the hut an altar had been set up, with two long candles and a glass vigil in the center, surrounded by bouquets of flowers," Swain wrote. "A straw mat was spread before the altar, and Santa Maria sat on it cross-legged, motioning for me to sit beside her. The candles were lit. Then she pulled a large bowl of freshly picked mushrooms from under the altar. . . . She gave me a cup with ten mushrooms. . . . No sooner had we eaten them than the three men behind us began vomiting and spitting. . . . I felt no nausea.

"Within half an hour the mushrooms began to take effect. First there were vivid flashing colors. Then a clammy chill came over me and I began shaking. . . . I pulled my collar tight around my neck and sat there, shaking," Swain continued.

". . . Intricate art motifs appeared in vivid colors. . . . Then they formed a spiral and we traveled down the spiral. . . . Our consciousness changed many times during the night. . . . I attributed this to the control Santa Maria exerted over us.

". . . Then there appeared before us dancing celestial eagle gods, with all their plumage. . . . They became ecstatic. We too became absorbed with them. It was wonderful.

". . . The dancing soon came to an end and the music stopped. The eagle gods vanished. A new scene quickly took shape. . . . We were in the center of a vast, endless desert . . . the 'Land of Eternal Waiting.' Yes, it was clear to me that we were waiting there eternally. . . . I was losing my identity. I felt it might be a hypnotic spell. . . . I felt I had lost contact with life on earth.

". . . Silence had become part of me, . . . but I roused myself and forced myself to speak. To my surprise, the Mazatecs answered in English. I swear it. It shook me up a bit. There was some kind of telepathic communication between us. . . . I was later told it sounded to them that

I spoke in Mazateca."

Frederick Swain heard them say, " 'Yes, we really are in the Land of Eternal Waiting. . . . Your life on earth never really happened. It was only a dream. . . . This alone is real.' "

The attack on the visitor had become very severe. Like Carlos Castañeda, who threw a rock at the sorcerer, Swain found it necessary to take rather violent action to break the grip it had taken on him.

"I began to get mad, really hot," he continued. "I turned to them and shouted, 'You're all crazy, and so am I.' . . . I felt I was being tricked. . . . The situation called for drastic action. I really had to get away if I were going to maintain any sort of emotional balance. I threw back my head and willed myself out of that place by sheer force of concentration.

"I don't recommend the mushroom to anyone . . . , many people would be terrified at the loss of identity caused" by it, Swain concluded.

A reporter, a man of unusually forceful character and exceptionally strong will, asked my advice but did not go by it. A week later he came by to tell me how wonderful his first LSD experience had been. Two weeks later he had a different story.

"I thought I was losing my mind," he said. "I felt I was coming under the power of this guy who was guiding us. It got so bad I didn't know if I could ever get back."

A girl in California took up marijuana at seventeen, went along on it a few years, then tried LSD. "We lay back on the floor and it was a good trip. We rolled on the floor, and we laughed and the room filled up with gold fog and we swam through it."

A week later she tried it again: "I began to shake and sweat, and I felt like someone was pulling a band tight around my head." Three days later: "I was still trembling and crying all the time and everything still had that nightmare comic strip look." When a reporter saw her nearly two years later, she had not taken any more LSD but "she was still trembling and unable to work."

The young woman was suffering from mental, physical, emotional, and nervous effects produced as a result of taking a devastating drug—a chemical supernatural agent.

Distorted perspectives may have a certain novelty, but they can result in a perspective permanently and irreclaimably knocked out of focus.

You would not let a person come along and crack your skull or break your arm; it is just as unwise to permit this kind of damage to be done to your inner being. You have only one mind. You can never get another. To guard it, you will be smart not to take something into your body that can devastate your brains.

The son of a wealthy and well-known family came to Columbia College, where friends introduced him to social drug use. He was no heavy user, but one morning he was found dead in his dorm room. Examination showed he had taken a drug and liquor in a fatal combination. The fellow was put down into his grave short of twenty years old. No, it does not always happen like that, so fast, but it did, and it can.

"Crack—It Reaches Your Brain in 8 Seconds," the headline read over a report on a potent form of cocaine by newspaper columnist Sydney H. Schanberg. In an interview Dr. Peter Pasternack, a heart specialist, said that cocaine may attack the body in a variety of ways—sometimes one way at a time, sometimes all of them at once. A few snippets from his findings:

"Cocaine causes an adrenaline surge that can make you restless, excited . . . anxious, confused . . . with [subsequent] headaches . . . abdominal pain. . . . You can experience delirium, shallow respiration, convulsions" and may lapse "into unconsciousness and death from respiratory and cardiac arrest."

The doctor said that with high dosages "the vital nerve centers of the brain stem are depressed—the nerve signal centers that . . . keep the heart and lungs working automatically, without us thinking about it." In some cases, the result can be "a stroke or a cerebral hemorrhage" or a wild racing of the heart.

The drug is a vasoconstrictor that "closes down arteries," so while it is making the heart beat faster and faster at an erratic rate, the vessels that carry blood to the heart are constricting and denying it the blood it must have to function. This combination "can produce almost instant death," the doctor said.

The drug imposes its tyranny by giving the user a pleasing jolt. Another report said: "Upon snorting cocaine one feels almost instantly more awake, alive, and alert. . . . One gets a sense that he is coming down almost as soon as he is aware that he is high at all; this creates an almost immediate desire for more."

A report on medical research in *The New York Times* said that two New York biochemists seemed to have found the long-sought scientific reason alcohol can cause behavioral changes "ranging from euphoria through drunkenness to hallucinations." Dr. Michael Collins and Gerald Cohen said that the body "probably converted alcohol through a series of complicated steps to substances chemically akin to morphine, peyote, and other opiates and hallucinogens."

Dr. Collins said that "heavy and chronic drinking was known to produce changes in the nerves and brain" sometimes resulting in tremors, delusions or hallucinations due to "the formation in the brain of an alkaloid named isoquinoline [which] exerts its effects on the brain and nerve endings."

These alkaloids were found to be "of a type called tetrahydro-isoquinolines," which are "found in desert cacti, most notably in the families that contain mescal buttons and peyote." So here in the biochemical laboratory researchers traced the hitherto hidden chemical relationships of alcohol and some of the most powerful hallucinogens.

Taking LSD may be one way to wreck a child before he's born. The prospect of genetic damage caused the March of Dimes Birth Defects Foundation to warn that "it is especially important that men and women in their reproductive years avoid using LSD." Breaks or other abnormalities in chromosomes are seen in roughly three quarters of persons who take the drug, the *Times* reported.

Chromosomes are the tiny, threadlike particles of material buried in the nucleus of every cell, which transmit hereditary factors from one generation to the next. They carry the instructions that form new life.

In its assault on the body LSD, among many other things, apparently penetrates to the very nucleus of the cell and attacks the chromosomes.

At the University of Oregon Medical School, as Bill Davidson reported in an extensively researched article on "The Hidden Evils of LSD," eight young men, all users, volunteered blood samples for microscopic inspection; six of the eight were found to have damaged—broken—chromosomes. Two of the six showed signs of "fatal chronic myelogenous leukemia," cancer of the blood.

Dr. Maimon M. Cohen, a geneticist at the State University of New York at Buffalo, tested normal human blood cells in a tube. "He added minute quantities of LSD and studied the chromosomes under a microscope. He was startled and alarmed to see the same kind of chromosomal damage that occurs with radiation." Next he examined the blood cells of three mothers, all LSD users, and their four children, and "the same frightening breakage of chromosomes showed up."

Chromosome damage represents a deep invasion of the inmost chambers of the body, piercing the most sensitive and delicate genetic messengers in the chain of life. LSD ranks with "certain violent factors, such as atomic radiation" in its battering effect on the chromosomes.

There is no necessary correlation between dosage and effects. Fragmentation and chromosome damage has been found in those who had only one dose. The kind of genetic damage caused by LSD can lead to an abnormality called the *cri-du-chat* syndrome, in which a baby cries like a cat, not a human.

"The results of this chromosome damage may have a delayed effect that may not be in evidence until the second or third generation of offspring," warned Dr. Howard A. Rusk, head of the Institute for Rehabilitation Medicine of the New York University Medical Center. Dr. Rusk found that the more immediate effects of the hallucinogens include a "possibility of permanent brain damage."

A dose or two of LSD now may be the cause of a child born two generations later coming into the world crippled for life. What potency that is! What a scheme for the maiming of the race. All of the supposed benefits of drugs—the trips, the kicks, the highs, the escape from reality into dreamscapes, the illusion of increased powers—are momentary and are offered in exchange for the chance to impose severe damage upon the user and deformities upon future generations.

What does the drug culture come to? Misery and sickness and untimely death for some. Despair and entrapment for others. Mental derangement in some degree for yet many more. When addiction spreads a visible demoralization of the culture occurs.

The narcotics trade is a ghastly conspiracy, nothing less than a modern day traffic in human slaves. To thrive it must create addicts and inflict serious injuries on human bodies. It takes the wealth it gains and bribes its way forward, breaking down law. "We will rule or ruin" is its message. Its tools are big payoffs and murder—each designed to paralyze the law. It is demonic in its operations and effects. Wherever it takes over, the blight of a curse falls across the scene.

A story in *The Times* began: "Down the circular staircase in the airless basement of the office of the city's Chief Medical Examiner on First Avenue, the day's consignment of drug abuse fatalities reposed on stainless steel slabs—five young men between the ages of eighteen and twenty-one who had been alive on Saturday and were dead on Sunday."

For each of them, we can be sure, the path to very early death began with a friendly offer, a temptation, a challenge to be daring, a false promise, or a surge of curiosity.

It was in their power, as it is in ours, to refuse to go along at the very first bid. That refusal, steadily maintained, in the face of anything and everything, is armor that lasts a lifetime for everyone who takes it. Decide on it now and hold to it and you gain a total assurance that none of all the dire things that can occur on the other side of this temptation will ever come your way.

**5**

**CALLED
TO
CONQUER**

# God, Government, and the Supernatural

To this point you have received an initial grounding in supernatural realities, as the Bible reveals them. We have gone, you might say, from a first-grade understanding through high school, with some glances at college-level knowledge.

That may be all you will need, but if you want or need more, it is available beyond the pages of this book, especially in a book called *War on the Saints* by Jessie Penn-Lewis and Evan Roberts, a classic on the Christian's spiritual warfare as it relates to the supernatural.

That book is available in two forms, a condensed edition as well as the original, unabridged text, from two Christian publishers. The shorter version will give any reader a good college-level *survey* course on the subject. The complete text is suited to ministers and missionaries and Christian counselors who come up against particularly resistant and perplexing difficulties in their work. Such matters may yield to the penetrating and precisely defined analyses that these brilliant and faithful writers impart.

There is no escaping the fact that two kingdoms are in conflict on this earth on which we live. That fact has consequences reaching from the individual heart, to the family, to our culture, to the nation and out to the world scene.

That conflict will continue and will intensify as both kingdoms bid for the allegiance of men and clash over the course of history. *Both* will reach their ultimate heights of realization on this earth in the form of *governments* with worldwide authority.

Satan's great thrust against mankind, the Scriptures plainly say, will be by the tyranny of a highly unified, virtually worldwide government under his sway. At its head will stand a counterfeit christ the Bible calls "the Antichrist" and the "man of sin." Energized by satanic power, he will affix himself upon deceived mankind, and will speak and act in utter defiance of God.

By this thrust Satan will say, in effect, to God, "You sent Your Son as the King and men rejected Him, but they will worship my christ and follow him."

Never think that Satan is uninterested in government. It interests him highly. It will be the means by which he finally imposes his will on much of humanity.

He will seek totally to interpose himself between God and mankind by means of that government, and to cut mankind off from God by it. Spiritually, on this earth, that will amount to a nearly total eclipse of God. Like any eclipse, it will be brief.

The Scripture describes the Antichrist as one who "opposes and exalts himself over everything that is called God or is worshiped, and even sets himself up in God's temple, proclaiming himself to be God."

His arrival on the world scene will create a sensation and "will be in accordance with the work of Satan displayed in all kinds of counterfeit miracles, signs and wonders, and in every sort of evil that deceives those who are perishing" (2 Thessalonians 2:4, 9-10).

If you know the Bible, you undoubtedly are aware of this future prospect. The point here is not that it will happen, but rather *what it tells us about our enemy.* The fact that he will ultimately nearly accomplish this short-term takeover tells us *what he pushes for.*

He is not just waiting for that day. He is straining toward it and seeking to bring it in. Understanding that can help us deal realistically, effectively, and spiritually with the world in which we live.

Satan is always at work to project and advance the interests of his evil kingdom to the maximum obtainable limits; one of the vehicles he seeks to ride is human government as a way of usurping and overthrowing lawful authority.

Never think that God is uninterested in government. Government is His idea. He ordained it for good (Romans 13:1-7). A governing authority is "God's servant to do you good," we are told, and, "He is God's servant, an agent of wrath to bring punishment on the wrongdoer."

A ruler's God-appointed role is to make room for what is good, protect law-abiding citizens and to punish and stop the evildoers. Knowing its power to affect conditions across a whole society, Satan seeks to twist and pervert government so that it does the opposite—actually punishes and persecutes the godly while protecting and elevating evildoers.

The living God has tremendous plans for government through His anointed Son, who was born to save and also born to rule:

"For to us a child is born, to us a son is given, and *the government will be upon His shoulders.* . . . Of the increase of His government and peace there will be no end. He will reign on David's throne . . . with justice and righteousness . . . forever" (Isaiah 9:6-7).

That is assured but we are not there yet. We are living short of the ultimate governmental expressions of these two conflicting kingdoms.

Until the day when "the kingdom of the world . . . become the kingdom of our Lord and of His Christ, and He will reign for ever and ever," as Revelation 11:15 portrays it, there will be a continuing dynamic tension between good and evil reaching for government power and wielding its authority. The difference between the two, and the effects they produce, is immense.

It is literally true that, "When the righteous are *in authority,* the people rejoice; but when the wicked rule, the people groan" (Proverbs 29:2, rsv). History teaches that conclusively.

Apart from the true church, there is no greater earthly agency for good than government. Without it, crime, thievery, and murder would run rampant, unchecked. There would be little stability, little assurance of life itself, much less property and liberty.

Christians are commanded to be both obedient and honestly submissive to government. A key passage concerning that is Romans 13:1-7, which affirms that the authorities "have been established by God."

Here is the stated purpose for which they exist:

"For rulers hold no terror for those who do right, but for those who do wrong. Do you want to be free from fear of the one in authority? Then do what is right and he will commend you. For he is *God's servant to do you good*" (13:3-4).

Though it is hard to understand how they can be so one-eyed and dense in understanding, some Christians flatly apply God's sanctions to all governments in all places at all times—with no regard to the verses that define the God-given role and purpose of government, the very *why* of its existence.

A government is meant to be "God's servant, *an agent* of wrath to bring punishment on the wrongdoer." Government is to roughly approximate at earth-level the justice of God. How profoundly perverse it is when government reverses that function and acts as an agent to advocate, promote, and enforce evil, even to become a terror to those who do what is right.

The parents of Moses pleased God when, after the ruling Pharaoh had decreed that all male Jewish infants be killed, they hid the child by faith and "were not afraid of the king's edict" (Hebrews 11:23).

When the evil King Herod thought to kill the infant Jesus, whom the wise men told him was "born king of the Jews," the visitors were warned in a dream not to let Herod know exactly where to find Jesus. Then "an angel of the Lord appeared to Joseph in a dream" and told him to flee to Egypt, so "he got up, took the child and his mother during the night and left" abruptly for Egypt (Matthew 2:2, 12-14).

This fact stands as an historical rebuke to some of the boldest platform overcomers of our day, who mock and belittle the power of Satan and tell God's people how readily they can defeat him: when God's own Son—in whose life and body all the authority and purposes of heaven were invested—was endangered, Joseph was not told that the child was supernaturally invulnerable. There is a difference between presumption and faith. In this case, faith fled.

There *was* supernatural intervention: the wise men were warned in a dream and an angel told Joseph to get up immediately and escape. There was divine protection, but it consisted in obeying the angel's warning. When Herod lifted the sword of government and killed all the boys in Bethlehem and its vicinity who were less than two years old, Jesus was not there to be murdered (Matthew 2:13-18).

Government, when it is evil in what it decrees, is not always to be blindly obeyed. When the apostles were hauled before the Sanhedrin (the supreme court of the Jews with religious, civil, and criminal jurisdiction), they were told, "We gave you strict orders not to teach in this [Jesus'] name."

"Peter and the other apostles replied, 'We must obey God rather than men!'" (Acts 5:27-29) It is only when there is a *direct* contradiction between the law or will of God and the laws of men that believers must choose to obey God above the will of government. Not to do so in that circumstance is to become bound by evil.

We must live under government, and it must possess and *use* the sword of enforcement spoken of in Romans 13:3-5. But *which way* the sword of government cuts makes all the difference.

"When a king sits on his throne to judge," Proverbs 20:8 says, "he winnows out all evil with his eyes." He distinguishes between what is evil and what is good and removes or puts away the evil.

King David is seen governing in this biblical cameo: "David reigned over all Israel, doing what was just and right for all his people" (2 Samuel 8:15). In Romans 13:6 we encounter this lovely fact: "the authorities are God's servants, who give their full time to governing."

The worst state of society occurs when evil rises up and takes hold of the very centers of government power and uses them to decree evil and enforce it. That enthrones lawlessness and gives to it all the organized authority and force of law. Evil can then have its way, with none to stop it.

The vocation of Satan is as a deceiver and murderer and destroyer (see John 10:10), and he endeavors to accomplish these very things through the power of government anywhere in the world that he can.

Whole governments, holding power over millions of citizens, have officially declared that there is no God, that the Bible is a deceptive fiction. They systematically indoctrinate children with atheism in state schools, hound believers (Jews also and others) mercilessly, sometimes sending them to slave labor and sometimes to death, breaking up families, ordering armed soldiers to disrupt worship meetings with rifle-butt violence, shutting church buildings and tearing them down.

Sometimes such governments, as with Nazism and Marxism, slaughter people by the millions in pursuit of their evil ends.

Seeing what government is meant to be as a force for good, and what it can become under satanic inspiration and usurpation, can we afford to be indifferent to government, just to let it be whatever it will be? In a free land, it is our privilege as Christian citizens to participate as directly and vigorously in government affairs as the unbelievers constantly do.

## Peace by Conquest

The fateful relationship between government and the supernatural is sometimes readily evident, and sometimes not. Moses was given supernatural power by God to overcome the resistant will of a headstrong Pharaoh and also to overcome his wonder-working magicians, whose powers were occultic and set against God's purpose to liberate His people.

Daniel is a book of the Bible that portrays the life of a godly man who worked at the very touch-points of government and the supernatural. Daniel, a Hebrew exile in Babylon, was a prophet. Yet he spent all of his adult life as a high government official in two great Gentile kingdoms, Babylon and Persia. In each he stood successfully and fearlessly for righteousness and truth.

King Belshazzar of Babylon became wanton and godless and sinned his way to judgment. It was God's man Daniel who stood at the crux of the transition. A wine-drenched banquet was the king's final act. Judgment fell swiftly and by openly supernatural means. Some handwriting appeared on the wall before the king. He called immediately for his pagan advisers, "the enchanters, astrologers and diviners" and wise men but they could not figure it out. Then Daniel was brought in. He pronounced judgment:

"But you . . . O Belshazzar, have not humbled yourself. . . . Instead, *you have set yourself up against the Lord of heaven.* . . . You did not honor the God who holds in His hand your life. . . . Your kingdom is divided and given to the Medes and Persians."

A great kingdom was brought to a sudden and irreversible end: "That very night Belshazzar, king of the Babylonians, was slain, and Darius the Mede took over the kingdom" (Daniel 5:22-31). Darius immediately appointed Daniel to be one of three top officers of the new government.

Daniel received remarkable revelations from God concerning a series of future kingdoms and governments all the way forward to the governments of the Antichrist and of the Lord Jesus Christ.

You can see the transition from the short-lived government of the Antichrist, based totally on presumption and evil, to the everlasting reign of the Messiah Jesus in Daniel 7:8-14.

Daniel shows the rise of the Antichrist, his blasphemous boasting on the earth, events going on in heaven, the sudden death of the Antichrist—then "one like a son of man, coming with the clouds of heaven. . . . He was given authority, glory and sovereign power; all peoples, nations . . . worshiped Him. His dominion is an everlasting dominion that will not pass away, and His kingdom is one that will never be destroyed."

Satan is ambitious to rule. He seeks to do so on the earth through a series of evil men, antichrists, leading ultimately to the Antichrist, who will almost as completely embody satanic evil in human form as Jesus Christ embodied divinity and truth.

According to 1 John 2:18, "the Antichrist is coming," yet "even now many antichrists have come." The final Antichrist will be a religious and a political figure, who will also control the world economy (see Revelation 13:16-17).

The powers of darkness gain a measure of control on the earth by locking into human sinfulness at the level of government. Satan knows, as God's enemy and man's enemy, that the *single most powerful instrument for the suppression of truth,* and of *persecution against believers and the church* is government when it is perverted, because it holds nearly total authority. So he goes for government, aware that government, twisted to evil, can multiply evil and darkness and death as nothing else can.

Hitler, filled with raging anger and worldly lusts and great false dreams of glory, told his people they were members of a master race. He promised them European supremacy and national grandeur—a Reich (German Empire) that would last for 1,000 years.

Instead, he remade Germany into a police state and a great war machine, and led them straight into a bloodbath. He gave vehement expression to Satan's historic hatred for the Jews. When he took power, he turned evil doctrine into official policy and set in motion a vehicle for the systematic murder of 6 million Jews.

German cities were bombed to rubble. The toll on Germans alone was 4,250,000 deaths, including about 3 million young men who died in Hitler's vain and empty cause. The man gained authority chiefly by the power of inflammatory speech, illustrating the biblical truth that "the tongue is a little member and boasts of great things. How great a forest is set ablaze by a small fire!

"And the tongue is a fire. The tongue is an unrighteous world among our members, staining the whole body, *setting on fire the cycle of nature,* and *set on fire by hell"* (James 3:5-6, rsv).

Hitler, a satanic messenger to his people, boasted of great things. His tongue was set on fire by hell and it, in turn, set the cycle or course of nature on fire. A paroxysm of blasting destruction and death swept across the continent. Europe went into flames.

Out of one man's wicked designs, eventually tens of millions died, and graves were dug across the face of Europe. How awesome is the power of government for evil when it is seized and held by evil men!

Our spiritual enemy is not playing games with mankind or with history. He is in dead earnest, and he works as widely and as wickedly as he can against God and man.

In this section we have gone beyond the dynamics of the godly and the evil supernatural in relation to individuals to consider its impact on the wider scale of nations.

Consider the next few lines of the highest importance. If you grasp them and understand their implications, you will have a key to understanding what is really at stake in the world.

Our enemy has a policy for this world, and he has a strategy to back it up. If we can see what that strategy is, we will be able to take steps to overcome it.

Satan, through his demonic agents, is "the *spirit* that is now *at work in* the sons of disobedience" (Ephesians 2:2, RSV). This speaks of his spiritual access to sinners and their susceptibility to him. He uses them to carry out his will, as far as they will allow him to.

He does all he can to inspire, energize, and propel sinners forward to be publicly influential for what pleases him, to make a mark on their time.

Then he does all he can to lull believers into inaction or less-than-adequate action, to call them down from their highest privileges in Christ, to make them less than they actually can be for God in their generation.

His two-pronged attack is to *maximize* the one while *minimizing* the other. It is to lift up evil (whether raw and flagrant, or delicate and philosophical) and exalt it, and to keep righteousness in a corner. It is to *activate* unbelievers in his cause, while inducing *passivity* in believers. He invites us to enjoy peace short of the battle line, so that we will not know the true peace of conquest.

That is why, in spite of nearly total liberty for Christians to spread the Gospel and truth, we have seen a waning influence of biblical truths and biblical standards in North America.

Here is the heart of it:

The policy of Satan is the suppression of God's *Word* and God's *work* to as nearly a total degree as possible.

That captures the very essence of his nature, his consuming desire, his working strategy, and his unceasing objective. It is that policy, and the strategies that affect it, that Christians, acting as overcomers, must defeat if we are to have a major influence on our time.

Among the strongholds that must be broken into spiritually in the reversal of the effect of that policy is his denial of the Gospel to millions who live in Muslim lands under Muslim law, probably the single tightest hold against saving truth in our world, even greater than that of Communism.

We have heard talk of the coming of "a New Age." It is said of the Antichrist in Daniel that, "He shall speak words against the Most High . . . and shall think to change" two things—"the *times* and *the law*" (Daniel 7:25, RSV). It is the desire of the supplanter to bring in a new order, a new age, and to cast down God's changeless truths and moral-spiritual laws and replace them. He is, in a sense, always knocking at the world's door.

Jesus said, "Watch out that you are not deceived. For many will come in My name, claiming, 'I am he,' and '*The time* is near.' Do not follow them" (Luke 21:8). "For false christs and false prophets will appear and perform great signs and miracles to deceive even the elect—if that were possible" (Matthew 24:24).

It should be no surprise to informed believers when false doctrines are attended by supernatural signs through demonic workings. We are told to expect this.

Even after he is shut up for the 1,000 years of the messianic reign, "Satan will be released from his prison and will go out to *deceive the nations*" one last time (Revelation 20:7-9). Prison will not reform him! His tactics often change, adapted to varying circumstances, but his nature is changeless.

He is presently hindered in his reach for total world power, according to 2 Thessalonians 2:7-8 (rsv), which tells us that "the mystery of lawlessness is *already at work*"—at work now—but cannot reach its full expression until God removes that which is restraining it.

Whatever the situation, whatever stands against truth, whatever the challenge, we who are believers are called to conquer in our time.

"*He who conquers*" was the risen Christ's word to members in every one of the seven churches that are spiritually described in Revelation 2 and 3. Even to backslidden, lukewarm, failing Laodicea:

"He who conquers, I will grant him *to sit with Me on My throne,* as I Myself conquered and sat down with My Father on His throne" (Revelation 3:21, rsv).

What a promise! What a purpose! What a prospect!

It is beyond our strength, but not at all beyond our reach. In Christ we receive the power to conquer even while we are in our earthly bodies. If that were not true, He would never have told us to arise and do it.


At a Radcliffe college commencement, a young woman named Susannah H. Wood prayed:

"We do not feel like a cool, swinging generation—we are eaten up inside by an intensity that we cannot name.

"Help us to prepare a kind of renaissance in our public and private lives. Let there be born in us a strange joy, that will help us to live and to die and to remake the soul of our time."

*Let there be born in us a strange joy!*

Remarkable words for a secular campus ceremony, but full of an accurate sense that what needs to be done outwardly—"to remake the soul of our time"—must begin inwardly with a birth and must also pass through the matrix of death. There is a distant echo here of Paul's profound secret, "I die daily" (see 1 Corinthians 15:30-31 and Galatians 2:20).

To be free in life, do as the vibrant soldier-poet David did: find out what God wants you to do and do it.

If you discover the joy that only God can give, your own life will be wonderfully enlarged, and you will be able to help remake the soul of our time in ways of which you cannot now even guess, because they are beyond you.

Hear these words: "Ho, every one who thirsts, come to the waters; and he who has no money, come, buy and eat! Come, buy wine and milk without money and without price. Why do you spend your money for that which is not bread, and your labor for that which does not satisfy? Hearken diligently to Me, and eat what is good, and delight yourself in fatness.

"Incline your ear, and come to Me; hear, that your soul may live; and I will make an everlasting covenant with you, My steadfast, sure love for David.

"For My thoughts are not your thoughts, neither are your ways My ways, says the Lord. For as the heavens are higher than the earth, so are My ways higher than your ways and My thoughts higher than your thoughts.

"For you shall go out in joy, and be led forth in peace. The mountains and hills before you shall break forth into singing, and all the trees of the field shall clap their hands" (from Isaiah 55, RSV).

If you have never heard the mountains singing, or seen the trees of the field clapping their hands, do not think because of that that they don't. Ask God to open your ears so you may hear it, and your eyes so you may see it, because, though few people ever know it, they do, my friend, they do.

## A Final Note

If this book has been a help to you, if it has made you wiser to important supernatural realities, you might consider giving it to a friend, especially a young or new Christian, who can be helped by it and enabled to stay out of traps and false experiences so readily available in our culture. For some the difference between a safe walk of blessing, and big trouble, is knowing what step not to take because the biblical warning sign has been posted in mind and heart.